MIRROR MIRROR

MIRROR, MIRROR ON THE WALL WHO IS THE FAIREST OF THEM ALL?

Ask a dementia sufferer or their families and carers, if they believe the NHS is fair in the way it treats people with this dreadful disease.

THIS IS NO FAIRY TALE

This is the reality and the truth
Look behind the NHS or see its reflection in
the mirror and what you see is SHN
SHN stands for:

STOP HYPOCRISY NOW

Oxford English Dictionary defines 'Hypocrisy' as . . .

The practice of professing standards, beliefs etc contrary to ones real character or actual behaviour, especially the pretence of virtue and piety.

Why has this group of people been singled out to be ignored, abused, forgotten and robbed?

TOGETHER WE CAN MAKE A DIFFERENCE

Published by Ink!

2023 Text @ David Allott
2023 Cover design @ Helen Braid 2023

The author has asserted their moral right under the Copyright Designs and Patents Act, 1988, to be identified as the author of this work.

All rights reserved. No part of this publication may be reproduced, stored in retrieval system, or transmitted, in any form or by any means without the prior written permission of the publisher, nor be otherwise circulated in any form of binding or cover other than that in which it is published and without a similar condition being imposed on the subsequent purchaser.

A CIP catalogue for this book is available from the British Library.

Typeset in Garamond Classic 11.25/14 by Hewer Text UK Ltd, Edinburgh

Paperback ISBN: 9781399935166

ink! By The Author School
Kent, England, United Kingdom
Email: inkpublishingservices@gmail.com
Website: www.inkpublishingservices.co.uk
Twitter: @services_ink

Mirror Mirror: Facing the hard truth of "dementia care" for sufferers and their families in the UK

By David Allott

A DEDICATION TO MARGARET ALLOTT
(2ND JUNE 1952 – 7TH JULY 2023)

The telling of the final chapter of Margaret's life, contained within this book, will be her lasting legacy.

Just as her life was one filled with love and happiness and wherever she was able, she had a desire to help others whenever she could.

So too that after her passing she would be thrilled to know that for all that she had to suffer, it would not be in vain, as others would gain from her experiences and in so doing, ease the pain that inevitably falls not only to those stricken by Alzheimer's or other dementia diseases but also on their loved ones.

When times look bleak and life seems hard, above all else remember, that the sufferers of these dreadful diseases are reliant upon the ones who love them, to keep them safe and free from harm, protecting them from the injustices that are perpetrated against them.

THE POWER OF LOVE
Love is an amazing thing
It is like a bottomless coffee pot
No matter how much you give
Even when you give "All Your Love"

It does not diminish how much you have left for someone else
Love is something that gives as much pleasure to give as to receive.
Love is extremely powerful; it can change people's lives for the better.
Love can overcome hatred in the hearts of others.

Love can bring compassion where it is lacking.
Love can bring out the best in people.
Love can right injustices where they exist.
Love binds people together like the strongest glue.

Love is like a rubber ball; it keeps on bouncing back.
Love for another person brings such happiness.
The only price we pay for such love is that of deep sorrow on that person's passing.

Love is an emotion like no other.

Better to have experienced the true meaning of love than
never to have had love in your heart.

When laws are made, the objective behind them should be to secure the citizens of this country a future which is better, fairer, and safer than it was without them, otherwise what would be the point in having them? For laws to be effective their content and meaning must be conveyed to those to whom they are applicable, with the expectation that the conduct of those involved will follow the law. When this doesn't happen, then the responsibility for upholding them falls upon those whose job it is to ensure they are enforced and when found wanting to bring the perpetrators of such crimes to justice.

To complete this circle and ensure the effectiveness of the laws it makes it is ultimately the responsibility of Parliament through those members who its citizens have elected to represent them, to ensure that the laws they have made are enforced.

THIS IS ALL I ASK IN LOVING MEMORY OF MARGARET, A WONDERFUL PERSON WHO DESERVED TO BE TREATED WITH LOVE AND RESPECT BUT, LIKE SO MANY OTHERS IN SIMILAR SITUATIONS, FELT THE FULL FORCE OF THE IGNORANCE OF THE LAW OR A DESIRE TO WORK WITHIN ITS CONSTRAINTS.

This is the height of HYPOCRISY to say one thing and do the exact opposite and why it is appropriate to look at the mirror image of the NHS in order to see the truth behind the name SHN - help "STOP HYPOCRISY NOW".

PREFACE

This book originated in trying to get justice for my wife who suffers from that dreadful disease known as Alzheimer's. In doing so it throws a spotlight on the very many inadequacies of the National Health Service and Continuing Healthcare (CHC), from its denial that it doesn't even recognise dementia sufferers as being covered by this part of the service, and the continuing denial that through lies and misinterpretations there is a determined effort to rob the innocent of their life savings.

It explores not only the whys of this outrageous conduct but looks at how successive governments and the UK's healthcare system have conspired to allow this to happen, be it through total ignorance or a wanton desire to hide the truth, and the denial that it is a broken system not fit for purpose. It looks at the way they have chosen to redefine the very meaning of some parts of the English language just to suit their own ends.

It offers some suggestions as to how we might come together to affect a change in the system for the benefit of all dementia sufferers, and aims to provide a better understanding of CHC and the means to fight for your rights through the telling of our own experiences.

There are useful tips and advice on the essential actions that must be taken to make it possible for the reader to give their loved ones the help that can only come from them.

For too long dementia suffers have been treated with disdain and in some instances their life's work and achievements are being used to subsidise not only their own care in their hour of need but the care of others who have been awarded CHC or local authority-funded care. Now is the time to reset the balance and force the establishment to come good on their promises of "A Free at the Point of Access Healthcare System" for everyone.

CONTENTS

1	INSURANCE	1
2	KNOWLEDGE AND EXPERIENCE	11
3	JUSTICE OR INJUSTICE	18
4	NHS CONTINUING HEALTHCARE	23
5	WHO REALLY PAYS	44
6	TRYING TO FIND SOLUTIONS	57
7	THE THINGS YOU NEED TO KNOW AND DO	74
8	THE USE OF PROFESSIONAL LEGAL SERVICES	86
9	OUR EXPERIENCES FROM THE START OF THIS TERRIBLE JOURNEY	96
10	THE MULTI-DISCIPLINARY ASSESSMENT FOR NHS CHC FUNDING	161
11	WHO PAYS: SELF FUNDING OR SOCIAL SERVICES?	213
12	PEOPLE'S RIGHTS AND WHO REALLY KNOWS WHAT ABOUT CHC FUNDING	219
13	MY HOPES AND ASPIRATIONS FOR THE FUTURE	265
14	JOINING THE FIGHT AND SPREADING THE WORD	271
15	SOME ADDITIONAL FOOD FOR THOUGHT	273

ACKNOWLEDGEMENTS

My love and appreciation to my son Benjamin for his advice and help in so many ways, without which I would have undoubtedly found it more difficult to get the help his mum needed and the rights she was entitled to. Not forgetting that this acknowledgement extends to his lovely wife Claire who we have always regarded as the daughter we never had and who has always been 100% supportive. We love you both, and of course our lovely grandsons Lewis and Stanley of whom we are extremely proud.

I recognise I am extremely lucky to have such wonderful immediate family who, through their telephone calls and visits, give me the needed added strength to know that, not only are we both loved, but also we are not alone in our struggles. So my personal thanks to all sisters and brothers: Margaret, Jean, Eddie and Carol, Kath and Fran, Lena and Dave, and Paul and Karen.

To Sue Webb, who we first met through The Memory Clinic in Milton Keynes in the earlier days of Margaret's diagnosis and subsequently in her new role as an Admiral Nurse, I offer my thanks and gratitude for the support you have given us and are continuing to give. Your advice and suggestions are always welcomed and of great benefit.

Thanks are also due to Sue's replacement at The Memory Clinic, Iona Charles, who has also shown great professionalism and care in helping us to get action from areas of the system that had been lacking in urgency to do what is expected of them.

To Jenny Trilsbach from social services, my thanks for organising the twice weekly sessions where I now have a lovely lady in Amie Barrow who sits with Margaret, allowing me a little time for myself and to do the essential shopping. Without this I don't know if I would be able to cope, so this is of tremendous help to me – so thank you Jenny.

To Penelope Makuwe, the student social worker, I acknowledge your help and trust that your desire to help others will never be compromised by others who have less noble intentions.

It would be wrong of me to not mention the role played by TOPAS in looking after my beloved especially after the appalling treatment she received at the hands of the NHS in Hospital X. To those good and caring personnel at TOPAS I say thank you for your dedication – you know who you are. It's a pity I can't say the same for all your colleagues.

In addition to the management my special thanks must go to the individual carers who attend to my wife on a daily basis, without whose dedication I would find it almost impossible to cope. Obviously some of those listed visit on a more frequent basis to others and naturally shoulder a greater responsibility than their colleagues, having gained a better understanding of Margaret's needs. To each and everyone, I have tremendous respect for the work you do and admire your abilities and positivity; you are truly at the pinnacle of your profession.

Thank you Estelle Brown, Pam Brown, Tanya Kenny, Kelly Steel, Amie Barrow, Carly Sadler, Del Draycott, Stacey Bushnell, Maria Grey, Barbara Otto, Leeann Demwell, Lorraine Parker, Shannon Ackland, Vicki Gellard and Scott Rose.

Finally, not forgetting my own parents Geoff and Joyce Allott and Margaret's parents Bill and Mary Evans, who both in their own ways gave each of us the opportunities, education and freedom to learn right from wrong and the tenacity to fight against injustices as and where we have the ability to do so.

1

INSURANCE

"An arrangement by which a company or the state undertakes to provide a guarantee of compensation for specific loss, damage, illness or death in return for payment of a specified amount."
(The definition given in the Oxford English Dictionary.)

So let us start by looking carefully at what insurance really means to us all and the various types of insurance we all come across in living our daily lives.

In simple terms it could be said that insurance falls into one of two main categories, but all have one important principle in common and that is the insured must have paid the required premium prior to any incident having occurred to which the policy refers.

Anyone found to be attempting to take out a policy after the event and subsequently making a claim against that policy is guilty of attempting to defraud the insurance company for which there can be severe penalties, which can include not only financial penalties but also the risk of being detained at His Majesty's Pleasure, and of course a criminal record.

Within the first category fall all those types of policies which we as individuals can choose whether to take out or not. We can form our own opinion of whether or not we wish to protect something we already have by taking out a policy that will compensate us in the event of loss or damage to all manner of things that we have acquired throughout our lives, subject to an insurance company offering us a policy.

In some instances we may feel that the premium could be too costly and, in any event, the item to be insured may have a limited life span. It could be that the premium for, let's say, a particular electrical item may be a high percentage of its actual replacement cost, and therefore the decision is to save the premium and put those savings towards a new purchase when the time comes.

On the other hand there may be items we own that we would never be able to replace in the event of a complete loss, and therefore the decision not to insure them may well be foolhardy and not worth the risk. Probably the prime example of this is one's own house that may be worth many hundreds of thousands of pounds, and in this context the premium can appear to be very reasonable as a small percentage of its actual worth.

Most insurance companies are no different from most other companies in that they exist to provide a good rate of return for their owners'/shareholders' investment, and hopefully a good living for their employees. The product being sold is merely a vehicle to provide them with sufficient funds to ensure their outgoings and liabilities are far less than their income.

Income £2— outgoings £1—result happiness
Income £1 —outgoings £2— result misery

In order to provide an insurance policy the providers must take into account many factors to determine the premium they need to charge to ensure, as far as is reasonably possible, that they can cover any claims made against them and still remain in the "Happiness Zone".

WHAT IS THE RISK?

Such elements as age of applicant, where they live, their history of claims, how likely they are to have an accident, how many other people they are insuring for this type of policy, whether their family members suffer from certain illnesses, what they do for a living, how often they use the insured item, how likely the insured item will breakdown, what it is used for, and many, many more questions and answers determine the level of risk.

Having determined that a policy will be offered the company will offer the customer such policy based on certain conditions often referred to as the small print. In every single case the onus is on the insured person to tell the truth about disclosing the information required. Not to do so will in the event of a claim more than likely invalidate the policy.

Remember this - it is important - there is no room to lie about anything.

You would reasonably expect this to be a two-way street; in other words, that there would be an expectation that the insurance provider would also have the same obligation to tell the truth and not lie to the insured person.

In my experience this has been far from the reality and seemingly with no consequences for the provider under certain insurances, and with massive consequences for me.

In all these types of policies we as individuals have the right to form our own opinions as to whether we spend some of our income or savings to protect what we already have.

However, the second category to which I referred is completely different, where we do not have a choice as to what we can or cannot do. These categories of insurance could be classified as compulsory: you have to pay, whether you like it or not.

This book is not about insurance in general, but it is important to see the difference between different types and how each is handled differently and how these differences may affect you or your family.

Let's take motor insurance as a good example of compulsory insurance. If you choose to drive a vehicle on public roads then you must be insured, no ifs, no buts; you don't even need to be involved in an accident or make a false claim. If you drive a motor vehicle on the road without insurance, you are breaking the law and can be fined or imprisoned for failing to get the correct cover.

Most law-abiding citizens would probably agree that this is a good law and that it is there to protect the innocent third parties; after all, a motor vehicle is a potentially destructive force that has the power to take lives and cause carnage to innocent people. (Well, when it comes to driving a motor vehicle, it is.)

Insurance to protect the innocent – very commendable. We are a society who looks after the innocent, aren't we?

Another similar example of compulsory insurance may be seen as that of public liability, needed by most organisations and businesses who in carrying out their daily work need to do so in a professional and safe manner. Again, it is there to protect the public against accidents and negligence that also has the potential to cause serious loss and/or injury or even death. Again, very commendable in a society that looks after the innocent.

Time now to turn our attention to a government-imposed compulsory insurance which should have the same aims as the others: looking after the innocent. If only this were true.

Remember that two-way street we talked about? No lies, only the truth, serious consequences for those who don't abide by the rules. One rule for us, but a completely different set of standards for the provider of this insurance.

They make their own rules; they change them when it suits them. They ignore them, lie about them, interpret them in different ways and even change the recognised meaning of the English language, all to achieve their own interpretation in a determined bid to achieve what they want. They renege on their obligations and act in a God-like way with little or no detrimental consequences to themselves. They will steal from you, your life savings, your children's inheritance, without so much as a second thought, and that includes even the home you have spent thousands of pounds over your lifetime protecting with insurance premiums. They decide who will get what, not you, not your loved ones. They will decide who will get paid out under their policy and who will get nothing.

So what is this dreadful policy that you have no option but to pay into over a lifetime of work, contributing tens or even hundreds of thousands of pounds with an expectation that you are covered in the event of needing to call upon it in a time of greatest need?

They refer to it as "National Health Insurance". There is no monetary payout from this insurance; instead it is claimed that it provides the resources to fund what we know as the National Health Service (free at the point of use).

We have looked at the meaning of the word "insurance" as described by the Oxford English Dictionary, and now we must turn our attention to the definition as to what is meant by "national" and "health".

"National (adjective): of involving or relating to a nation as a whole" or "a citizen or subject".

In the context of the National Health Service, this is just not the case. How can it be described as "national" when the rules and conditions are not applied evenly and fairly throughout the whole nation, to every single citizen or subject?

Firstly, we are all aware that with the establishment of the devolved parliaments or Assemblies of Scotland, Wales and Northern Ireland, the citizens of these areas of the so-called United Kingdom enjoy all manner of improved services not available to those citizens of other areas: free prescriptions, free parking at hospitals for patients and visitors, certain treatments and medications etc. In addition to these anomalies we also have to endure further unfairness in the system by virtue of the fact that the country is still further divided into even more regions controlled by different Clinical Commissioning Groups (CCGs) who pretend to be applying the same standards and rules as their counterparts in other areas.

In reality this is just not the case, as they are left to interpret the rules in different ways. Hence we have a situation that has become known as a postcode lottery, where two identical cases in different areas can be treated in entirely different ways. Dependent on the boundaries of these authorities it is possible for one person to receive treatment, and for another person living in close proximity or possibly even on the same street to be denied that same treatment. Not only is this grossly unfair, but it also does not conform to the principle of providing a "national" service which is equal and available to all those who are in need of it. In some cases this can be the difference between life and death, and it is certainly not in line with the idea that society is looking after the needy.

We now turn our attention to the word "health" contained in the very name of the National Health Service.

Once again let's look at how this word is defined by the Oxford English Dictionary:

"The state of being bodily and <u>mentally</u> vigorous and free from disease."

"The general condition of both body and <u>mind</u>."

It will be noted that I have purposely underlined the reference to "mentally" and "mind". Why, you may ask, have I found it necessary to highlight these two words in the definition provided by the OED? To put it simply, the NHS has in too many cases chosen to redefine their interpretation of "health" as not being inclusive of mental diseases or ailments, or at the very least choosing instead to concentrate their service on other bodily ailments to the detriment of those many people who are suffering from totally disabling diseases and conditions of the brain and mind.

This is at the heart of what this book is about: a fight for justice and an attempt to get those in power to recognise that the time for wheezily words, lies and denials is over. Time for honesty, compassion, fairness and above all to truly act as a society that recognises that the majority need to care for the needy, no matter what disease has affected them or what part of their body or organs no longer function as they should.

I offer this thought. Whilst hundreds of thousands of people stood on their doorsteps to clap the NHS, I believe this institution is not worthy of such adoration. The people who work in the institution, probably the majority, but certainly not all, are the ones who deserve our thanks for their hard work and dedication throughout the Covid pandemic and I applaud every one of those making up this majority, but certainly not the institution for which they work. Let us not forget it was the politicians, having noted what some people were already doing, who decided to suggest that we all got out there and clap for the NHS. In reality this was just another way of getting us to believe that this government-funded institution is all good and without fault. This is simply not so; it has many flaws that politicians from both sides of the house don't want us, the citizens, to know about. No, better to have us believe, with their propaganda, that it is a wonderful national treasure for which we should all be eternally grateful. Just more spin from our elected officials. Try asking the thousands of families who have already seen and experienced the dark side of this institution.

So remember its very name is neither national nor looking after all our health needs, and it is certainly not funded by the so-called insurance policy it purports to offer every citizen throughout this land.

It fails on all three definitions that are used in making us believe it is something it is not.

So the question is, how do we protect ourselves in the event that some dreadful disease, like the many forms of dementia, befalls ourselves or our loved ones in the future, or indeed those who are currently experiencing the trauma? Knowing that the insurance and taxes we pay throughout our lives means for nothing without sticking up for our rights and having to fight every step of the way to get a change that is fair for everyone.

If you are let down by an insurance company to which you have been paying premiums, and they fail to honour their commitment and refuse to settle your claim – what would you do?

Well, you would at least have some options open to you:

- Never use them again and move your other policies to other companies at renewal time
- Tell everyone you know or even people you don't know how bad this company really is
- Plead your case with them, and if that fails
- Go to the Ombudsman, or
- Sue them in court – this could be a tricky or expensive option dependent upon the size of the claim involved. However, bear in mind they are the experts at assessing risk and often a threat to go to court may be sufficient to get the matter settled.

On the other hand, with this government-funded policy, the first option is not available to us; we can't take our business elsewhere (other than taking out a private health policy, but we are still liable for NHI contributions and taxes).

So the big question is: can we do anything else to protect ourselves against this social injustice?

Fortunately, the answer is YES. It can often be hard, but there are ways to make it easier.

If you insure your property and your accumulated belongings against total loss, then you already know the value of doing what is necessary to protect your family and yourself against such a disaster.

You know it makes sense to have such policies in place. Imagine that there are people out there who haven't heard of insurance. It could be said that they are foolish, uneducated or, to put it another way, they lack the knowledge about how to protect themselves. If this were the case, they must live in trepidation of being robbed or their house burning down. We see this type of thing on a large scale in what we refer to as third-world countries where hurricanes, earthquakes, floods, droughts, volcanic eruptions etc. literally rob the whole population of an area of absolutely everything they have spent a lifetime working for.

We are fortunate that we don't live in such a place and in the main are not subjected to such a degree of devastation by acts of nature.

We do, however, have diseases like dementia that can rob us of absolutely everything, because our government allows one of its own institutions to engineer a way to deprive these sufferers of the other things they have spent a lifetime working for.

My wife is suffering from late-stage Alzheimer's. She can no longer feed herself, go to the toilet, walk unaided, read, write, understand a conversation, talk, dress herself, know what is dangerous, recount past times, know who is who or remember anything. In fact, she exists with nothing to look back on and nothing to look forward to; her life is literally one of sleeping and sitting in a chair, staring into space.

I think she has lost enough, but oh no, the state has decided that it is not enough; she should lose all of her worldly possessions, her savings, her house and belongings too.

Their interpretation of their rules is that her needs are not medical but social.

Shame on them; it is a disgrace. So why is this the case? To put it bluntly: money. Social care is means-tested, whereas NHS care is not. This means they have the power to take almost every last penny. But it is even worse than that: not only are they expecting this group of people to fund their own care, but as you will learn, the system means that you will also help to part-fund the care of complete strangers.

The only way to fight against this injustice is through knowledge and experience. The knowledge is out there, and the experience of others will be of great help to you and your loved ones.

The next chapter covers certain aspects of these, with apologies to any reader who may at times think some things are obvious; but bear in mind the only obvious things are in themselves obvious by virtue of the fact that they are the result of having gained the knowledge.

2

KNOWLEDGE AND EXPERIENCE

> "The facts feelings or experiences known
> by a person or group of people."
> "The state of knowing."
> "Awareness, consciousness or familiarity
> gained by experience or learning."
> "Erudition or informed learning."
> "Specific information about a subject."
> (Definitions given in the Oxford English Dictionary.)

We all enter this life with no knowledge, save for inbuilt instincts such as suckling at our mother's breast, or alternative. If all goes well we look forward to a lifetime of learning, be it through learnt instinctive responses, observations, chance, looking, listening, tasting, hearing, smelling, reading, watching etc. We learn through our experiences, by chance or by choice, and we can have the determination to obtain the facts about certain subjects if we are inquisitive enough to find them out. Some things interest us, and some things don't; we are thankfully all different in the things we like or don't have an interest in. We can make a choice about what knowledge we acquire and ignore things that don't seemingly hold any interest for us.

One of the ways of learning about something is to ask questions and listen to the answers, providing of course that you ask the right person. It's no good asking someone a question about a subject they know nothing about. However, what if you don't know what questions to ask? If you can't ask the right question, you will find it extremely difficult to get the right knowledge. You are then reliant on gaining knowledge purely by chance. In other words, you will remain ignorant of certain facts.

Remember this: the NHS, contrary to their obligations, do not necessarily inform you of your rights or what you may be entitled to. They most certainly work in some instances on this principle of don't tell and you won't ask. After all, you can't ask about something you don't even know exists.

Sometimes we need to be motivated to make the effort to learn about certain things. That motivation can be for a wide number of reasons, and sometimes different reasons bring forth similar results. Maybe going on to further education is motivated by the desire just to learn more about a subject that really interests you, or maybe you feel it is the only way to improve your chances of getting a certain job. Could it be that what job you ultimately do is less important than how much they will pay you for doing it, or your choice to go to uni is based purely on the understanding that you've heard it's great, party time, freedom from parental control, a chance to make new friends and fool around before having to get serious about earning a living?

How many times have you spoken to people who have said things like:

- One day I'm going to learn how to X, Y, Z
- When I retire I'm going to do a certain thing
- If only I had the time I'd love to learn X, Y, Z
- When I can afford it I'm going to X, Y, Z.

In other words, there are desires that people have, but they do not feel they are sufficiently committed to them at this moment in time. Now that may well be because they are overcommitted in other areas, be it through time constraints or lack of funds.

However, it could be that their priorities may be wrong and the real reason they are putting off doing what they really want is through lack of motivation.

It is hard to devote time to the things you want to do and learn about and even harder to think about having to gain knowledge about a subject that you may never have use for. But what if you do need that knowledge, that fate deals you a blow that you never expected, and then you wish you had gained the knowledge you then need?

It is probably appropriate to use the example of the London black cab drivers, as their learning is both time consuming, not easy and has to be done whilst earning a living in another way. In order for them to succeed in becoming one of the elite they have to learn and pass the test: "the knowledge". They do so not knowing if they will succeed, but they devote many, many hours to their objective. Why? Because they are highly motivated.

It is my hope that I can help you, through this book, to become highly motivated to learn all you can about how dementia patients (Alzheimer's in our case) are unfairly treated because the stakes are so high.

The chances are that in time you will ultimately and sadly know someone who gets this dreadful disease. That person could be your own partner, the love of your life; it could be your parents, your brother or sister, aunt, uncle, cousins, your best friend or maybe your next-door neighbour or even your own son or daughter. Whoever that person is will need your help to fight for their rights against a corrupt system.

History is littered with instances of when a certain group of people use their knowledge to their advantage, which you may say is just the way of life. After all, if you have the knowledge to fix something that someone else doesn't know how to do, then you can possibly build yourself a very successful business based on servicing the needs of those people who don't have the knowledge of how to perform a particular task.

However, ask yourself this question: if that knowledge should be freely available to those who not only need it, but have contributed to its very existence, then they are effectively robbing you of what you are entitled to. In the worst-case scenarios, they enrich their lives at the expense of yours.

Let us consider the acts of war throughout time. Generally speaking, the side that has the biggest and best weapons with the best strategies and possibly the biggest armies are those most likely to win. In other words, because of their knowledge they are at an advantage to the opposite side. It matters not which side is on the side of right or wrong. In some instances, their advantage can be defeated by a determination to do the right thing but only through a concerted effort of coming together and improving their own knowledge of how to defeat the enemy, because a common goal for the good of its people enables things to happen which might otherwise not be the case.

"Necessity is the mother of invention."

"It takes only one good person to do nothingto allow evil to prevail."

We must also consider how greed forms the very basis for what are in themselves acts that could be described as evil. Think back to the very worst cases that caused the financial crises of the 1990s or the collapse of the world banking systems of the 2000s.

Those with the knowledge engineered a change to the system that allowed them to do away with regulations that had been in place to protect the innocent, purely so they could profit to the tune of millions if not billions. Why do these evil people need so much money? Just how many homes, apartments, Learjets, fast cars, swanky yachts, art works or jewellery etc. does one person need? The worst part of this is that in order for them to have these things, hundreds of thousands of people lost their homes and their life savings. If only a few good people had had the courage to blow the whistle, all this might have been avoided. Sometimes it is very, very hard to be on the side of right from wrong especially if you appear to be a lone voice in the wilderness and the establishment is against you by gagging you with something like the Official Secrets Act.

It seems to me we look down on whistle-blowers with disdain when we should be applauding them for their courage, certainly when the subject matter should not be a secret but where the citizens have a right to the truth.

If there is anyone reading this book who is of the mind that they do not have the power to change anything and that they will live their lives in such a way that the easiest thing to do is to just accept that the cards they have been dealt are the ones they must play in this game of life and death, I would ask two things:

(1) That you consider that there is a possibility that you may find yourself in a situation, in the future, that would change your outlook and that you may be grateful that other people made the choice to fight for something that you will ultimately benefit from.

(2) Please pass on this book to someone else who may be grateful to you that you did.

Before we move on to the next chapter, I would like to recommend a mix of documentary films that highlight certain issues in fairly recent history, each one dealing with different subject matters and incorporating different types of evil behaviours, but with the common thread that they all required a good person to do something extraordinary to counter the injustice, greed and determination of people who acted purely in their own self-interest without a single thought for the consequences their actions were having on other human beings.

These true stories are all worthy of watching and each one highlights the fact that trust is something that cannot be taken for granted. Trust is something that has to be earned, but it must also be maintained. When taken for granted, the greedy will help themselves to not only their rightful share of the "pie", but they will consume yours, your family's, your friends' and many other people's as well.

(1) *Dark Waters* - A story about a mammoth conglomerate, DuPont, who knowingly, for their own financial gain, made the choice to continue to produce a product that they knew was poisoning and destroying the environment at great cost to animal and human lives.

(2) *Spotlight* - The incredible story of how the Catholic Church covered up and allowed the continuation of sexual abuse against minors on an incredible scale. Make sure you read all the credits at the end of the film; they truly make for disturbing reading.

(3) *The Trial of the Chicago 7* - A true story of the injustice metered out by the establishment for political reasons by the very offices of state who were there to uphold the law but chose instead to use it for their own gains.

(4) *Inside Job* - The story behind the financial crisis of the early 2000s.

(5) *Dirty Money* – Fraud within the banking systems of one of America's largest, oldest and most respected banks.

(6) *Official Secrets* – The whistle-blower who leaked a top-secret NSA memo exposing joint USA and UK illegal spying operations.

I hope that through watching these excellent productions you will not only enjoy their entertainment value, but that you will be wiser and more motivated to play your part in helping to find justice for those in need of it.

3

JUSTICE OR INJUSTICE

"The quality or fact of being just."
"The principle of fairness that like
cases should be treated alike."
"A particular distribution of benefits and
burdens fairly in accordance with a particular
conception of what are to count as like cases."
"The administration of law according to
prescribed and accepted principles."
"Conformity to the Law; legal validity."
(Definitions given in the Oxford English Dictionary.)

"INJUSTICE"
"The condition or practice of being unjust or unfair."

The Old Bailey court building in London is topped by a statue of Lady Justice, based on the Greek Goddess Themis, honoured as clear sighted, and the Roman Goddess Justica, honoured as representing the virtue of the morality of the justice system.

She holds in her right hand a sword to symbolise the power of justice, and in her left she holds a set of scales to represent the impartiality of the court's decisions.

When giving evidence in court the first thing that must be done is to swear an oath to tell the truth and nothing but the truth. There are basically two options open to the person giving evidence: one for those who are prepared to swear on the Bible, and another for those who are not prepared to do so.

No matter what choice is made the witness is bound by the law to be factual and tell the truth at all times. The seriousness of this expectation is enforced by the law finding someone guilty of perjury when it is proven they have lied under oath. Perjury is a serious criminal offence which will likely lead to a term of imprisonment.

Regretfully, there is no such vehicle to force people not to tell lies about almost anything outside a courtroom. Some people can lie with impunity outside this setting and will do so just to gain advantage over another person or group of persons. They can tell you almost anything in the hope or expectation that you will believe them and acquiesce to their way of thinking.

Now, some lies are worse than others, and undoubtedly some liars are worse than others. Sometimes we have an expectation that the person we are talking to will be telling us the truth. We may never even have met this person before, or indeed never even have heard of them. So why would we take what they are telling us at face value and believe it to be the truth?

Simply, they may well be in a position of trust with a fancy title or letters after their name. Doctors enjoy this sort of privileged position, and many people will accept what they say because they see them as highly knowledgeable, educated and trustworthy. Do not be fooled; these are the worst kind of liars: if they take the opposite view to you, they probably think you are not knowledgeable, maybe not well educated and can easily be led into their way of thinking.

They may sometimes think that they are better than you and even look down in a superior way at what you are saying or asking about. On the other hand, the misinformation they are giving you may indeed be through their own ignorance of the subject matter being discussed. That does not excuse them; in fact, it may be worse if this expert should have known the correct information, in which case they are being negligent, with far reaching consequences for you and themselves.

Getting justice is all about doing what is fair and just which, dependent upon what the subject matter is, can often be hard.

Again we look back in history to unjust practices that took place without a second thought. Things that we can now hardly comprehend ever took place because they were so unjust, that we still find difficult to understand how they came about in the first place.

How could any human being have ever thought it right to enslave other human beings, take them away from their home and country, put them in chains, ship them to another continent and treat them like a commodity to be bought and sold, with little or no feelings for their happiness or welfare?

How could the male of our species believe they were all wisdom and without fault, to the extent they wouldn't recognise women should have equal rights and be able to vote, enjoy equal pay etc.?

How could, and even to this day, can certain well-off sectors of the community enjoy life to the fullest extent without compassion for others less fortunate?

As a nation I believe we are in the main a caring and loving society which is evidenced by the donations given freely to hundreds of charitable organisations both home and abroad.

The question is, should some of these really exist? Should some of the cost of the work carried out by these charities not have fallen on the shoulders of the many, not the few?

Without doubt, change can happen with the intervention of just a few people, sometimes from high profile individuals, but sometimes just through sheer guts and determination of dedicated, otherwise ordinary individuals.

In other cases, change can only occur because the ground swell of opinion for a particular cause becomes so great that resistance against change can no longer be sustained.

My fight for justice is for the individuals who have had inflicted upon them probably the most serious loss any human can imagine. Not only have they lost their present, but they have lost their future and their past, their dignity and in some cases their ability to do almost anything at all, even to communicate their needs.

The injustice is that it seems this group of people have been singled out to be forgotten other than when their assets are sufficient for the state to use to enhance their failing system and assist in the care for others for whom the state has no other option but to fund their care.

Injustice can and often is caused by the very system designed to uphold it. When a dispute arises between two parties and neither party is prepared to accept the viewpoint of the other, then the chances are that the only way to resolve those differences is for the offended party to go to court and prove that it is their assessment of the differences that is correct, not those of the opposing party.

Unfortunately, this process can be lengthy and extremely costly. Let us suppose that we have a dispute over the use of a parcel of land, clearly owned by Party A, but Party B has decided they wish to have unfettered access over it. In the first instance B requests permission from A to install a door in their property so they can freely use the land owned by A. This permission is denied and so starts a dispute that B is determined to win.

B begins by ignoring the lack of permission and goes ahead by installing the door anyway. A informs B that they must block up the new doorway and return the area to its original position, otherwise they would be leaving A no choice other than to seek redress through the courts.

Now, here is the interesting thing. Party A is undoubtedly in the right, but B is so determined to get what they want that they are prepared to tell numerous lies in an attempt to get A to back down and acquiesce to their demands. Their lies know no bounds and include threats, bully boy and scare tactics and a whole host of made-up stories.

The problem is that each party seemingly judges each other by their own standards.

Party A is honest and genuinely means what they say i.e. they will take the matter to court if B does not remove the door.

Party B, however, is used to getting their own way, by telling whatever lies they need to. So the judgement of B is that A is only issuing an idle threat about going to court. (This is B judging A by their own standards and believing A is just lying about going to court.) On the other hand, A judges B by their own standards of honesty and integrity and believes that B will see sense to avoid a court case.

The result of this was that a long and expensive battle between the parties took place, resulting in A finally issuing proceedings against B. This resulted in B making an offer to settle the case prior to going to court on the understanding that the door could remain in place. The offer of £17,500 was insufficient to cover A's legal costs to date. A responded by agreeing that the door could remain in place for use in an emergency only, providing it was fitted with a break glass mechanism to avoid any unwarranted use and conditional on payment of £23,000. This figure would cover the legal costs of A in full and a small amount in compensation. This counteroffer is accepted and the dispute is resolved.

The moral of this true story is, when you know you are in the right and have taken the time to get the required evidence in place by being knowledgeable about every aspect of the case, don't be intimidated by another person's lies. Do what is right.

Without doubt, B's attitude of trying to get something they wanted that they were not entitled to, at the expense of someone else, probably cost them well in excess of £30,000 when you factor in their own legal costs.

Justice can prevail but only through determination and knowledge.

4

NHS CONTINUING HEALTHCARE

Are you familiar with the meaning of this phrase or, probably more to the point, have you ever heard of NHS Continuing Healthcare?

It would not be unusual if this is the very first time you have heard mention of what has become known as the "Best kept secret of the National Health Service". So secret, in fact, that if we didn't know better one begins to wonder if those in the know have been asked to sign the Official Secrets Act.

Firstly, we need to understand that CHC is part of the NHS and is therefore subject to the same principle of "free at the point of use".

The difficulties we encounter are numerous and start with the basic understanding that you can't ask for something if you don't know it exists. Well, it does exist, and the fact is it never seems to be offered but relies on the patient asking about it and how it works. So let's be honest about this: the fact that it is so secret immediately denies a significant number of patients the opportunity to avail themselves of this service, even when they would be entitled to it.

Let us refer to this as the NHS CHC first line of defence.

CHC is operated under a set of guiding principles set out in a 167-page document known as *the National Framework For NHSCHC and NHS Funded Nursing Care*.

(I would recommend that you invest in the time, paper and ink to familiarise yourself with its contents. Remember how we discussed the need for knowledge? Well, this is so important because you will learn that in many instances these guiding principles are either ignored, misinterpreted or lied about and all to your disadvantage.) The guidance was revised in October 2018 and replaces the previous framework of November 2012. There is so much content contained within this framework that it would be impossible to mention every little detail as that would in effect be merely a duplication of the actual document itself. I will therefore try to confine my comments to the areas I see to be of the most importance and in particular those areas where I have experienced the greatest deviation from the truth.

Page 3
Read here the reasons for the revised edition and its objectives and take particular note of the final paragraph: "All those involved in the delivery of the NHS CHC should become familiar with the whole framework etc."

The reality is that those involved who I had the displeasure to have to deal with had *not* become familiar with the whole framework. Remember, you are effectively putting the future life of your loved ones in these people's hands. You would not knowingly get on an aeroplane with a pilot in charge who was not fully familiar with how to fly the plane and what to do in an emergency, would you?

Page 6
Read here and learn who is entitled to this service, and I would ask you to take particular note of paragraphs 3, 4, 5, 6 and 8. Having done this you will note that there is an inbuilt limitation of accessibility which enables them to have a way out of providing this service. This is referred to as the assessed patient needing to display a "primary health need".

(Note OED definition of primary: first in importance, degree, rank etc. Fundamental, basic.)

Also take particular note of the fact that these regulations are to be referred to as the "standing rules" and require Clinical Commissioning Groups (CCGs) to have regard to the National Framework.

Page 7

(1) Take particular note of the fact that NHS CHC is not determined by the setting or by the type of service delivery.

(2) Paragraph 2 of the key definitions refers to NHS-funded nursing care. Note the fact that the funding is based on a single band rate. This is extremely important when we move on to talk about how the government has conned the nation into believing people will not have to sell their houses in the future to fund their continuing care. More about this later.

(3) Paragraph 3: read the last sentence and understand its significance.

(4) Paragraph 4 Clinical Commissioning Group (CCGs): note they are ultimately legally responsible for all eligibility decisions in accordance with the rules.

Page 8
All relevant but take note particularly of paragraphs 13, 14 and 16.

Page 9
Note paragraph 19 on joint funding. This is effectively the fallback position for denying CHC funding. It is a little bit like the Scottish courts, which are not confined to finding a person guilty or not guilty; they have a fall-back position of "not proven".

Page 10
Rules and responsibilities of CCGs.

Take particular note of paragraph 21 item (a): CCGs. are responsible for "promoting awareness of NHS CHC".

This is the NHS CHC's second line of defence.

My experience at Hospital X and at the specialist unit my wife was admitted to after being sectioned was that they did not display any signs, posters or leaflets showing any information about the existence of NHS CHC, even though it is a responsibility of the CCG to do so. Remember, you shouldn't have to ask for information as this is again impossible to do if you are not aware of its existence. This point is again reaffirmed on page 13 in paragraph 32, and even after having to demand a screening assessment I was still not offered a copy of any leaflet or information on CHC.

Page 14
Legal content.

Pay particular attention to paragraph 37 and note under key legislation paragraph 38 (a): the physical and *mental* health of the people of England.

Page 17
Health Need and Social Care Need.

Take particular note of paragraphs 50 and 51.

Pages 19–23
Primary Health Need.

It is important to read and digest the entirety of this section but take particular note of the following paragraphs: 54, 55, 59, 60, 62, 63, 64 and 65. Probably the most important of these is 63 where I was personally informed my wife would not be eligible because I wanted to take her home, even though this paragraph clearly states that "Eligibility to NHS CHC is not determined or influenced either by the setting where the care is provided nor by the characteristics of the person who delivers the care. The decision-making rationale should not marginalise a need just because it is successfully managed – well-managed needs are still needs. Only where the successful management of a healthcare need has *permanently* reduced or removed an ongoing need, such that the active management of that need is reduced or no longer required, will this have a bearing on NHS CHC eligibility."

Page 22

Core values and principles.

Think about the impression given by this phrase; it gives the reader a sense that at the heart of this process is a determination, willingness and desire to be fair, honest and compassionate when dealing with the needs of those unfortunate individuals who come within the process of the rules contained in the Framework.

Words, words, words: they are not enough, especially when they are used glibly to convince those in need that those in control have your best interests at heart.

Paragraph 67

"Individuals being assessed for NHS CHC are frequently facing significant changes in their life (correct) and therefore a positive experience of the assessment process is crucial (absolutely not correct, my experience was most certainly negative). The process of assessment of eligibility and decision-making should be person-centred. This means placing the individual at the heart of the assessment and care-planning process."

Paragraph 68

This goes on to reinforce these commitments by describing some of the elements to a person-centred approach. Clearly those involved in my wife's assessment had not bothered to read this section, or failed to see the importance of it.

Paragraph 69
This says assessment decision-making should be fair and consistent. (In my wife's case it was certainly not fair and if it was consistent then there are an awful lot more people out there who have been treated unfairly.) It goes on to state there will be no discrimination of any type, including the type of health need, and gives an example as "the need can be physical, mental or psychological.

Paragraph 77
Please note the final sentence: "A third party cannot give or refuse consent for an assessment of eligibility for NHS CHC, or for sharing information, on behalf of a person who lacks capacity, unless they have a valid and applicable lasting power of attorney (Health and Welfare), or they have been appointed as a Deputy (Health and Welfare) by the Court of Protection. The importance of having a lasting power of attorney cannot be over stressed and will be covered in Chapter 7, "The Things You Need to Know and Do".

The next section of the Framework beginning on page 29 is headed "Screening For NHS CHC Using The Checklist Tool - What It Is And Why Is It Used".

Please read and understand fully this section, pages 29 through 37.

A brief summary of this is:

- This screening assessment is used to determine who qualifies to go forward for a full assessment, which uses a "Decision Support Tool"

- Although this could in itself be seen as the third line of defence, you will note that there is yet another (let's call them obstacles from now on) to overcome. I would refer you to paragraph 91: "There will be many situations where it is not necessary to complete a checklist". Situation One: "Where it is clear to practitioners working in the health and care system that there is no need for NHS CHC at this point in time. Where appropriate/relevant this decision and its reasons should be recorded. If there is doubt between practitioners a checklist should be undertaken."

This is exactly what happened in the case of my wife. When I enquired as to whether an assessment had been carried out, her doctor, Dr G, informed me that no, one had not been carried out as it was not necessary as she would not be eligible for CHC. He went on to say it would be futile, which I felt was an unbelievable statement for a doctor to make and along with his misguided reasons for denial, it made me aware of two very important things:

(1) As a senior clinician it was his responsibility to understand and be fully familiar with the rules laid down within the Framework. Due to his answer it was clear he lacked the knowledge to make such an important decision.

(2) It certainly brought it home that if I was to get justice in the form of what my wife was entitled to have, I would have to fight for it. This led me to take the view that there may well be many other people working in this area of CHC who were also not up to speed on their responsibilities of applying the rules in a fair and consistent manner without prejudice or discrimination.

You will have the opportunity to read for yourself in Chapter 9 the correspondence which took place between Dr G and myself, which should in itself help with your motivation to ensure you gain the knowledge you may need.

- The Checklist has eleven care domains broken down into three levels of need. High level of need, medium, low or no need. The level of scoring will determine either a negative assessment and therefore no eligibility for a full assessment, or positive meaning an entitlement to go forward to the full assessment. At least with this checklist there is a pre-determined level for passing or failing.

A full assessment for CHC is required if:

- Two or more domains are selected as high level, or
- Five or more levels are selected as medium, or
- One domain is selected as high but which also carries an asterisk which denotes a priority rating, of which only two domains carry this significance. The scoring in other categories can be any number of selections in the other two levels.

WARNING

(1) Do not expect that the person carrying out this assessment will do so in a completely honest way. They can use this tool to ensure your loved one is not scored sufficiently high enough to meet the criteria as listed above

(2) Make sure you or someone authorised by you is present at the assessment. You have the right to be

there and you have the right to put your case forward if you disagree with their assessment.

In my case after fighting to get an assessment (after being told it was futile) one was conducted without my knowledge or involvement (again, contrary to the rules) and I had to insist on a second assessment where my son and I were present and able to get a far more realistic scoring that allowed for a full assessment to take place.

We now come to pages 34 to 37 – when and where to screen and assess eligibility for NHS CHC.

As you will see from reading about my experiences, when asking for this assessment I had been misinformed by two care home managers that my wife should have been assessed on admission to hospital and that before any care home would accept an admission they would need sight of these as well as conducting their own assessment. I was later to learn from reading the Framework that the former was in fact not the case, which is just one more example of people who should be knowledgeable about the workings of the system not being fully clear on the subject.

Assessment of eligibility for NHS CHC using the Decision Support Tool. Pages 38 to 44.

This is the part of the process that will help decide the financial fate of your loved one. Remember, if you are ultimately assessed as being entitled to CHC then the NHS will pay for your loved one's care fees in total, or if they are being cared for at home it is possible to be granted a personal care budget which once agreed you can spend how you see appropriate, providing of course that it is used for the provision of care. On the other hand, if the outcome is that your loved one is assessed as not being entitled to continuing healthcare then you fall within the local authority social services department. This is a wholly different matter as their services are only provided at their expense if you can prove that the patient has insufficient funds to pay for their own care. This is referred to as "means tested".

The assessment is carried out by a team consisting of at least two professionals who are from different professions, or one professional and one who is responsible for assessing persons who may have needs for care and support under Part 1 of the Care Act 2014.

This team is referred to as a Multi-Disciplinary Team, or MDT, and should usually include both health and social care professionals, <u>who are knowledgeable about the individual's health and social care needs, and where possible have recently been involved in the assessment, treatment or care of the individual.</u>

In the case of my wife's assessment by video conference, the assessment was carried out by a lead nurse from the CCG and a senior manager from social services, both of whom had never met my wife prior to the meeting. Also in attendance was a senior nurse from TOPAS, the facility run by the NHS, where my wife resided and was treated for the four weeks of her sectioning under the Mental Health Act and subsequent time there for a further period approaching an additional two months under DOLS (Deprivation of Liberties). In addition to these was the university student to whom my wife's case was allocated whilst getting work experience, and my son and me. Whilst five out of the six people present contributed to the discussions that took place, the student said nothing beyond introducing herself at the beginning of the meeting. I found there to be nothing unusual about this as she was there to observe and learn from the experience. However, to my utter amazement, disgust and anger I was later to discover that her manager had got her to sign off in agreement with the decision made by him and the lead nurse that my wife was not entitled to CHC. (I believe this was done to help convince the CCG that their decision was the right one, as agreed by _three_ professionals, not the two as was actually the case. After all, three people singing from the same song sheet is more convincing than just two.)

Due to my past experiences both at Hospital X and the misguided views of Dr G, I was concerned that the assessment may not be conducted in a proper manner in accordance with the rules laid down by the Framework. I concluded therefore that I should make a statement prior to the assessment starting, and ask certain questions of them, the answers to which should have given me confirmation that the assessment would be carried out in the way it was intended. More about this in Chapter 10.

It is important to understand how the assessment is conducted using what is referred to as the Decision Support Tool. Equally, if not more so, is the absolute need to know everything you can about your loved one's case, their history, their condition, their abilities and, above all, make sure you are fully familiar with how the assessment should be conducted within the rules of the Framework.

Whilst the ultimate aim of the assessment is to determine the person's eligibility (or not) for Continuing Healthcare, it does so through determining their needs by establishing whether or not they have a primary health need. This is supposedly measured by establishing the complexity and intensity of those needs across the twelve domains listed and the unpredictability and intensity of each of these by ascribing a level of need to each one.

- *Four categories (the most serious) carry a rating under six levels of intensity ranging from no needs, through low, medium, high, severe and priority

- Five categories rate up to five levels between no needs and severe
- *Three categories rate up to four levels between no needs and high.

The twelve care domains are:
   (1) Breathing......................up to Priority
   (2) Nutrition......................up to Severe
   (3) Continence ....up to High
   (4) Skin Integrity ....up to Severe
   (5) Mobility ....up to Severe
   (6) Communication ....up to High
   (7) Psychological/emotional ....up to High
   (8) Cognition ....up to Severe
   (9) Behaviour ....up to Priority
   (10) Drug therapies and medication ....up to Priority
   (11) Altered states of consciousness.....up to Priority
   (12) Other significant health needs.....up to Severe

Domain Twelve is to be used where a person has particular care needs not covered by any of the other eleven.

There are a number of things that are imperative that you do prior to the assessment.

(1) Download a copy of the DST and do your own assessment of your loved one's needs. This is probably best done with another person who has knowledge of their situation and can critique your own thinking, to arrive at what you consider to be a realistic view. You need to be honest and make the necessary notes as to how you formulated your decision. Where possible give examples of occurrences and dates of incidents etc. This endeavour

will best be served by keeping a diary on a daily basis to record such things as changes in behaviour like forgetfulness, aggressiveness, falls, lack of appetite, ability to communicate their needs; instances of unusual behaviour such as talking to people who don't exist; in other words, anything at all that deviates from the ordinary.

(2) Order some more printer ink and paper. It is a small price to pay to arm yourself with all the knowledge you will need. Contact your doctor to get your loved one's complete health records. In my case this amounted to nearly 600 pages, hence the need for the ink and paper. However, remember that health records are private and confidential and to obtain them for someone else, you will undoubtedly be required to produce evidence that you hold power of attorney for the person, in this case attorney for health and welfare. This can only be done at a time when your loved one still retains such ability to freely give their consent for you to act on their behalf and the documentation has been registered and approved by the Office of the Public Guardian. I will give you more information on this in Chapter 7, "The Things You Need to Know and the Things You Need To Do". If your loved one has spent time in hospital or a care home, you might also need to obtain their records in the event that not all information has been updated onto their health records. Unfortunately, having read about many other people's experiences it would appear that some care homes are not as efficient as they ought to be in keeping detailed records.

(3) Make sure you have read and understood everything you can about how the assessment should be conducted in line with the National Framework. If

you happen to be as unlucky as me then unfortunately you may well discover that even when confronted with the facts they still refuse to accept what you are saying. The important thing is they will know you are not someone who is going to acquiesce to their way of thinking and this will aid your case should it be necessary to appeal their decision. Where possible quote the relevant paragraphs within the framework to help make your case. Please remember that the following rules should be adhered to in the assessment and do not be afraid to quote them.

a) Page 42, paragraph 139: "Where deterioration can be reasonably anticipated to take place in the near future, this should also be taken into account, in order to avoid the need for unnecessary or repeat assessments."

b) Page 43, paragraph 142: "The decision-making rationale should not marginalise a need just because it is successfully managed; well-managed needs are still needs. Only where the successful management of a healthcare need has permanently reduced or removed an ongoing need, such that the active management of this need is reduced or no longer required, will this have a bearing on NHS CHC eligibility."

c) Page 39, paragraph 124: "A good quality multi-disciplinary assessment of needs that looks at all of the individual's needs 'in the round' – including the ways in which they interact with one another – is crucial both to addressing these needs and to determining eligibility for NHS CHC." "The individual or, where appropriate, their representative should be enabled to play a central role in the assessment process."

d) Page 19, paragraph 55: "Having a primary health need is not about the reason why an individual requires care or support, nor is it based on their diagnosis; it is about the level and type of their overall actual day-to-day care needs taken in their totality."
e) Page 122, paragraph 30.1: in answer to the question "Can associated needs be recorded in more than one domain on the DST? Yes, needs associated with a single condition can be reflected in more than one domain." "The belief that there is 'NO DOUBLE-SCORING RULE' is a common misconception." "Paragraph 24 of the user notes of the DST makes it clear that the DST is a record of needs and a single condition might give rise to separate needs in a number of domains." "All of which should be recorded and weighed in their own right."

These five quotations from the National Framework are used as examples of areas that you may well have a need to quote based on my own experiences, but are not intended to be an exhaustive list, as you may well feel the need to be aware of other things contained in it that may also be applicable to your needs.

(4) Set up a filing system with an index so you can readily access the information you may wish to refer to at the assessment meeting.

Hopefully, you will by now appreciate the need to furnish yourself with your own copy of the Framework and be sufficiently motivated to read it and highlight the most relevant and important aspects of it.

There are many other subjects covered therein, not least how to appeal a rejection of entitlement to CHC funding which I sincerely hope you will not need to do. Unfortunately I fear that the chances are that, given the statistics and the obstacles they seem to use, this will more than likely be the case.

I do, however, wish to point out the other provision contained therein which is referred to as "The Fast-track Assessment".

In essence this "end of life care choice commitment" is used in the case of those people who have been identified as having reached this unhappy point in their lives as their condition starts to rapidly deteriorate.

Rightly so, this fast-track assessment is designed to be less onerous in its assessment as indeed time is most assuredly of the essence. In fact, this could be construed as being the sign of a caring and compassionate system being operated by a part of the NHS in exactly the way it was intended and living up to its boast of being "free at the point of need".

Whilst I take no issue with this provision for those people who have reached this point in their life span, my issue is with the application of CHC for those people who are not judged by a flawed system to be in need of this level of care at a time in their lives when such help is desperately needed.

The real difficulty I personally have is that there are no qualms at refusing help to those in need, which is backed up by lies and non-conformity to the rules. This is despite the fact that it is stated in the Framework that any decision on eligibility should not be made on any financial constraint or judgement. If limiting a service or need for care requires a change in the application of those rules to allow those reaching the end of life, then it must be clear that this in itself is a judgement that has been taken to limit the cost to the NHS and therefore is taking into account financial costs, contrary to the rules laid down in the Framework.

The NHS issues a press notice on NHS CHC and NHS-funded nursing care data on a quarterly basis and it makes for some interesting reading with reference to the statistics provided therein.

In view of the fact that Covid has played such a large role in the operation of the NHS over the past two years, I felt it was appropriate to look at their reports over a three-year period, being 2018/19, 2019/2020 and 2020/2021.

The first table headed "Referrals" gives the number of incomplete standard NHS CHC referrals that exceeded the goal of twenty-eight days as stated in the National Framework. Whilst one could reasonably expect a delay in dealing with some of these referrals, especially in 2020/2021 due to Covid, there seems to be no reasonable or similar excuse in the figures for 2018/2019 or the excessive numbers in the four-twenty-six-week range and for those over twenty weeks. Where is the care and compassion in dealing with these?

Exceeded By	2018/2019	2019/2020	2020/2021
Up to 2 weeks	525	709	766
Between 2 and 4 weeks	377	406	533
Between 4 and 12 Weeks	557	555	1070
Between 12 and 26 Weeks	422	286	823
Over 26 Weeks	672	273	816
TOTALS	2553	2229	4008

This next table shows the total number of persons found to be eligible for Continuing Healthcare both through the standard assessment and the fast-track processes, with their respective conversion rates.

	2018/2019	2019/2020	2020/2021
Eligible by Standard Assessment process	56,395	53,886	46,255
Conversion rate	19%	18%	20%
Eligible by Fast-track process Conversion rate	104,461	111,752	88,988
	96%	95%	96%
Total found eligible for the year	160,856	165,638	135,243
Total number of CCG contributing	195	191	135

It should be noted that the significant reduction in the number of CCGs contributing is, as I understand it, due to an amalgamation of some CCGs through reorganisation and probably due at least in part to the forthcoming scrapping of the CCGs in the near future.

Although it is not entirely clear whether the conversion rates are for the entire year or just the last quarter, as there is consistency within the figures to within 1% or 2% it is not unreasonable to use these to calculate the total numbers.

This table shows the total number of assessments that took place using the figures from the previous table with the total number of persons who had their applications rejected.

	2018/ 2019	2019/ 2020	2020/ 2021
Total number of Standard Assessments	296,815	299,366	231,275
Total number of unsuccessful assessments	240,420	245,480	185,020
Total number of Fast Track Assessments	108,813	117,633	92,695
Total number of unsuccessful assessments	4,352	5,881	3,707
Overall numbers	405,628	416,999	323,970
Overall numbers of unsuccessful	244,772	251,361	188,727
Overall percentage of those people who had their application for CHC rejected	60.34%	60.27%	58.25%

So what conclusions, if any, can be made from these statistics? What is that saying ... "Statistics, statistics and damn lies". I guess the meaning being that different people will inevitably have a different conclusion from an identical set of figures dependent upon their viewpoint and what they wish to prove.

For my part and for what it's worth I would make the following observations.

(1) The fast-track option is only available to people who are not currently receiving NHS CHC. It would therefore follow that people who qualify to be considered under this option must come (in my opinion) from one of the four following categories:
   a. People who have suddenly experienced serious deterioration in their health, who previously did not require help of any kind, which could have been the result of being infected with a life-threatening disease or as a result of sustaining serious injury through an accident.
   b. People who have been getting care through other agencies other than NHS CHC, whether funded through those agencies or through self-funding.
   c. People who have previously applied for and been denied NHS CHC due to the fact that their CCG through the recommendation of an MDT did not consider their needs to be sufficiently serious enough to classify them as a primary health need.
   d. People who were denied the right to even have an assessment for NHS CHC, either because they fell at the first hurdle of being denied even a screening assessment, or because of the lack of public promotion were not even aware of its very existence.

(2) In view of the above there can be little doubt that the majority of those given the fast-track are made up in the majority by persons who were previously denied NHS CHC by the other normal route.

(3) The figures show that over the past three years only between 18% and 20% of the standard assessments have been approved for NHS CHC. However, these figures do not include those denied a full assessment

for the following reasons and for which it does not seem possible to obtain any actual numbers.

a. What was the total number of screening assessments that took place in the same period and how many of these were in fact rejected as not being worthy of a full assessment?
b. How many people who knew about the process were informed that their loved one's condition was not covered by CHC and consequently even denied this initial screening?
c. How many people were told that their needs were simply social needs and therefore also denied this initial screening assessment?
d. How about the unknown numbers of people who, through the lack of promotion by CCGs, fell at the first hurdle because they were totally unaware of its very existence?

One can only hazard a guess at what the true scale of the numbers are in relation to those people who are self-funding their loved ones' care.

It may well be that the system is set up this way because of the enormous costs involved in providing care.

That does not however excuse them from their legal obligations or give anyone the right to tell lies and effectively rob those hard-working families who throughout their lives have contributed through their NHI payments and taxes.

If NHS CHC is unaffordable then surely there can in reality be only two solutions: one is to find the way to make it affordable for all those who should be entitled to it, or be honest and tell the nation the reality of the situation. It will never be right to lie and cheat, but it is disgraceful to place the burden on the shoulders of only one sector of the population.

Try as I might, I have failed to get any information on the statistics that would show or indeed prove beyond doubt whether or not people with dementia are unreasonably denied NHS CHC in relation to the awarding of funding to other persons suffering from any other physical disease.

Unsurprisingly, the Framework makes it perfectly clear that the diagnosis of any particular medical condition has nothing to do with the awarding or not for CHC funding. It centres on establishing "a primary health need". This in itself makes it possible to argue that there is no need to keep such records, as diagnosis of a particular condition has nothing to do with establishing who is entitled to CHC funding. Now that is convenient, isn't it.

We are left therefore with making a judgement without the full facts. However, we do know that there are firms of lawyers who specialise in helping people fight against this injustice of being refused CHC funding. Take a look at as many of these firms as you like and note through their advertising and case histories that in the main they are dealing with cases involving any one of the mental diseases that fall under the umbrella of dementia. That is not to say there are not also injustices that affect people with other non-mental diseases, but is the scale of these anything approaching that of dementia patients?

A very wise man once told me at a very young age that "the true cost of anything is the price you pay for the alternative". This little phrase has remained with me throughout my life and has helped me to make all manner of decisions from little ones to life-changing ones. To those people who may think this is stupid and makes no sense I give you this thought.

If you can afford only one of two things that you want, at a particular point in time, then your choice is this or that; it will never be both without either having to borrow the money for one item or stealing it from someone else.

This brings me nicely onto my next chapter: Who Really Pays?

5

WHO REALLY PAYS

I'm starting this chapter by asking you to think about a well-known puzzle that many readers will immediately know how to solve, but in the event that there may be some people who have not come across it before, I believe it has relevance to what our situation is all about, and that is:

Draw a square with a cross in the middle where the two diagonals join the opposite corners of the square. The only proviso is that this must be done by using straight lines only and not removing your pencil from the paper and that no line must be repeated by going over it again. We will return to this later on.

You may recall that in Chapter 1 I talked about most companies merely being vehicles to provide the owners and/or shareholders with a reasonable or good rate of return on the investment they had made. How successful they are in this endeavour is either being in the "Happiness" or "Misery Zone".

The institution we all know as our National Health Service does not generally feel constrained by this need to keep its shareholders in the financial "Happy Zone". Maybe that's because it's an institution funded by the government and those people needing to avail themselves of its services appear to care nothing about how it's funded, what things cost, and if things could be achieved in a more efficient way. I well remember when the subject of foreign nationals was in the limelight. Some doctors were interviewed on national TV news and documentary programmes and were quite open about their reluctance or refusal to ask patients for the reimbursement of their treatment costs, or to even complete the necessary forms to record such activity which would enable the NHS to at least have a fighting chance at getting some payments from people who had not contributed to the system. In many cases those individuals may well have had private health insurance prior to coming to our country, just like most of us would do if travelling abroad for business or pleasure. These doctors seemed to suggest, in defence of their position, that they were there purely to aid the unwell and those in need no matter from where they came. They seemingly felt they had no obligation to their employers, who in the end are all the taxpayers and contributors to NHI.

So on one hand we have some doctors who are seemingly quite happy to deprive the genuinely needy who have contributed to the system, through their refusal to even give a screening assessment to some of their patients for NHS CHC. At the same time some of their colleagues do the exact opposite and are happy to provide services free of charge to anyone they choose.

One can only hope that a third group exists that plays by the rules and understands that "the true cost of anything is the price you pay for the alternative".

I would now like to talk a little bit about the big differences in the operation of some businesses, the relevance of which plays a major part in who ultimately pays for goods and services, but more importantly how much you pay.

We are all familiar with the fact that businesses either provide goods or services in one form or another, or indeed a mixture of the two.

In most cases there is a common bond that binds them together with an overhead and challenge they have to manage to ensure they stay in the Happy Zone.

One way or another, their vehicle for making a living is at risk through their stock in trade. Some sell goods that go off, or have a short shelf life, like fresh food, or goods that can go out of fashion or become obsolete through advancement of science and technology etc. Then of course there are goods and services with a longer shelf life, like dried, frozen or tinned foods, but these too have a shelf life, albeit a longer one. Even some services or skills can have an end date; maybe the advice that people are willing to pay you for becomes obsolete, and a change in the law may be enough to wipe out your business. Just how many Coopers (Hoopers) are there left making wooden barrels?

Some businesses are undoubtedly more at risk than others and also have to contend with what they politely call shrinkage, or to you and me, theft. In the end any loss of stock for whatever reason has to be paid for one way or another, which probably means we all pay more for what we purchase to cover the cost of these losses.

Naturally there are always exceptions to any rule; if your business is in fine wines then maybe your stock actually becomes more valuable in time. Some garden centres will benefit from certain stock items that didn't sell one season, then purely because the trees/shrubs etc. have gained another year's growth, they can be increased in price the following year.

You may well be asking yourself why I am talking about such obvious things and what relevance it has to the subject of care!

There are other businesses that don't fall into this generalisation but can be grouped together by virtue of the fact that their stock in trade is specifically time sensitive, on a day-by-day basis.

An unsold train, bus or aeroplane seat is gone for ever once they leave the station or airport. A hotel room that remains unsold for any night is lost for good for that night; it has in effect perished.

For these reasons we see last minute bargains, particularly from airplane operators and hotels; after all, better to get something rather than nothing. The trick is to do it in such a way as to not devalue the product or upset the travellers or guests who have paid full price. The cost of selling those last-minute bargains could result in you finding that your regular customers start to delay making their booking in the future, for which they pay full price, in the expectation of getting a deal.

Now we come to the reality of the situation and the reason why I chose to call this chapter "Who Really Pays".

A care home is nothing more than a specialist hotel which by its very nature has no need to provide some of those things you would expect in a normal hotel, but obviously needs to provide other services you wouldn't find in a conventional hotel.

Remember it is still just a vehicle for the owners/shareholders to make a good living and remain in the "Happy Zone".

In order for me to make the point about what you need to know, I am going to give an example using simple figures that may or may not represent actual cases, but rest assured any reduction or increase in numbers, percentages or costs does not change the reality of how the system operates.

Let us begin by imagining that we are looking to start a business and we believe a care home would be a good business.

Firstly we would do a business plan, which would identify all normal things expected such as location, market, set up and running costs, availability of personnel, suitability of premises etc.

Within this plan we would do a projection of likely expected income, which in simplistic terms would be:

- The number of bed spaces or rooms
- The expected bed/room occupancy levels in percentage terms
- The daily/weekly charge rate for that room.

Let us imagine that our plan shows us having 100 rooms with an average weekly occupancy rate of say 90%, and that having looked in detail at all fixed and variable expenses and included loan costs and returns on capital invested we conclude that the charge rate we need to stay in our "Happy Zone" is say £1,000 per week per room. We know we have given ourselves a margin of error and the opportunity to do even better if we can increase our occupancy level above 90% with the spare ten rooms at our disposal.

So prior to opening our business we set about marketing and promoting our business to make the public aware of our existence. We realise that social services will be a good source of recommendation for those people who will be self-funding their loved ones' care but also that social services are a source of direct placement for individuals who are funded directly by the local authority.

Oops, the local authority tells us that they are indeed always looking for suitable placements for people who come under their care, and inform us they could within a short period of time look to place say forty people within our care.

However, their budget has constraints and with the numbers on offer they will only pay £500 per week.

This is a double-edged sword in that if socially funded persons are rejected then it is unlikely they will recommend those persons who will be self-funding their own care.

So using this as an example we need to look again at our business plan in terms of income.

Desired: 90 rooms occupied x £1,000 per week = £90,000
Achievable: 50 rooms x £1,000 per week = £50,000
 +
40 rooms x £500 per week = £20,000
 = £70,000

Result: in the "Misery Zone" to the tune of £20,000 per week.

This would be unsustainable, so you can guess who pays the shortfall. Simple – those people who are self-funding; their costs have now increased by £400 per week (i.e. 50 x £400).

No wonder care home fees are so high, because those who are deemed to be able to afford it are not only paying for their own care but they are also subsidising the care of someone who could be sat right next to them in the home and paying nothing.

Are we not led to believe that it is prudent and sensible to save for our old age, when in fact the opposite may well be the wisest thing to do!

However, the story doesn't end there; we've not mentioned that old devil called greed. In their attempt to get a good deal for the public purse, the local authority has inadvertently skewed the market. The going rate for a week's care and accommodation has risen by £400; we'd be mad to think that all the other care homes who don't have socially funded guests now see that they can charge more for their services.

Remember this phrase: "Everything is relative to comparison".

I would ask you the reader to think carefully about the cost of a stay in a modern, clean hotel, inclusive of a full English breakfast. Compare this with the average daily cost of a care home.

So, who really pays? Now you know, or you think you do.

Maybe you watched the two-part documentary presented by Ed Balls, where he went to work in a care home in Scarborough, Yorkshire, and sampled first-hand not only what it was like to provide the care, but also the impact it had on the families whose loved ones were being cared for.

I thought it was refreshing to hear an ex-politician admit that he regretted not doing more when he was in a position of power and how he appreciated that the system needs a complete overhaul for the benefit of both the cared for and those providing the care. The documentaries touched on the fact that some residents were subsidising the care of other residents, but I think the interview he conducted with the owners of the care home he was working in was even more so. In fact for me I think it could be described as a lightbulb moment.

The father and son who owned and managed the care home that Ed Balls was working in, along with three others in the town, explained how their occupancy rates had slumped, caused part by the sad demise of a number of residents due to Covid.

They went on to state that if occupancy rates didn't improve substantially in the near future their business model would be unable to sustain the losses and would inevitably lead to closure or bankruptcy. Amazingly in the second programme it was reported that the vacancies they had been experiencing had mainly been addressed and the homes' occupancy levels were then back up to acceptable levels.

Now I understood.

From my very first meeting with my wife's doctor, Dr G, in the facility where she had been admitted following her sectioning under the Mental Health Act, he was quite firm in his belief that my wife should be discharged into a care home and, even though my preference was to have her come home, which he thought not to be wise, he did say he would sanction this in the first instance to see if I would cope.

All along from that point in time it was assumed that we would be self-funding with the allocated social worker (a student on work experience) asking me to complete financial disclosures etc., all of which I refused to do on the basis I felt the cart was being put before the horse because of the lack of willingness to complete a screening assessment.

Because I was unwilling to acquiesce to these demands until I had at least had the opportunity to get an assessment for NHS CHC, it was agreed that my wife could come home for a few hours, accompanied by two members of the Occupational Therapy team and the social worker.

This visit consisted of the OTs, accompanied by me, doing an assessment of our home to see if they felt it represented any risks to her. Quite understandably comments were made about such things as rugs being trip hazards, the need for additional grab rails in the shower, toilet frames etc., their principal concern being that they thought it was possible for her to fall over the balustrade, being the standard height for such a safety feature and approved by building regulations.

I had no hesitation in confirming to them that I would have a new balustrade fitted at an increased height and a door fitted at the top of the stairs and remove all rugs. On their part they would arrange for toilet frames and a grab rail to be fitted.

Following this inspection the OTs then aided Margaret up and down the stairs to assess how they felt she would be able to cope. They expressed concern that she would be unable to do this on her own, and I immediately informed them that there would never be a need, as I would always be here to assist her and would never dream of leaving her in a position where she could attempt this on her own.

After this visit it was agreed that a further visit would be made the following week with a repeat of the stair assessment.

On this second visit Margaret was again accompanied by the two OTs, but also in attendance was the case nurse from The Memory Clinic and a more senior social services team member.

While the OTs went ahead with their stairs assessment I was left to talk with the other two personnel about my position.

Suffice to say that I was told by the senior social services team member that in her opinion I would not be entitled to funding through the NHS CHC as she had seen many, many cases of patients in a far worse condition than my wife who had all been refused funding. I pointed out to her that this had no relevance to my situation, and these other people's rejection for funding didn't necessarily mean that they were correct. The conversation turned to the need for me to complete a financial assessment, as I would no doubt be self-funding. Again, I refused such a request and confirmed that I did not consider it appropriate to do so at that time.

The OTs reported back that they had grave concerns for my wife's safety and also that of myself in negotiating the stairs on a daily basis. They then made an alternative suggestion of moving her bed downstairs into the lounge.

I refrained from stating how stupid I thought this suggestion was, in view of the fact that it would require both of us to sleep in the lounge if I was to properly care for her 24/7.

I informed them that this was not a solution as there was no shower downstairs, but stated that I would look into getting a lift fitted to overcome this objection.

It does have to be said it felt very much like they were trying to find ways to persuade me that my wife would be better off in a care home.

As the care industry is mainly reliant upon private enterprise, it doesn't take a genius to realise that a crisis will inevitably occur if these private businesses are unable to maintain a viable income by having high occupancy levels. With so many deaths over a short period of time during the Covid pandemic, this situation must have been arising throughout the length and breadth of the country.

A severe reduction in the number of care homes would present serious problems for the future of this sector. So what is the solution? Either the government must prop them up by way of subsidies, or find a way of getting more people into care who have sufficient assets to be able to pay for their own care.

It is my firm belief that the latter option was embarked upon, and I have little doubt that many people reside in care homes who shouldn't or don't need to be there.

Again, the honest hard-working individuals who, throughout their lives, have paid their taxes and made their contributions to the so-called NHS through NHI are being treated like a cash cow for a sector that successive governments have failed to tackle. For too long, governments, no matter of what political persuasion, have treated this as a hot potato in the hope that their opposite numbers will tackle it when they get into power.

I have no particular allegiance to any particular party; in the main each party does whatever they think is necessary to attract sufficient votes to remain in power or to snatch it from their opposition. What is the saying? "Power corrupts and absolute power corrupts absolutely."

We have seen how the Conservatives, under Margaret Thatcher, embarked upon a policy of selling off the public utilities into private ownership, on the basis that they would be better managed and more efficient with greater choice for the consumer. That coupled with their policy of selling off the public housing stock at a knockdown price was all aimed, in my opinion, at believing that those people who benefited, in large numbers, substantially from such policies would be eternally grateful and continue to vote for their party. We all know how this turned out. Utilities owned in part by foreign governments and greedy capitalist companies, not to mention the vast numbers of people who are now reliant upon private landlords with inflated rentals, and in some instances vastly inadequate standards of quality.

It didn't work, did it? The New Labour Party promised better, and enjoyed a decade of power. They embarked upon, amongst other things, another way of getting voters to be forever grateful to them, by encouraging mass immigration, again believing these new breed of voters would remain loyal to their party; but that also didn't work, did it?

We now have another Conservative government who are making claims to have limited the cost of care to the extent that people will no longer be forced to sell their houses to fund their care by limiting that cost to a little over £80,000+, after which the state will step up and be responsible.

Let's face it: this is yet one more example of putting a positive spin on something that is claiming to be something that it's not.

The reality is that a person going into care will still have to fund the "hotel" element of their stay in a care home. The package is split into two specific elements, care and accommodation, the latter being the cost of providing those things that are needed by everyone, be they young, old, rich, poor, healthy or unwell. The former being those things specific to persons who are far from healthy, people who need assistance to carry out basic functions of the body just to exist, and which will eventually be covered by this new £80,000+ limit.

In simple terms, providing meals is a hotel function; getting the food into the mouth of the resident is a care function.

I pose this question: who determines the true costs involved in what is provided under each element?

Let's say we thought about this as a hotel that offered a package which included accommodation, all meals and, let's say, free use of an adjoining golf course, where the course is provided by the state and looks only to recover the running costs from the hotel owners.

Under this scenario the course is a non-profit-making endeavour, whereas the hotel is a fully commercial undertaking with owners and shareholders looking for a return on their investment. Imagine the state has agreed with the hotel owners that the cost of running the golf course will be £X,000 per annum, but if it exceeds this amount then the state will pick up the shortfall. Let's add to this scenario that it has been determined by the NHS that a long stay in such a place with daily exercise in the form of walking around the golf course will have health benefits for the individuals they deem to be in need of such treatment.

The hotel will provide the accommodation and meals and will determine their own running costs and decide what in their view a reasonable profit is for the owners and shareholders.

An unlikely scenario, I know, but the point is the reality of this new part-funded package being proposed by the government is just as crazy.

Who determines the cost of the care element of the package?

If it is left up to the NHS then it is clearly in their interests to keep this to the absolute minimum; after all, the smaller the sum the longer it will take to reach the threshold of this magical £80,000+ figure before they have to fund it. This also has massive implications for the cost of providing care for those people who are not self-funding and are solely their responsibility. We have already learnt that this principle is currently in play with social care driving down their costs to the detriment of those who are self-funding. Importantly, the longer this figure takes to reach the threshold the longer the patient will be funding the entire package.

How can any reasonable-minded person boast that there will be no need for anyone to sell their house in the future under this "amazing new initiative"? There are too many unknowns to make such claims e.g. the cost of the hotel element, the length of time before the ceiling for state aid is reached, the assets a person has accumulated, the value of their property and not least how long they are likely to live.

It may well be a step towards trying to provide an answer to this long-lasting dilemma on how to look after an ageing population, but it is a very small step, when in reality it needs to be a giant leap to truly make a difference.

There are pretty much always alternative ways to solve any problem by looking at each one from a different viewpoint.

We should look at problems as an opportunity to find a better solution.

The next chapter offers some thoughts on these opportunities; some you will find to be completely outrageous, but I make the point that with determination and the will to make a change, maybe we can all find a way to move towards a more equal and just society.

6

TRYING TO FIND SOLUTIONS

Let's start by looking at a solution to the puzzle that was posed at the beginning of Chapter 5.

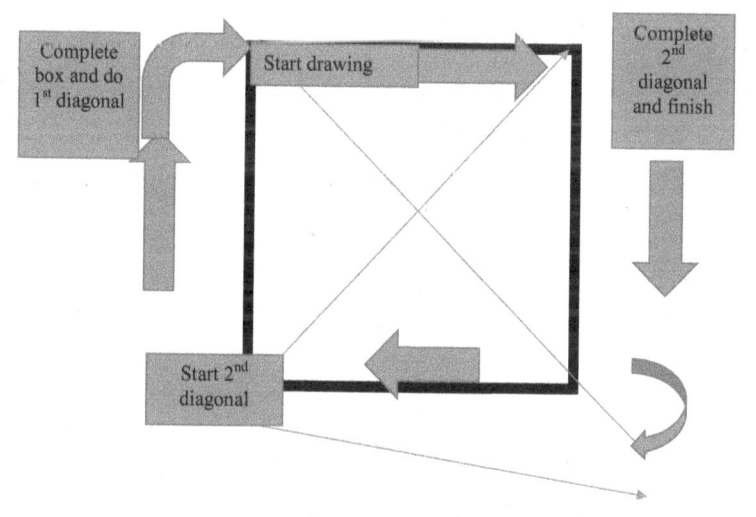

We have now completed the task set without removing pencil from the paper. This typifies the meaning of thinking outside the box.

Just because something has always been done in a certain way does not mean that it is the only way to achieve a certain result, and it may well be that there is a better solution to be found by other means.

We are governed by a system that we refer to as being democratic; each and every eligible citizen has the right to vote for who they think will do the best job at running the country by forming a majority party from which to form the government. Every so often we are given the opportunity to think again and cast our vote in what we feel is then appropriate at that time.

I am truly tired of hearing the same old clichés from politicians who claim to have entered politics with the one desire to make a change and make this a better country to live in and a fairer and more compassionate society.

How can so many people with such similar noble desires keep failing all manner of different sectors of our citizens?

It can be particularly galling to hear them calling each other "The Right and Honourable Lady or Gentleman from X constituency". In some instances, these people are often not right and not honourable in what they do.

I do accept that there will be "bad apples" in any large organisation or group of people, be they lying politicians, bent coppers, uncaring carers, unhelpful and unwilling doctors, thieving and shoddy tradespeople, rude and ignorant service providers; the list is endless. However, whilst I also appreciate the custom of calling each other right and honourable is seen as having respect for each other no matter what political leaning they have, it amazes me that there is very little evidence of cross-party agreement on matters which should be common to all no matter what party is making the proposal. It almost feels as though if one party says this is black the others will argue that it's white, blue, yellow, red, grey, almost anything to disagree.

Finding a better way of doing something and becoming more profitable in the case of businesses need not always be about increasing turnover or selling something for a higher price. Making savings on costs, reducing wastage and generally being more efficient as well as treating the workforce with respect and appreciation can all make for a more profitable outcome.

Can such practices translate from business into mammoth institutions like the NHS, or other government-funded services?

With a little more out-of-the-box thinking, I'm sure they can; after all, politicians seem to be very adept at out-of-the-box thinking when it comes to trying to justify their own actions when they get exposed for doing things they shouldn't.

We live in a crazy world, with mixed messages coming from our elected leaders. On one hand we are advised to save for our retirement and old age, but on the other hand we are encouraged to get out there and spend to help the economy. I can well remember Gordon Brown substantially increasing the road tax rates for fuel-guzzling cars, all justified by the belief that this would encourage consumers to purchase smaller and lower fuel consumption vehicles. It was not long after this that Jaguar/Land Rover was sold to the Indian company Tata who was subsequently bailed out to the tune of millions of pounds to save the company and jobs by keeping production in this country. Get rid of the gas guzzlers – oh no, wait a minute, we need the jobs . . . Make your mind up!

On a similar subject, we saw the scrappage scheme introduced to save jobs and production and give a boost to the economy. Why didn't they give more thought to the consequences of their actions? This disastrous policy resulted, in my opinion, to various negative effects, not least:

- A substantial cost to the taxpayer, money that could have been spent on other more worthwhile causes

- The loss of many good and serviceable vehicles that had not come to the end of their useful lives

- The carbon footprint of their original production was replaced by yet more in the production of new vehicles

- The expectation of a younger generation was altered to believe that they could have it all. Borrow the money and buy a new car, or lease a brand new one; after all, there were less old cars for them to purchase. Remember, the true cost of anything is the price you pay for the alternative

- Why do we hear so many moans about how life is unfair to youngsters of today because they can't get a foot on the property ladder; could this not be connected to the fact that they have made a choice like driving around in a new car, drinking expensive coffees, always having what they want when they want it? "Everything is relative to comparison." Maybe the introduction of credit cards has had the most detrimental effect on society in modern times. Being able to spend the money you have not yet earned comes at great cost as it immediately devalues the money you will earn in the future by virtue of the fact you have to pay back what you borrowed at a high rate of interest.

I can recall talking to a thirty-year-old man whom I was working alongside, and I asked him if he was married. His reply was quite shocking. He didn't feel he would ever be able to afford to get married as he was still living with his parents and had debts of over £40,000. At the time I know I was shocked and asked him how he had managed to get into such debt; after all, with no mortgage, no furniture to buy etc., living at his parents' home and with no expensive car, I honestly couldn't imagine how he was spending his earnings. He explained that he liked to live the "high life" and loved to go on expensive holidays. He went on to tell me that only recently he had obtained a new credit card with a limit of £3,000 which he had spent within a week by going to

London, staying in a posh hotel, drinking champagne and eating expensive food.

Clearly, he was not using his common sense in managing his affairs; he was, in effect, living for the day with no regards for his future happiness. Clearly a path to disaster and inevitably misery.

One more example is when I was stood behind a lady at the checkout, waiting to pay for the fuel I had just put in my car. She was purchasing no fewer than 100 x £1.00 lottery scratch cards, telling the person serving her that "she had now got it sussed". Can you believe it? Well it's a true story and yet we had a government at the time that was embarking on the madness of lifting all manner of restrictions that had previously been in place to protect people from themselves when it came to gambling. What do we now have? An industry that preys on the vulnerable, with advertising across the many types of media, which encourages people to enjoy a little flutter on this or that with the pretence they are doing the right thing by adding the strapline "Gamble responsibly". Gambling can become addictive and lead to misery for not only some gamblers but their families when it gets out of hand. The addiction is real with real consequences, especially when the addict starts to believe that chasing their losses is the only way of resolving their problems. Because of the unending advertising that now forms part of so many popular sporting events it exposes young minds to the belief that it is quite normal to gamble on the outcome of who will win and who will lose. If it was right to ban advertising for tobacco products why was it right to lift the ban that had been in place for many years on gambling. Does this really make sense?

All this was sold by the New Labour government as giving the public freedom of choice; after all, is this not what people want? Let's get rid of the nanny state! Unfortunately, not only do some people need to be protected for their own good, but they also need to be protected for the benefit of the rest of society. What is the true cost of this gambling epidemic? With family breadwinners spending their wages in the hope of getting a big win, working and middle-class people driven into poverty, children going without food and clothes because Mum and or Dad had a flutter! How many well-to-do people do you know who lost a fortune by gambling? There are no doubt some, but not many, of that I'm sure.

The phrase that springs to mind is that by the acclaimed French writer and philosopher Voltaire, back in the eighteenth century: "Common sense is not so common", and yet here we are over 250 years later, believing it is possessed by everyone!

The reality is that society has the ability to care for everyone in need; the problem is that there has to be a willingness to find the way, and it all comes back to "The true cost of anything is the price we pay for the alternative."

Just imagine what could be achieved if everyone paid the taxes that were due and lessened the burden on those who have no choice but to do so. Generally speaking those people who work and come within the PAYE system have no option but to pay their dues, this being taxes on income and contributions to NHI. When making payments for goods from most companies they contribute further by payment of VAT or possibly other taxes such as import duties etc. In fact, the only way they may cheat their tax liabilities is in getting someone to give a service or provide goods by making a cash payment (off the books).

Hereby hangs the main problem: cash. It's not easily traceable, so the taxman finds it difficult to get at his fair share, which ultimately means some members of society are not only richer than they should be, but their improved lifestyle is funded by those paying their fair share. This is similar to the example of those funding care homes.

As we inch forward to a cashless society the ideal would be to do this in a much more determined and speedy way.

I would recommend reading *The Curse of Cash* written by Kenneth Rogoff, a Harvard economist. It offers an insight into the effects of still using a system of payment and reward that is now outdated and costly to society as a whole.

Amongst many other things he argues that cash enables at least three things to thrive:

(1) Massive criminal activity where cash is a medium of exchange which is highly favoured by criminal enterprises throughout the world, be it drug-related, people smuggling, counterfeit goods, bribery and corruption etc. to name just a few

(2) Those people who, in what public finance economists refer to as a "horizontal equity problem", work for firms who use cash to get around all manner of laws designed to protect the public. These may include such things as anti-pollution laws, the use of illegal workers and production of illegal or inferior goods etc. Their use of cash enables them to not only dodge their liabilities for taxes but at the same time gives them a competitive advantage over their competition, all of which drives down wages for the honest domestic worker

(3) Payment by cash, by otherwise law abiding-citizens, enables them to get something cheaper than would otherwise be the case, but such actions help others avoid their tax liabilities.

It is roughly estimated by the economist Friedrich Schneider that the size of the underground economy in Europe, excluding most illegal activities, would be in the region of $3 trillion (for 2016). He estimated that the United Kingdom's underground economy as a percentage of GDP averaged at around 11% for the 2003-2016 period.

Just imagine the amount of additional taxes that would be paid if this underground economy ceased to exist, but more importantly what the additional tax revenues could fund.

So the answer is simple: get rid of cash and make all payments by bank transfers, something a lot of people are already doing. With contactless debit and credit cards and the increased upper limits, it has become a better option for those people who only receive their income directly into their bank account. No more fumbling for change or waiting for it, no more trips to the bank or cash machines to restock on cash. Not such a good option for those who don't currently pay their share of taxes.

If only it were that simple. There are a number of things that make the ultimate move away from this ancient system of payment difficult to achieve, not least would be:

- It would require determination and global agreement to make such a move away from a system that has serviced the human race well for a very long time. If only a few countries tried to go it alone, we would no doubt just see a flood of other countries' currencies being used as an alternative

- There would no doubt be a great deal of reluctance to accept such a system, not only from those who benefit from its existence and work in the underground economy, but many law-abiding citizens who have an understandable mistrust of the banking system and a fear that they could lose everything. (Hmmm sounds familiar; that would be like being a victim of dementia, without the dementia.)

- The criminal fraternity would be forced to look for other ways to transact their business and would no doubt use some of their wealth to persuade some of the most powerful decision makers that this would not be a good idea.

There are probably many, many more reasons that could be cited for keeping cash as a global means of exchange for goods and services. Each and every one would require out-of-the-box thinking and a determination and willingness to find the answers; the fact is, the rewards are high, not just in terms of the extra taxes this would inevitably bring, but more importantly what those taxes will pay for, for the benefit of society as a whole.

As we have previously said, "Necessity is the Mother of Invention". What could be more necessary than reducing crime, increasing the number of people who pay their due taxes and helping those people who are in need? Surely this is the measure of a civilised and compassionate society?

As human beings it is in our DNA to look for improved ways of doing things; if it wasn't, we would still be living in caves, scratching on the walls with bits of stone and clubbing other species to death in order to survive.

Each generation picks up the ball and runs with it until it is the time of the next generation to inherit all that their forebearers have learnt and improve upon it.

I am still amazed by the achievements of the human race and in particular what improvements, inventions and innovations have taken place in just the past 120 years. Imagine what your great grandparents, or even your grandparents (dependent upon your age) would make of the world we live in today; they wouldn't believe it. It's hard to imagine where we might be in another 120 years.

The Wright brothers are credited with being the first to fly a small engine plane in 1903 and yet it was only sixty-six years later that Neil Armstrong and Buzz Aldrin were walking on the Moon. Incredible.

In World War Two we saw the sowing of the seeds of things that today we take for granted. Allan Turing was laughed at, belittled, disbelieved and vilified for what he believed in. Yet he persevered, he believed in his own abilities, and with a small group of others who also had faith in him he gave the world the first computer, and in so doing probably saved thousands of lives. He of course was not alone in having faith in his own abilities; who on earth could have imagined a bouncing bomb? Barnes Wallis did, amongst his other achievements. There were many other inventions and the formation of different ways of doing things that owe their very existence to men and women who truly thought outside the box without the worry of being seen to be stupid or crazy. They knew the true reality of not being confined to a set way of doing things and were able to produce what many others believed to be impossible.

I mention these achievements because I believe many people will see the idea of scrapping money as unachievable, therefore not worthy of a second thought. No doubt some will say that to get the whole world to agree to a major change in the way we do something is in itself an impossible task. I don't agree; it just needs to be enough people who see the advantages to give their support to the idea. I doubt very much if there aren't millions of people who, for a variety of reasons, feel it would be better for society to spread the burden of taxes amongst us all and at the same time help towards reducing crime on such a massive scale.

This got me to want to find an example of a modern-day equivalent, where the world has adopted a different way of finding a more efficient way of doing things, which also may have originally started out as a necessity in a small way but grew at a rapid pace to where we are today.

There are of course many examples of advancements in technology which have been adopted by the citizens of the world and have become almost essential to modern-day living. However, most of these didn't require a determination on the part of governments to make them happen, and certainly not all at the same time. If we think about the growth in the use of mobile phones, computers, the internet etc., all of these required a certain amount of capital investment by governments for them to be truly global, but the demand grew by the initial investment of private enterprise and a growing demand from the populace.

So is there an example, in modern times, of a change in the way we do things, that essentially gives us an example of how all nations can pull together if the rewards and incentives are great enough? Something that required massive capital investment in infrastructure and a willingness to see the rewards that such a change could bring, something that was so big a change that it became obvious that the only way forward required every large nation on Earth to participate? A truly global co-operation that was committed to throwing out the old way of doing things and bringing in a new and exciting alternative?

Although this idea had its roots in the past, it was mainly born out of necessity and, as is often the case, through the vision and determination of one individual.

The man widely hailed as the inventor of the most important element of this change was Malcolm McLean, a truck driver and road haulier. It was after the Second World War, in 1952, that McLean saw an opportunity to improve the way goods were transported which would not only speed things up but also cut costs. During that war the United States and Australian Military had used standardised wooden containers to speed up supplies to their forces.

McLean sold his haulage business in 1956 and purchased two World War Two oil tankers and converted them into the world's first container ships, setting sail in April 1956 with fifty-eight containers on board.

The new containers were made of steel with reinforced corners, which made it possible to stack them without causing any damage.

Next came the Vietnam War in the late '60s with the US military needing to get equipment to the troops in a speedy and efficient way. It was McLean's containers that provided the solution with the added advantage that the empty containers could be used to ship back goods from Japan to the USA.

The modern container and an ISO standard was born in 1968 (ISO 668) with seven standard sizes.

Goodbye to the old way of loading ships; the labour intensive, expensive and slow ways of the past were soon to become history along with transporting goods in barrels, crates, boxes, pallets etc.

Hello to the new way. It would now become viable to ship almost anything around the world, goods that in the past were just too costly to get from A to B.

Hello to globalisation, welcome to a whole new world, and all because of a simple steel box that could be loaded, secured and shipped to anywhere in the world. Well, almost anywhere, to countries who embraced this new way of thinking and wasted no time in being able to accommodate ever larger ships and the means to unload them quickly.

Of course, this was not without cost. In order for this exciting new world to become a reality it could be said that it was not what could be fitted inside the box, it was what needed to be accomplished outside the box.

Britain's first containerised port was New South Quay at Felixstowe opening on 1 July 1961 and later renamed Languard Container Terminal. Since then expansion has taken place in the '70s, '80s and '90s with the final completion of this phase being in 2004. Growth has continued with the opening of berths 8 and 9 in 2011 and expansion in 2015, which involved the reclaiming of land from the river Orwell. It is now one of the largest container ports in the whole of Europe and handles over 3,000 ships per year with 4 million TEUs (Twenty Foot Equivalent Units).

In order for this to have become a reality it required a massive investment by different governments throughout the world, the scale of which was almost unprecedented. When you start to think about the scale of it, it cannot be denied that when the rewards are high enough, the funding can be found.

We have a more recent example of how the world has co-operated in coming together: to find a solution to the Covid pandemic. With so many lives lost, all stops were pulled out to find a way of affording the way forward to ensure that this did not become the catalyst that could conceivably be the end of our species as we know it.

Imagine what had to be invested for this new way of transporting goods.

- Millions of containers had to be manufactured
- Thousands of new ships had to be built
- Hundreds of thousands of new trucks to be manufactured
- Hundreds of new ports with all their associated infrastructure, such as storage, new cranes designed and built, handling equipment designed and built, new systems developed for recording and logging the movement of goods, new security systems; the list goes on
- New roads and railways with new rolling stock

- Retraining of personnel
- New warehouses built to cope with the handling of the containers and storage of their contents and the increase in volumes.

This is not an exhaustive list, and then of course other problems needed to be overcome, not least:

- The obvious objections from those who had the most to lose, like the traditional Stevedores or Longshoremen, and other dockworkers who would no longer have a job
- All those associated tradespeople whose services and skills would no longer be required
- A need to find a new use for those docking areas that would no longer be able to operate in this new environment
- The means to redevelop these areas into a useful and sustainable feature for the future
- Employment for those individuals who would inevitably lose their jobs.

Maybe the vast majority of us are driven by what we see as being in our own self-interests. Who could blame those dockers and other associated workers from trying to save their livelihoods by resisting the change? Don't we vote for the political party who we think will serve our needs better than the alternative? Maybe the prospect of saving a few quid here and there or even a few hundred or thousands by paying for something with cash is justified in our own minds simply because we believe we already pay enough in taxes, and something saved in this manner enables us to afford something else.

Whatever the reason, in the end when change is inevitable it will happen no matter how hard it is resisted.

Sometimes, one's own self-interest must not be put before the best interest of our family, relatives, friends, neighbours, work colleagues, acquaintances and even people we have never met or are likely to meet. Indeed, we have experienced such overwhelming evidence of this fact in the way the majority have abided by the rules throughout the Covid pandemic. Thankfully, the majority have taken the view that wearing masks, staying distanced, self-imposed isolation and generally doing the right thing for not only ourselves but for the benefit of complete strangers, is a price we had to pay. There is now little doubt that the vaccinations developed so quickly and with such skill and dedication by very clever people have played a mammoth part in helping to reduce the death rates from this terrible virus.

Everyone has a right to freedom of expression and to their own beliefs as to whether or not the vaccine programme was something they personally wished to participate in. However, with that right comes the responsibility to ensure that only the facts are used in the pursuit of trying to persuade others to their way of thinking. To use scare tactics and unsubstantiated claims is not only unfair but can have devastating consequences to others. Not only have they, in their own way, contributed to an increase in the death rates, but their actions have and will continue to cause still further suffering from those who have been denied the love and affection from family members who unnecessarily became just another number in the statistics.

Yet another quote from Voltaire: "Those who can make you believe absurdities can make you commit atrocities." How wise he was.

Just look at what President Donald Trump managed to get others to do through his alternative truths. Yes, some of his claims were absurd and this culminated in the storming of the US parliament, which not only caused severe damage to the building and its contents, but also loss of life and a loss of faith in democratic elections.

By now you are possibly asking yourself what all this has got to do with the way our own government and the NHS handles patients with dementia diseases. The reality is that the system is nothing more than absurd; it pretends to be something that it is not.

It makes the pretence that it is available to everyone, but it can't even be honest enough to tell you that CHC exists; worse still, they lie about entitlement. They don't even follow their own rules, they conveniently change the very meaning of the English language to suit their own agenda and, as we have said previously, they are devious and determined that you will not get what you are entitled to.

That's the "absurdities" part; the "atrocities" element is the harm and damage caused to thousands of people who are either suffering from this terrible disease or have loved ones who may feel helpless in being able to get justice for them.

Too often big institutions or companies get away, literally, with murder, and in the end it all comes down to money and greed.

Is it not time to realise that no matter how big an institution or a company gets, it is not these organisations that make the policy and the decisions? No, decisions are made by flesh and blood, breathing human beings who need to be brought to task and punished where they have knowingly misled, mistreated, conned, stolen from, degraded or even contributed to the death of another human being. Earlier on we mentioned that one of the key objections to a change in the way we do things could be a mistrust of banks. There is nothing wrong with banks, only the people who run them and the fact that, seemingly, no matter how greedy these people get, they are allowed to keep their millions or billions, when in reality their actions should have been rewarded only by free board and lodgings at His Majesty's pleasure.

I say to all those politicians who claim to have entered the profession with a strong desire to make life better for society, please get on with it. There are far too many injustices which are desperate to be resolved. It is no good publishing manifestos and making outrageous promises, some of which are so grossly over-exaggerated as to never be achievable, at least not until you fix the system so everyone contributes in a proportionate way.

I ask this question: why is income tax calculated as a percentage of what the person earns, but when a person chooses to not play by society's rules the penalty they will pay will be the same no matter what their wealth? I do not believe anyone could reasonably argue that this is a just and fair system. A fine for one person may mean no food on the table for a period of time, but to someone else it is just pocket change.

I once worked for a boss who took the view that double yellow lines should be treated as his own private parking space. He was seemingly happy to pay parking tickets on a daily basis. In fact he was personally known to the local traffic warden who greeted him with a "Merry Christmas" and "have this one on me".

Why not make all fines a simple percentage of an individual's annual tax liability based on the severity of the offence? (E.g. speeding/parking could be 1, 2 or 3%.)

We will look further at out-of-the-box ideas, but the next chapter is so important that I don't wish to delay any further in giving you the things you need to know and, even more importantly, the things you need to do.

7

THE THINGS YOU NEED TO KNOW AND DO

- The very best time to put one's affairs in order will always be today, never tomorrow, as there is always a tendency to put things off until it is too late, and as the saying goes, "Tomorrow never comes"

- Have you done your will? Should something happen to you, without warning, do your loved ones really know your wishes, and importantly what evidence are you leaving them to prove who you want to get what and does the law recognise these wishes?

- Are you confident that the advice you are given is the right advice? Or maybe you haven't even sought advice

- Have you considered what may happen if your demise is sudden and possibly at an earlier age than you could have imagined? Leaving everything to your spouse or recognised partner may deprive your children of their rightful inheritance. What would happen if your partner remarries and you have left everything to them? Maybe your children even lose their family home. Uncomfortable conversations to have but nevertheless important ones to have

- Getting advice on trust funds amongst other things should be part of your financial planning

- What about your principal asset, your house – how is it owned? Is it owned jointly and equally with your partner, and how is it registered with the Land Registry? Did you know that when one partner pre-deceases the other and the ownership of the house lies 100% with the remaining partner, this can result in the whole asset being lost to the state in the event that the remaining partner has to go into a care home or even being cared for in the family home, and deemed to be self-funding? It is therefore imperative that the ownership is registered as being (I believe the terminology is) "as Tenants in Common". Essentially the difference is that each partner owns 50% of the property and can freely choose what they wish to happen to their half share. This makes no difference to the rights of the remaining partner's ability to stay in the property after the death of the other. It may be that both partners choose to leave their share to the same people, but providing the will has been legally completed and registered, neither one will have cause for concern about the benefactors wanting to sell their share and make them homeless

- When one partner is deemed to be in need of care and if (as is most likely without a fight) their application for NHS CHC has been denied, you should be aware that their local authority, through their social services, cannot take into consideration any value contained within the principal property, so long as their partner is still living there. You also need to understand that they also have no rights to defer any costs they may incur in providing services by imposing a repayable loan against the property while the partner is still in residence. If you should happen to own a second property in the form of, say, a holiday cottage, then regretfully they can force the sale of such or impose a loan against that property to get their hands on the share belonging to the person requiring care

- As social services is means-tested, they will require you to disclose all assets owned by the person in need of care. Failure to do so will be deemed as acceptance of the fact that you will be self-funding. Should your experience be similar to that of mine and my wife's, they were very keen to start the process at the earliest opportunity, even when she was still in a hospital environment and before we had even secured the initial screening assessment. I personally took the view that they were trying to put the cart before the horse and had concerns that if they had any sense that we would be self-funding there was even less chance of getting the screening assessment and the full assessment for NHS CHC. It will inevitably be your decision as to whether or not and at what point in time you choose to divulge this information

- You will be required to provide copies of bank statements, held in the name of the person requiring care; likewise, copies of joint accounts where it is considered that such funds are held in equal share by the account holders and any other funds held in their name such as insurance policies, ISAs, other shares, savings and building societies etc. This is in addition to disclosing any income derived from any source including pensions, earnings from dividends, work etc

- You can reasonably offset any household expenditure, and I suggest you take the time to make this as exhaustive as possible. This list will include all the usual major items of expenditure such as utility bills, council tax, TV licence, insurances, repair costs, car expenditure including road tax and repairs, insurance, fuel costs, loan costs, car parking etc. Then of course there is your weekly/monthly shopping costs and expenditure on clothing/takeaways etc. The greater the detail you are able to provide the less the opportunity you will give them to query your figures. For my part I was fortunate to have charged most of our expenditure to a credit card which was settled in full each month and could prove where and when monies had been spent as well as itemising each transaction

- I read somewhere that just because you know someone with Alzheimer's doesn't mean that you know the effects of the disease. I think this was a way of saying that the effects of the disease and its manifestations and speed of decline is wide-ranging and different in many ways between different individuals. However, I have also noted that it is not uncommon for sufferers to simply deny there is anything at all wrong with them. This was certainly the case with my wife for some considerable period of time and any attempt to suggest anything to the contrary resulted in her becoming very upset with me and made her suspicious of my motivations. I mention this because the reality is that you need to ensure that you get in place the two further legal documents that will protect the best interests of your loved one and yourself

- A power of attorney will be required for "Health and Wellbeing". This is, in order for you to make decisions on their behalf when it becomes necessary to act in their best interests in matters concerning anything to do with procedures of a medical nature. Without this in place, your opinions and desires will not necessarily be considered and will remain with the doctors or through the courts by The Court of Protection. Obviously, your loved one has to be of sound mind and give, of their own free will, their permission by signing a legally binding document. They have to understand what entering into such an agreement means and what power and responsibility that bestows on you. It goes without saying that this requires complete trust by the individual in their chosen attorney. This could prove more difficult as the patient's condition continues to deteriorate, whilst at the same time having it in place becomes more and more important. Before I was able to access my wife's medical records, or even to demand her rights to an assessment, I was required to produce copies of the POA. Prior to attending the MDT meeting for assessment of NHS CHC I was again required to furnish them with yet another copy. These are difficult conversations to have and may be easier to have well before there are any signs of dementia, not forgetting that they can be cancelled in the future should that be necessary through changes in circumstances, such as divorce or separation

- The second power of attorney which is of equal importance is that for property and financial. All the same principles and conditions apply to those for Health and Wellbeing, but gives the appointed person the authority to deal with the appointee's finances and investments, without which the Court of Protection will likely appoint solicitors and/or accountancy firms to handle these at considerable cost

- By way of example I can repeat a true story that at the time was very distressing to one of the beneficiaries of her mother's estate. Circumstances were such that the mother's intentions on formulating her last will and testament were no doubt made with every good intention to "do the right thing." The elderly lady who remained in the family home and attached to the family farm had just one daughter and two granddaughters whom she wished to ensure were well cared for after her demise. I think she may have had concerns that as her daughter was divorced and was then currently courting a person some fifteen to twenty years her junior, that leaving her whole estate to her may see the family wealth transferring out of the family after her daughter's death. Maybe this drove her decision to leave her estate in three equal parts to her daughter and two granddaughters. Following some substantial losses in wealth, the daughter moved back into her family home and continued with the farm's principal activity. Regretfully, her youngest daughter, who herself had two children, suffered from a mental illness that caused her to be sectioned under the Mental Health Act. Having not appointed an attorney for neither Health and Wellbeing nor Property and Finance it was left up to the Court of Protection to appoint a firm of solicitors to act in her best interests. The appointed attorney made the decision that it was in the youngest daughter's best interest to liquidate her share of the assets bequeathed to her by her grandmother. This of course could not happen without either her mother's agreement or that of her elder sister who was living abroad at that time in what amounted to a kibbutz. Consequently, she too thought it to be to her advantage to cash in on her share of her inheritance which enabled her to have a change in her lifestyle. In order that the mother could maintain her home and business, she had no alternative but to mortgage the property and business to pay off her daughters and at the same time embark on the daunting task of developing a new business to service the loans she by necessity had taken out. Having no other family to bequeath her assets to, and with her relationship by then having come to an end, she saw the irony in the fact that her daughters would in fact receive their inheritance twice over. If there is a moral to this story then it must be "to think carefully and get good advice on how to word your will – don't live or die to regret it"

- It is not unusual for partners in a loving relationship, whether it be short-lived or long-lived, to have wills that mirror each other, each partner leaving all their assets to the other on the demise of the first (with the exception of the joint ownership of the principal property if owned as Tenants in Common). There are maybe other things to consider if, God forbid, one half of the partnership is struck down by a disease such as one of the various categories of dementia. Remember that it may be necessary to adapt certain clauses of your will and to leave your assets to your children in the event you predecease your partner. There would be little point in leaving your assets to a partner if in reality this just enables your local authority to assess that they then have the means to be self-funding. Consider also the possibility that you may inherit other assets, such as your parents' home or business or cash, that would fall into the hands of the local authority unless you change your will accordingly. Finally on this point remember that as a beneficiary of your parents' will, you can always apply for a Deed of Variation which may enable you to divert some of your inheritance to your children or grandchildren, which could be tax-beneficial in the event of your demise. This must be actioned within twenty-four months from the death of the benefactor. Remember, I am not a solicitor, accountant or financial advisor and therefore recommend that you seek the correct advice should you find it necessary

- In hindsight I can now look back and realise there were a considerable number of incidents and changes to my wife's behaviours which were initially small and subtle in nature but should have indicated to me that all was not well. My wife was always the life and soul of family gatherings and parties, always willing and keen to engage in conversation and debate on all manner of subjects. Over time it seemed that she could nearly always be found in the kitchen doing the washing up and generally tiding up. I later realised that she was avoiding putting herself in the position of having to engage in conversation or the embarrassment of forgetting what she had said or who she was talking to

- Apparently it is not uncommon for sufferers to deny there is anything wrong, whether that be because they genuinely don't know or because they are scared and find it more comforting not to accept the reality of their situation

- You may find it useful to keep a diary from the moment you observe a change in your loved one's behaviour. If all goes well I hope that you have only the occasional entry to record; the fewer the better. Unfortunately, if your loved one is developing signs of dementia, the chances are that over time the frequency and range of entries will increase. If this is the case then it may be necessary to approach the subject of going to see a doctor about what may be wrong. Don't be surprised if this suggestion is met with denial and resistance, but it may help to have a conversation about your diary, and your concerns that you need to put in place the powers of attorney and the writing of your wills if these haven't already been actioned

- Keep updating your diary, including such things as conversations you have with the doctors and memory clinic personnel. Remember, if it becomes necessary to fight against doctors' opinions then the more information you have at your disposal the better

- As soon as your loved one has a diagnosis of Alzheimer's or other form of dementia the clock is ticking; you must get your wills and powers of attorney sorted

- Time to assess how disabled-friendly your home is for someone with Alzheimer's or other types of dementia. Consider such things as:
  (1) Do you have a shower, is it large enough to accommodate a shower seat, and is it large enough for the patient and a carer to give assistance in showering? Is it easy to enter and exit, are there grab rails in appropriate locations for both patient and

carer? Is the shower hose long enough, can you switch off the water supply at the shower head hose? What about somewhere to store shampoo and shower gel which is convenient for the carer? Could it be more advantageous to replace a bath with a new larger shower cubicle?

(2) Look into replacing the patient's bed with one that lifts and reclines; this could be critical in helping them to have meals or snacks in bed or in assisting them to get out of bed

(3) Do some investigations into the various types of disabled reclining and lifting lounge chairs. I have personally found these to be of tremendous help in not only making my wife comfortable but in aiding her to get in and out of her chair

(4) In my case the occupational therapists who did an assessment of our property to deem its suitability for my wife to return home initially had concerns that she could fall over the balustrade, which involved me having to replacing this with one of two-metre height and a matching door at the top of the staircase. Having overcome this objection after their first visit, they moved on to their concerns in the use of the staircase. I was fortunate enough to have a "U" shaped staircase with half landing between the first and second set of stairs. This afforded me the ability to replace the whole staircase with a new "L" shaped one with three winder stairs, and free up sufficient space for a lift going from the hallway to the first-floor landing. This was not a cheap option: all in with the cost of stairs, lift, plastering, decoration and new carpets the expenditure was in the region of

£35,000, and that was having obtained relief from VAT due to my wife's disabilities. Her doctor had the audacity to suggest to me that I did "not consider that such expenditure could be a waste of money". To put it simply: NO. (I had an option of doing the best I could for my love and knowing without spending money in this way we would have been self-funding if we fell under social care in the event of refusal of NHS CHC.)

(5) Make sure you keep a detailed account of all expenditure incurred in purchases that you need to make because of the condition of your loved one. You will be surprised at how costs can mount up and just how many little aids there are that make a big difference to coping with everyday life.

- Take a look at the literature provided by The Alzheimer's Society, Dementia UK, and Age Concern. All of these organisations can give sound advice and recommendations of other contacts which can provide useful information.

  You will also find comments provided by other carers to their loved ones and in some instances their personal stories of how they were treated by the NHS CHC system. If these are not sufficient to convince you that it could happen to you then read on

- At some point in time you will without doubt need help and assistance in dealing with NHS CHC systems and procedures. Initially you may feel you have the time and means to handle the screening assessment then, subject to getting over this first hurdle, the more demanding actual assessment with the Multi-Disciplinary Team. Involving a family member to help you is invaluable, in that they can give another perspective on your opinions; they can maybe remember things of relevance that you have overlooked and can be a crutch to keep you going when things might look impossible. Having them test your presentation skills and critique your arguments can make all the difference, especially when you are up against so-called professionals who will no doubt have had a meeting prior to the assessment and will undoubtedly have a meeting to discuss what their report will contain after the event.

The next chapter discusses the options also available to us all in the use of professional advice through the use of solicitors.

8

THE USE OF PROFESSIONAL LEGAL SERVICES

We are all aware that the laws of the land can be complex issues and can be left to interpretation by those professionals who have studied hard to try and understand not only the legal jargon contained within them but in some instances to look deeply into what the formatters of some of these laws actually intended when they were being put into legislation.

From time to time some laws are not entirely clear and have to be tested by the finest minds to make conclusions which, when reaching these, may differ from past similar cases and consequently changes the way the law should be interpreted. When these cases are finally judged upon, they can create new accepted case law which may be quoted in subsequent legal challenges.

Due to the number of laws covering a multitude of issues and intentions it is unsurprising that lawyers tend to specialise in particular areas; better to be an expert in one area than to be master of none.

So far as I can see, due to this need to specialise in one or two particular fields, most law practices seem to work for a multitude of different businesses, organisations and individuals, who from time to time require their expertise, either working for the plaintiff or the defendant. However, it would not be unusual for some law firms to be retained by large organisations or institutions and gain a significant understanding of that client's business, probably by virtue of the nature of the operations carried out on a regular basis which in themselves could attract a regular need for legal advice and/or court proceedings. This situation by its very nature would limit the number of clients they would be able to deal with.

On the other hand it would be unusual to find a significant number of law firms acting for numerous plaintiffs who all have a very similar case and where the defendant happens to be the same business or organisation. This of course does happen where a significant number of plaintiffs all have the same grievance against a particular company or organisation; in some cases, this can run into hundreds and even thousands of plaintiffs. The similarities are so profoundly alike that it makes little sense for these to be heard over and over again in a court of law using the same arguments, witness statements, evidence and defence, only to arrive at the same conclusion. In the USA these are referred to as class action cases where the findings of the court can be binding on all parties who have agreed to join in the action. Here in the UK a similar type of procedure exists for collective actions to deal with multiple claimants; these are known as representative actions, or the court can manage these by applying the use of a test case. There are significant benefits to both sides of the dispute and to the courts. Collective actions can alleviate the inevitable clogging up of the country's courts and has the advantage of reducing the costs of such cases for both the plaintiffs and defendants.

One can imagine the shareholders of any large company seriously questioning the CEO and board about the running of the company if it was discovered that their business was the sole defendant in actions taken against them, by a significant number of law firms. Not that this is completely unusual, particularly for an organisation providing a unique service or product, but because of the sheer scale of the fact that many law firms have been set up to deal only with the grievances of its consumers. That in itself would ordinarily ring alarm bells, but add to this the fact that these law firms have been established for a number of years and have been successful in arguing that their clients have been denied a service which they were entitled to receive and therefore having been wrongly deprived of many tens of thousands of pounds and in some cases hundreds of thousands of pounds.

How would a CEO and the board explain the fact that there is an annual ongoing need to settle hundreds of cases each year, not only at tremendous cost in settlement, but the massive costs involved in trying to defend their actions? Without doubt such a high rate of disputes on an ongoing basis would indicate that the senior management are allowing their clientele to be defrauded on a regular basis, by personnel employed by them.

Clearly due to the length of time that such a situation has existed, and the need to authorise such quantity and scale of settlement payments, no CEO or board member could reasonably offer a realistic defence of such practices. Internally the board may be taking the view that settlement of these cases is necessary to enable them to keep operating by continuing to defraud hundreds of other clients as the stakes are so high that in the end it is cost effective to do so.

I would agree this is an unlikely scenario, but this is in effect how the NHS is operating the CHC funding liability that exists and for which they are responsible.

In reality it is not dissimilar to a massive Ponzi scheme: pay off the people who refuse to be conned with the money saved from conning fresh new victims.

Remember, I said that knowledge would be your most valuable weapon in trying to get the justice you are entitled to.

With this aim in mind I would implore you to look online at "solicitors specialising in NHS Continuing Healthcare".

You will note that we are not just looking at a couple of firms who specialise in this particular field; there are a significant number who do so, and remember, not only is this a true indicator of the scale of the problem, but they exist by virtue of the fact they have an unending supply of clients provided by a determined system to deny the most vulnerable people in society the help and care they are entitled to.

Please also look at independentliving.co.uk/advice/nhs-continuing-healthcare-chc/.

This article makes for some interesting but disturbing reading, so much so that I will repeat some of what is said.

Firstly, a gentleman called Philip Mathias, a retired Rear Admiral and former Ministry of Defence official, has been working hard in his determination to hold the DHSC and NHS to account for their failings in providing NHS CHC to people who are entitled to it. His efforts in this regard should be applauded by us all and any help we can provide him with in this respect would undoubtedly be appreciated.

He has been endeavouring to seek a judicial review to hold government to account, but reports that the judge assigned to consider this request has refused permission for this to proceed.

Understandingly he is extremely disappointed with this decision, which is no doubt echoed by so many of us who feel this disgraceful scandal has been going on for far too long and is nothing short of a stain on the character of our once-proud nation.

Apparently, this refusal was based on a range of complex legal reasons, most of which would be almost incomprehensible to the general public, including the retired Rear Admiral. He goes on to report the part that states that he doesn't have "standing" to bring such a case and that there has been too long a "delay" in making the claim.

(How unbelievable is such a statement in that the issues surrounding the need for a judicial review are ongoing, with thousands of very ill people still being denied their entitlement to Continuing Healthcare Funding? I personally am amazed that Gina Miller, as a private citizen, was able to get a Judicial Review over Boris Johnson's attempt to prorogue parliament, and yet someone of such high standing in public life was denied it.)

The judge in his/her actions is denying the public their right to hold the NHS and the Secretary of State accountable for their actions. It appears that Philip Mathias was able to shoulder some of the responsibilities of looking after the defence of our country and yet just one judge can act in a God-like way and has the power to deny him the right to fight against a system that is profoundly flawed and is operated outside the guidelines, set and intended to ensure fairness and compassion to the most vulnerable in our society.

The article goes on to give more details of such things as:

- The estimated shortfall in funding provided (£5 billion)
- The decline in funding given, even though the ageing population is increasing and the numbers of awards are decreasing
- The huge variations in successful applications throughout the country giving rise to a "postcode lottery" situation
- The NHS merely refers to CCGs with unexplained low award rates as "outliers"
- The NHS and DHSC simply claim that eligibility numbers have increased over the last few years even though there has been an 11% drop over a four-year period per 50,000 of the population

- CHC is not a discretionary award, it is a matter of law, and yet they offer no explanation as to why they simply state the opposite of the reality. Why do they not offer an explanation of their reasoning so it may be tested in a court of law?

- Philip Mathias wrote an open letter to Cressida Dick, the then Commissioner of the Metropolitan Police, making an allegation of misconduct in public office against the CEO of the NHS. She in turn took the allegation seriously enough to direct her specialist crime unit to review the evidence. He worked closely with the lead investigator for some three months. Whilst the investigator confirmed that the law does indeed require CCGs to allocate funding to individuals based on a set of fixed objective criteria, he concluded that given the high bar for criminal charges associated with this offence, for a number of complex and technical legal reasons it was not appropriate to proceed to a criminal investigation

- The investigator did however state that he was very aware and sympathetic to the scale of injustice and carefully implied that a case under civil law could be feasible

- Undeterred, Philip Mathias subsequently made a formal submission to the CEO of the Equality and Human Rights Commission (EHRC), providing extensive and irrefutable evidence of the thousands of old and vulnerable people who are being discriminated against based on age and disability and being a gross violation of their human rights. He reports that she was initially very positive and that she was aware of the growing significance and degree of immenseness of the issue. However, after six months her view was that the NHS and DHSC already had obligations to prevent unlawful discrimination and that the EHRC's strategic plan did not cover such an issue and that any legal action would not achieve a better compliance by CCGs

- Philip Mathias's comment is: "By any standard this was a woeful failure of the EHRC, bringing into question its credibility, not least given one of its three strategic goals is to protect the rights of people in the most vulnerable situations. How much more vulnerable can someone be if they are old, ill and suffering health-related disabilities, particularly those with severe cognitive impairment due to dementia?"

- The report goes on to itemise questions that need to be asked, all of which are relevant and the answers to which the public is entitled to know

- The reports of the extensive criticism and evidence of the failing and unlawful CHC system by the PAC (Public Accounts Commission), The NAO (National Audit Office), CQC (Care Quality Commission), CHC Alliance (seventeen charities) and the media

- Philip Mathias asks this very pertinent question: how can a minister of state justify the following statement:
    "The government does not believe that CHC is being mismanaged by CCGs."
    At this time I would like to add my own comments and feelings about all that you have just read.

- Firstly in re-reading the article referred to above, I have felt the anger arise within me and no doubt also my blood pressure. In my opinion NHS CHC exists only for a minority of people who are in need of it and that is mainly dependent upon where they live. Its denial of funding also preys on those persons who are unable to defend themselves and who become reliant on their loved ones fighting for them. Regretfully not everyone has the time, means or abilities to fight against this injustice. Some may even think that the system is so stacked against them that there is little point in trying to get justice. Who could blame them when you read that it seems no-one in authority is prepared to accept the true reality of the situation? The NHS, the politicians, the police, the judiciary and even the Equality and Human Rights Commission have all conveniently turned their backs on our most vulnerable members of society. To them I say: "Hang your heads in shame because you have by your actions chosen to be the very worst type of authority figures."

Maybe you don't have the backbone to do what you know is the right thing to do, maybe you enjoy such a privileged lifestyle that you don't want to put it at risk by disagreeing with your peers, or is it simply that you don't have the intelligence to know this is not how seriously ill people should be treated? Whatever the reason, to you all I would remind you of this fact:

Authority without responsibility is nothing short of being completely self-centred with no regard for those persons who have to shoulder responsibility without authority.

I am not generally prone to believe in conspiracy theories even though we all know that conspiracies can and do happen; some people in positions of power can do some terrible things. They are prepared to tell lies when it is to their benefit. I need not remind anyone of the many examples of such behaviours and when they are found out they finally end in, if they are lucky, getting away with it, or paying back their ill-gotten gains. The less lucky find themselves spending years in jail. People like Fred West and more recently Jeffrey Epstein chose the cowardly option of taking their own lives rather than taking the punishment due to them. Well, I am on this occasion prepared to make an exception and suggest that because of the comments made by such people in power that there is a high possibility that a conspiracy does exist when it comes to NHS CHC funding.

I believe we owe Philip Mathias a debt of gratitude for all he has done to date in trying to get this terrible situation resolved. To him I would say the blame for not getting anyone in authority to do anything lies not on his shoulders but on the shoulders of those people in authority who accept no responsibility for their actions or lack thereof. To use a military analogy, he tried to make the "generals" see sense, but when that fails the inevitable consequence is to bring on the troops who have the responsibility without the authority.

It is right to start at the top in the hope that solutions can be found which would then filter downwards; alas, due to their total reluctance to engage, there is little alternative but to then start at the bottom and work our way upwards.

Now clearly I am not the arbiter of the right or wrong way of doing things and although I will give my thoughts further airing in a later chapter, I hope that there will be many others with ideas and determination to offer their own thoughts on how we might best get justice for those in need.

Warning: if you do choose to use the services of one of these firms, choose wisely; my experience with my law firm was not a happy one, and would therefore not recommend them to anyone.

The purpose of employing them was to take the pressure off in making an appeal against the CCG's decision of Margaret not having a primary health need. Due to the inordinate length of time my law firm took to review all the paperwork, and their lack of addressing certain issues which I considered to be paramount, they left me very little time to prepare the appeal paperwork. Having lost complete faith in their abilities to do what they promised in a timely manner, I saw no benefit in spending a further £2,160 over and above the nearly £1,000 already spent with them which I feel was a complete waste of money.

My appeal letter of twenty-one pages and a further seventy-one pages of evidential information had to be compiled with just over four weeks until the deadline for appealing this decision, this being due to my law firm's broken promises and lack of urgency in carrying out the review.

9

OUR EXPERIENCES FROM THE START OF THIS TERRIBLE JOURNEY

I am recounting here our experiences, set out in three parts, in the hope that in so doing it may be of help to others who find themselves in similar circumstances.

There will undoubtedly be those whose experiences are better, which I sincerely hope is the case, but also those whose experiences are even worse than our own, in which case you have my heartfelt sympathy.

Whatever your experiences are, I hope that my thoughts and actions may be of some help to you, even if it is as simple as knowing you are not alone.

PART 1
THE START OF THE JOURNEY
The history of Margaret Allott's development of Alzheimer's disease.

Margaret was first diagnosed as a person suffering with Alzheimer's in January/February 2018.

This was not the beginning of the condition and in hindsight there were numerous indicators that should have suggested that all was not well and that changes in her behaviour were happening for years prior to diagnosis. Unfortunately, most of these were seen as minor incidents that did not give cause for concern at that particular moment in time.

I would suggest that these indicators probably went back four or five years in total, which in themselves gradually became more serious as time progressed and more frequent.

I am unable to pinpoint any one incident that I could say was a definite indicator until the defining moment occurred in August 2017. Margaret had a Ford Mustang Convertible motorcar that we acquired in February 2000, at a time when we were working in Florida, USA. She loved that car and looked after it with great care and attention, shipping it back to the UK on our return in April 2001. Over the seventeen years of ownership the paintwork became faded, the soft-top was well worn with signs of leaking and the interior carpets showed obvious signs of wear. Mechanically it was in good condition and the bodywork sound, so we decided to bring it back to excellent condition by replacing the soft-top, replacing the carpets and having it completely re-sprayed in its original red colour, complete with new decals along the sides and rear.

To this end it was booked into a specialist body shop for re-spray, with Margaret driving to the location by following me. When the work was complete, I took her to pick up her car and she asked me to make sure I showed her the way home as she was unsure of the way. I was able to reassure her that I would go slowly and keep her immediately behind me and signal in plenty of time when making any change of direction. At the first roundabout I signalled left and she followed suit by signalling and following me to the left turn.

At the next roundabout she was directly behind me. I again signalled left and made the turn, but to my horror she did not follow but instead went straight on. I had no alternative but to proceed to the next roundabout, do a u-turn and turn left at the roundabout to arrive back on the same road where she had gone straight on. Having got about halfway to the next roundabout I spotted her going in the opposite direction on the other carriageway.

Despite trying to catch up with her, I had lost her completely and returned home to see if she had found her own way back. Regretfully she had not, and I had to call our son and daughter-in-law to assist in looking for her. After about sixty minutes of the three of us driving around with no luck in finding her, I again drove home to see if she had found her way back on her own. Despite there being no car on the driveway I was pleased to find Margaret was in fact inside the house. She appeared to be quite distressed and explained that she had become completely lost and unable to find her way home. She did however have the presence of mind to park the car and get a taxi to bring her home. Fortunately she was able to explain roughly where she had parked the car, which our son and I were able to recover the following day.

As we had lived at our current address in excess of twelve years and Margaret had been driving to and from work, going shopping, visiting friends etc. with no problems, this was the defining moment when I realised something serious was happening with her memory.

Despite my attempts to get Margaret to visit the doctor's surgery, she was insistent that there was nothing wrong with her and the incident with the car was a one-time lapse in memory, and she did not want or need to see the doctor.

I visited our GP and explained the situation, requesting her to get Margaret to visit the surgery under the pretext of doing a medication review in order that she could ask her salient questions and make a determination about her loss of memory. This was eventually achieved with the outcome that the doctor would make a referral to the Specialist Memory Clinic for a more intensive investigation.

As I have said, in hindsight there were numerous small changes in Margaret's behaviour over many years, which to pinpoint just a few, included:

- Not noticing things that were immediately in front of her

- Despite always being the life and soul of the party, at family events, she would be more reluctant to make the effort to go to these events, or when we did, to join in the conversation by always offering to go and do the washing up or some other task that would remove her from the crowd

- Despite us purchasing a new touring caravan she would find ways to avoid us going away in it, such as "the weather's not nice enough", "it's too hot or too cold", "not in the school holidays"

- Outright refusal to accompany me to visit my elderly mother even when she was hospitalised

- Getting upset and angry if I was just a few minutes late in being home at the stated time

- Not wanting me to go and assist our son when he needed help with a DIY project

- Becoming argumentative over the smallest of things or differences of opinion.

Margaret has always been a proud and independent person with strong viewpoints on a vast range of subjects. From the outset she has never wanted to be involved in any group therapy meetings, clubs or discussions with other people in a similar situation. She has until recently been in denial that there was anything wrong with her and berated me for betraying her confidence with other members of her family, accusing me of being a traitor, even though I had not specifically told anyone that she had been diagnosed as having Alzheimer's.

From the moment of diagnosis, symptoms appeared to progress slowly at first with occasional moments of strange behaviours, not least of these being:

- No longer wishing to give our grandchildren their weekly pocket money on the basis that I was giving all her money away
- Believing that the house was hers and I had no interest in it
- All the money was hers; I didn't have any
- Believing she had promised our collections of various things to a woman in the village who was opening a museum
- Likewise, she thought she had promised to give away her Juke Box and record collection
- Not wanting me to go even outside into the garden or to the study in the garage
- Loss of interest in doing her crosswords or puzzles
- Even though an avid reader all her life, this ceased completely over time
- TV viewing was reduced to watching game shows and quizzes; only those programmes that did not require any memory retention of a storyline
- No longer able to remember where to find things in the house or where things belonged
- Remembering what each room in the house was used for or where they were located

- Following me around if I was to go to another room, say to make a meal

- False accusations would come out of the blue. At one point in time she believed I had another woman living in a room upstairs

- We could maybe discuss the need to purchase even the smallest of items and once agreed and purchased she would again accuse me of wasting her money

- Out of the blue she could turn aggressive and attack me, punching me, throwing things and screaming, slamming doors etc.

- Forgetting to put on her glasses and complaining her eyes were hurting

- A change in what she liked to eat happened just recently, with many of her favourite foods now things she doesn't like at all. It seems that chicken is now the only thing that she really likes.

This list is by no means exhaustive but gives some indication as to what Alzheimer's has robbed her of.

PART 2
The history of the change in behaviour of my beloved wife Margaret. Born 2 June 1952.

This account was written in July/August 2021 and was done so in an attempt to record where we were then and the progression of Margaret's symptoms of her Alzheimer's disease since official diagnosis approximately three and a half years ago.

It is furthermore a record of the appalling lack of support and help offered by the NHS, including what I consider to be serious and possible life-threatening incidents which someone in authority needs to take notice of, not only for the safety and well-being of Margaret, but for all those patients and carers/families who find themselves in a similar situation in the future.

Over time since her diagnosis of Alzheimer's the change in Margaret's condition has been gradual and manageable.

I would suggest that it could best be described as 90% OK. And 10% challenging.

During the 10% challenging period Margaret could get very upset, confused and disorientated, with the odd occasional bouts of violence, severe screaming, and almost total lack of understanding of reality.

There was a marked change in her behaviour around the end of April, beginning of May, of the year 2021.

So much so that I would now suggest the percentages have reversed, being 10% OK and 90% challenging, including increased acts of aggression with incidents of hallucinations and extreme distress. (This was prior to her admission to TOPAS (The Older Persons Assessment Centre) and changes in her medication.)

This behavioural change started with Margaret complaining of pains in her abdomen and her refusal to get out of bed. At this time she started to refer to herself in third person e.g. when asked what was wrong she would reply "she has a pain in her stomach and won't anyone help her". When I suggested getting up and getting changed to come downstairs this would be followed by her insistence "*she* can't get up because *she* can't walk", followed by a demonstration of her getting out of bed and being bent almost double, and having to hang onto furniture and prove to me that she was incapable of walking.

The peculiar thing was that when she needed to go to the toilet she seemed capable of doing so, although she would frequently not go to the en-suite bathroom in our room but go to the family bathroom which we never used.

At this time I phoned the family doctors and requested a home visit, having explained the situation. Thankfully this was agreed and a doctor duly arrived at our home to examine Margaret. The doctor did all the usual tests such as blood pressure, temperature, breathing etc. and announced that in her opinion there was nothing physically wrong with her and prescribed giving her paracetamol as and when required.

This I duly did with little sign of improvement during this three-week period when in the main she remained in bed, apart from the three or so occasions when she did get up at around 4pm. There was one additional occasion when she did get up prior to midday and we took the opportunity to do some food shopping at the supermarket. This was again extremely challenging as she would start to wander off when I was distracted for a moment when getting something from the fridge or freezers.

As no real improvement was being made, I once again contacted the doctors' surgery who informed me that there was little else they could do as there was nothing physically wrong with her. I was advised of certain telephone numbers I could call for help and advice together with the further advice that should Margaret continue to show violence towards me I should phone emergency services and ask for the police.

On Monday 31 May, a Bank Holiday, Margaret continued to refuse to get out of bed and was particularly distressed by my presence, not recognising me as her husband, believing me to be a complete stranger and wishing her and this other person some sort of harm. Once again, she would start to get agitated with screaming and physical attacks on myself.

Not knowing what to do I dialled 111 to see if I could get some help. I was informed that a doctor would phone me back, which he/she did within a reasonable period of time.

Having fully explained the situation it was confirmed that an ambulance would be sent to assist. I have nothing but praise for the crew that arrived; they were absolutely marvellous in their willingness to do whatever they could. The male and female crew did all the usual procedures such as temperature, blood pressure, ECG and examination, and determined there was no physical problem. From this point on they truly went above and beyond what might be expected of them. The female paramedic tried to persuade Margaret to get out of bed and offered her assistance in getting showered and dressed. It was at this point Margaret made her feelings clearly known, being that she would not get up whilst there were two strange men in the room, being the male paramedic and me.

The gentleman and I retired to another room where he proceeded to make numerous telephone calls to various agencies including social services. Having talked through the situation with the on-duty worker, he was informed right at the end of the conversation that, having given our address and postcode and our doctors' surgery address, we were in fact not within the boundary of responsibility for social care assistance and that we should contact the hospital. I found this to be most peculiar, given that our home and our doctors' surgery are well within the boundary of our area and our council taxes are all paid to that council.

The paramedic explained that he had come across this sort of situation before in this area and had experienced similar situations where NHS boundaries differed from council boundaries. Undeterred, he proceeded to contact elsewhere social services and once again explained the situation. The lady he was talking to asked to speak to me and reassured me I would get the help I needed, making it a priority when the offices returned to work the following day. That was 31 May; today is 9 July, with no assistance given.

Meanwhile, the female paramedic had managed to persuade Margaret to get out of bed and had assisted her in getting showered, hair washed etc. and dressed in clean day clothes, which I had been unable to achieve on my own. She brought Margaret downstairs, got her settled in her chair and made her a cup of tea. As I have said these two people were absolutely wonderful and by the time they left they had spent more than two and a half hours looking after us and doing whatever they could.

I was advised by them that I needed to get help both for Margaret's sake and my own. This was indeed sound advice, especially as it had become apparent that Margaret was unwilling to let anyone other than another female to assist her in washing and dressing.

Sometime between Tuesday and Friday (1-4 June), I contacted a retired Doctor who runs a voluntary care group in our area who in turn gave me the number for a care organisation. I also contacted social services to explain the situation with reference to the conversations I had with the paramedics. If my memory serves me correctly, the person I spoke to was a lady named Sandra who asked me what authority I paid my council tax to, and she confirmed that if I paid council tax to my particular council it would definitely be their social services department who would be responsible for our situation. It was further confirmed that a referral would be made for Margaret and me. To date no-one other than a lady named Fern who is a social care worker in the hospital has contacted me from the Care Department. I also phoned my doctors' surgery, requesting that I also needed to be referred back to the mental health clinic as the previous contact we had had (Sue) on her last visit said she was going to discharge us from their care for the time being, but should we need help in the future we would have to request a re-referral via our doctor.

Since coming back to the mental clinic I have learnt that our previous contact, Sue, has since left the employment of the clinic.

On Friday or Saturday 4 or 5 June 2021, I spoke to a lady we'll call 'J', the owner of the care organisation, to explain the situation regarding Margaret. It was agreed that her sister Vicky, along with one of their carers, would visit me on Sunday 6 June to discuss what sort of care needs would be appropriate. We agreed that we would start with a one-hour visit each morning to assist Margaret in getting up and showered/washed and dressed.

This service commenced on Tuesday 8 June with service provided by the carer I had met on Sunday. This first session seemed to go quite well, with the carer succeeding in getting Margaret up and showered, dressed and downstairs.

The second session did not go anywhere near as well. The carer went upstairs and within ten to fifteen minutes was back downstairs, telling me that Margaret had attacked or pushed her while she was trying to get her in the shower. She reported that she believed Margaret to be a physically strong person and as such she was unable to care for someone like her on her own. This left me a little perplexed as to what we would do next, but I was soon contacted by 'J' with reassurances that they would not give up on us and that they would try other carers with maybe a slightly different approach.

I have to say 'J' has been as good as her word, not only by providing three different carers who have had various degrees of success in getting Margaret showered or washed and into a change of clothes, but also instrumental in speaking to various people or agencies both prior to and after going into hospital.

On the following Sunday Margaret was insistent that she had to go home as she had two small children that needed feeding. This had started to become a regular belief in her mind once she had transitioned from staying in bed to getting up and coming downstairs for the day. I tried to reassure her that she did not have another house in the village and that she did not have any young children to feed. I could not persuade her to the contrary, even showing her pictures of our sons who were then aged fifty and forty-six, together with pictures of us and the fact that that year would be our fiftieth wedding anniversary.

When I left the room for a moment she was up and away through the front door and headed for the street. Despite my calling her she continued to walk at a faster pace than I was able to achieve given the state of my knees. Consequently she was getting further and further away from me, but fortunately a couple of the ladies from further down our road had noticed what was happening and kindly caught up with her and gently persuaded her to come home.

For obvious reasons I then found it necessary to lock the outside doors and make sure there were no keys left lying around. This had the desired effect of making sure Margaret could not run off again, but the downside was that because she still believed she had children to feed she then began to see me as an evil (her words) person who had imprisoned or kidnapped her. This increased her aggression towards me with bouts of severe screaming, throwing things and hitting me. She would threaten to call the police but was unable to do so as she had lost the ability to know how to use the telephone. After one particularly bad episode and violence towards me, I felt I had no alternative but to phone 999 and ask for the police service. After having spoken to the operator and being informed I could expect a visit from police sometime later that day, I became worried about what might happen to my beloved wife. I telephoned the police and explained that I wished for no further action to be taken, but was informed that a police officer would be phoning me the following day as their protocol was to follow up on such reports. This they duly did, but once I explained the circumstances they told me they would not be taking any further action, and emphasised that if I found myself in a similar situation it was perfectly acceptable to phone 999 and ask for assistance, which would be given in a caring and compassionate way.

On two occasions when Margaret was becoming particularly agitated, I offered to take her to this home she believed she had and where her children were who were waiting for her to feed them. This seemed to please her and she readily got in the car so I could drive her around the village to find the house she believed she owned. This involved us driving up and down every street in our town with Margaret stating it was not down this or that street. Having completely covered every street in our town I drove back down our street and it was then that Margaret announced "This is it", and immediately recognised our house as we drove into the driveway. Margaret was happy to enter the house and I was hopeful that she would settle and be calmer. Unfortunately, this calmness lasted for a matter of ten to fifteen minutes, when she then began to insist on going home to feed the children.

The care organisation continued to provide care through three different carers, all of whom were calm in their approach to dealing with Margaret and had varying degrees of success in aiding her to get out of bed and get showered or washed and dressed. I would suggest they were successful in getting her showered for more than 50% of the time.

On Wednesday 16 July Margaret's elder brother and his wife, along with her elder sister, came to visit us and left after lunch the next day. During this time she seemed happy to see them all and in the main I believe she understood her relationship to them. This afforded me the time to do some shopping and they reported that she had been reasonably OK during my absence. They did however report that she was once again saying she would have to go as she had to feed the children and that she had been kidnapped and imprisoned by me. During their stay they experienced some of the animosity that Margaret had been showing towards me. I think it would be fair to say that they were all surprised at the level of deterioration in Margaret's condition.

Fortunately, we were all able to enjoy a barbeque in the garden along with our son Ben and his family, although Margaret didn't seem to recognise Ben as being her son and was still adamant about going home to feed the children.

Margaret's younger sister and brother, along with their spouses, arrived mid-afternoon on Friday 18 June and stayed until midday Sunday 20 June. A similar pattern of events unfolded regarding feeding the children, needing to go home, being kidnapped etc. as well as screaming, and animosity towards me. It was decided that Margaret's brother Paul, Ben and I would go for a game of golf and leave Margaret in the care of her sister, sister-in-law, and brother-in-law on the Saturday afternoon.

During this time they took her out for a drive in the car and reported that she had seemingly had a good time, reminiscing about the past with a considerable amount of laughter being enjoyed by Margaret.

On their departure, Margaret couldn't understand why they were leaving without her or me, falling back into the regular pattern of wanting to go home and the need to feed the children.

The rest of that week remained a similar pattern of events, but bearable without too much animosity towards me.

However, Saturday proved extremely challenging with an increased amount of screaming at me and physical abuse.

Eventually we retired to bed around midnight, some two hours later than normal, as Margaret refused to go to bed.

On Sunday I awoke having had a peaceful night's sleep, which I should add is quite normal for both of us, save helping Margaret to the toilet once or twice in the night. I usually get up around 5 to 5.30 and use this time as a quiet period for myself or as an opportunity to do some household chores.

I was doing the ironing at around 6.30am when I was startled at the sight of Margaret stood looking at me and crying. I asked her what on earth the matter was and why she was so upset. Her reply was that she was scared and frightened because that "bloody" woman was trying to kill her; she was trying to drown her in perfume.

I managed to get her to sit in her chair in the lounge and went into the kitchen to make her a cup of tea and a piece of toast, which is usual each morning but normally around 8.00 to 8.30am, never as early as 6.30am.

We now moved into a whole new, frightening phase of behaviour from Margaret. This included physically and verbally abusing herself. She began to shout at this imaginary person using foul and abusive words, threatening to kill her, and began to violently attack herself, thinking her own arms and legs were somehow not hers but those of an entirely different person.

It was at this point that I realised I was unable to cope with this situation as when I tried to stop her harming herself by explaining that there was no third person and that she was attacking herself, this was followed by her once again turning her aggression towards me.

In view of this and not knowing what to do I telephoned our son Ben, who immediately came round within the following twenty to thirty minutes.

Ben, like myself, was distressed to see his mum behaving in such a manner and had the presence of mind to capture her behaviour on his phone whilst trying to calm her and convince her that there was no-one here other than the three of us.

Having been given a Crisis, Relapse and Contingency Plan by the mental health practitioner from the Specialist Memory Service, I followed the instructions of this advice to phone the Urgent Advice Line (located in London) on 0800 0234 650 for advice and support.

This call was made around 8.15am and answered by a recorded message saying that I was number two in the queue and to continue to hold. This I did and within five minutes or so the message told me I was number one in the queue. Finally, thirty-five minutes after calling this helpline, my call was answered by an operator asking how he could help me. I explained fully the circumstances leading up to the call and was told that I was being put back on hold. Two to three minutes later the line was disconnected.

My feelings were that this was far from satisfactory, especially given the length of time it had taken to get through to someone I could speak to.

As no help or advice was forthcoming, I decided to phone 111 and again went through the sequence of events before being told that because it was not physical I couldn't get an ambulance. Only through persistence I was put through to a nurse and again explained the situation. I was then told that she would contact a doctor who would come out to the house within the next two hours to do an assessment, but I should receive a call from said doctor prior to this to advise me of time of arrival.

Two hours later, no call and no visit from a doctor.

At this point the last resort was to telephone 999 at just before 11.00am. Once again, I explained the situation and was informed that someone would get back to me. At approximately 11.10am a call was received from 0186935001 stating that a doctor would call back within the next two hours.

At 12.35pm I received a call back from the urgent advice line to apologise for me being cut off. This was over three and a half hours since being cut off. My feelings are that this service is mis-described. I do not consider this length of time to be acceptable when something as serious as this situation was being treated with anything like the urgency that it warranted. I merely informed the caller of this fact and informed him that I was seeking help from an alternative source.

At 1.16pm, we (being either my son or myself) tried calling the number from whom we had had a call at 11.10am, only to discover that this number was blocked.

Consequently we re-dialled 999 explaining once again the

situation. Despite calling several times throughout the remainder of the afternoon and evening we were met with the same reasoning, being that there were no ambulances available for non-emergency cases.

As no help was forthcoming, by 10.00pm (our usual time for retiring to bed) I felt the best thing to do was to go to bed and see what we could do the following day. Sleep gives both Margaret and me an escape from these traumas, at least for a few hours. Ben returned to his family and home and we went straight to sleep.

Sometime between 10.45pm and 11.00pm, I was awoken by flashlights shining through the windows of our bedroom. I immediately got up and dressed, went downstairs and on opening the door was greeted by two ambulance crew members who stated that they were pleased to know they had managed to wake me as they were about to telephone the fire brigade to bash the door down. I asked them why they would do such a thing and was informed this was protocol in an emergency. My only comment was that we had been told all day that we were not regarded as an emergency for the past twelve hours, yet all of a sudden after just ten minutes or so on the premises we were now deemed as an emergency.

Within a few minutes our son Ben arrived back, having being contacted as the paramedics had initially been unable to awaken me.

The crew were very nice and informed us that they were instructed to take Margaret to Accident and Emergency. I explained that she was now settled and asleep and therefore I did not intend to awaken her at this time as this would only cause her further stress and upset. In addition we explained to them that we were told a doctor would visit to assess her and have her admitted straight onto a ward, so we were not happy with the thought of her having to go through even more trauma in A&E. Having experienced on far too many occasions the shortcomings of waiting in A&E, both my son and I did not wish to subject Margaret to this.

The ambulance crew were sympathetic to our viewpoint and agreed it would be better to wait until the following day. As one of the crew was only part-time in this role he explained that his day job was of a more senior role in the ambulance service and that he would reschedule an ambulance for the next day, as he put it, on the docket for 8.00 am the following day.

Our son Ben called round at about 7.30am and we awaited the arrival of an ambulance, expecting that this would be sometime between 8.00 and 9.00am. As no ambulance had arrived by 10.00am Ben telephoned the ambulance crew member from the previous night on the number he had given us in case of any problems.

He was sorry to hear that no ambulance had arrived and said he would look into it and call us back. Approximately five to ten minutes later he called back to apologise that someone had removed the booking from that day's docket and regretfully we were left with no other choice but to re-contact emergency services and start again. This we did and explained the situation regarding the previous night and our expectation of an ambulance that morning.

An ambulance did eventually arrive at around 11.15am and the whole situation over the past twenty-four-plus hours was explained to them. Margaret was once again seen to by the crew, who eventually left our home around two hours later.

It was explained to me that they had no alternative but to take us to A&E but that I was able to accompany Margaret in the ambulance.

Having arrived at A&E we were shown into a side room with soft seating and informed that a nurse would be along in a short time to take her blood pressure, temperature, and bloods. The first two were achieved on the first visit, although Margaret became a little distressed by the pressure created by the arm cuff whilst taking her blood pressure.

Approximately four hours passed before Margaret was seen by two doctors from the mental health team. During this time I took Margaret to the toilet four times, each time giving her the funnel and bottle, which I explained how to use; each time she was adamant that I was not allowed in the toilet to assist her and each time she forgot to take a sample of her urine. Margaret got agitated with me whilst waiting in this side room and showed aggression towards me both physically and verbally. At one point she got up and went for a walkabout in the wards of A&E announcing that I could F*** ***, she would do what she wanted. Obviously I was concerned not only for Margaret but also the other patients lying there in various states of distress of their own. Despite trying to calm her down and get her back to the room this was clearly not working and so I called out for help from any one of the many people working there. I believe my words were "Would someone please help me?". Now here's the shocking thing: not one person came to my assistance, not one person said a single word to me; absolutely everyone there ignored my pleas for help.

This incident was followed by Margaret walking out of the A&E department, heading towards the outside door, and yet again no-one from the clinical staff so much as battered an eyelid or came to my assistance.

Fortunately an ambulance crew were booking in another patient and told me not to worry, that they would get her back, which they thankfully did.

On arrival of the two mental health doctors, one of them, presumably the most senior, started asking Margaret various questions e.g. did she know where she was, what was her date of birth, did she know how she got here etc. The doctor then turned to me to ask me some questions about Margaret's behaviours. It was at this point I explained that if I answered his questions honestly this would no doubt cause Margaret further stress and was likely to cause further reactions from her. I suggested it may be better if I explained the situation in a more private setting away from Margaret. I was told not to worry, that wouldn't be necessary. Surprise, surprise, Margaret then jumped up, fists clenched, calling me a b******. At this point she once again headed for the door onto the wards and had to be brought back into the room by the doctors. I was told to go and sit in a waiting area and that the doctor would come to speak to me later.

After approximately forty-five minutes the doctor took me to a small consulting room and told me he didn't think Margaret would be able to go home today. (Really, I thought!) I explained that we had had to fight hard to get Margaret to the hospital, she needed professional help, and there was no expectation on my part that I wanted to take her home in her current state of distress.

I left the hospital around 7.30 with my son giving me a lift home.

The following morning I telephoned the hospital to enquire as to Margaret's whereabouts and condition. I was informed that she was on an admissions ward and that later on she would be moved to an appropriate ward.

I subsequently found out that she was on Ward 3 and telephoned to ask as to her well-being and if there was anything I needed to bring in for her, such as night clothes, toothbrush, change of day clothes etc. but was assured that there was no necessity for these items as the hospital had all the requirements needed. I enquired as to visiting and was advised that it may be better to leave it for a couple of days to give Margaret the chance to settle in.

This was Tuesday 29 June, and by Thursday 1 July on my telephoning the ward to enquire about how Margaret was doing I was told that it would be OK for me to visit her from Friday 2 July.

Subsequently, I had done so each day since and tried to give her some stimulation by reading to her and going through our old photo albums, and I took in a bag with a change of clothes, pyjamas and personal hygiene items, toothbrush, soap etc.

On the third or fourth visit I enquired as to why it was that Margaret was still wearing the same clothes that she had on when admitted to hospital and if she was getting changed into her pyjamas at the end of the day.

I was told that she had refused any assistance to get washed or changed and that she had in fact been wearing these clothes 24/7.

My wife has always taken extreme care of her personal hygiene and appearance, and to see her in this state was of great sadness and distress to not only myself but I have no doubt that somewhere in herself she too would not be feeling right about these issues. Bad enough to have to contend with the effects of this terrible disease, but it appeared that she now had to contend with the loss of her dignity.

Imagine my delight to find that she had been showered and changed when I visited the following day.

Less than one week later I was informed that she had been washed and changed again, but subsequently once again this week I had to request that she be given more encouragement to shower and change her clothes. Again I was informed that Margaret continually refuses assistance in getting showered and changed. I explained that since having carers at home to assist her in getting up in the morning and showering or washing then dressing, that they too experienced resistance, but with some gentle cajoling they achieved the desired result in excess of 50-60% of the time.

Once again on the following day's visit she had been showered and changed, proving that it is possible to persuade Margaret to undertake these important personal hygiene tasks.

My feeling is that it should not require me to have to bring this to the attention of the nurses on the ward before they do anything.

On a far more serious matter, at the end of Margaret's first week in hospital I enquired of one of the nurses as to if or when the doctors from the mental health team would be seeing my wife. The nurse I spoke to consulted a piece of paper and informed me that she had already been seen by said doctors. I enquired as to why I had not been informed of this fact and was directed back to the side of my wife's bed to await word from the on-duty doctor.

In a matter of just a few minutes a doctor arrived, pulled the curtains around the bed and started by asking me, "What makes you think your wife has a mental health problem?".

I could not believe what I was hearing, and I believe my response was, "I beg your pardon?", to which the doctor restated her question.

This felt like a real kick in the gut to discover that a doctor on the ward on which my wife was being cared for had no clue as to why she was in there. I proceeded to demonstrate to this doctor, in actual detail, how Margaret had been abusing herself by hitting myself on the arm and legs just as she had been doing.

The doctor responded by telling me not to do that and said she would have to consult with the rest of the team later on.

I had not left the confines of the hospital grounds when I received a call from the same doctor to apologise for the fact that she claimed not to have read fully my wife's notes prior to speaking to me. You may well imagine I was very concerned that my wife was supposedly being cared for by people who seemingly didn't even know why she was in there. I did, however, discover that the visit by the mental health team doctors, that the nurse had referred to, did not occur whilst she was on the ward but during the admission process in A&E which I have described earlier.

The following day I contacted our Health Professional Access contact from the Memory Clinic, not only to appraise her of the previous day's happenings, but to enquire as to whether or not she had any further information with regard to the appointment of a social care worker that she had previously informed me would be allocated in-house by the hospital to handle my wife's case.

I learnt that the clinic had been informed by the hospital's Mental Health Team that they would not be attending on Margaret whilst in the hospital as it was their view that as the clinic had been dealing with Margaret's case for some time, they felt it best for the clinic to continue to do so as they knew the patient better than they did.

I was further informed that the clinic had only one full-time doctor (who was currently off sick) and one part-time doctor. She personally was not aware of what authority she or anyone from the clinic had in respect of visiting Margaret on the ward. I further learnt that a social care worker named Fiona had been allocated to Margaret's case.

Once my son and I had spoken to Fiona we understood that she would try to arrange a meeting with us, the mental health team doctors and herself. Regretfully this meeting did not take place prior to Fiona leaving for a one-week vacation period.

I did at one stage enquire as to whether or not Margaret had had a brain scan and was informed that her records indicated that she had a scan, but no information was forthcoming as to when this had taken place, or the results of such a scan.

My concern was that, due to the rapid deterioration in Margaret's condition, I needed reassurance that there was not something else going on in addition to the Alzheimer's disease.

I was beginning to feel that I was being treated like a mushroom, being kept in the dark, whilst not confident that my beloved wife was getting the best treatment and care that she deserves.

In desperation I decided to visit my GP surgery with the intention of speaking to the practice's senior doctor. On arrival at reception I was informed that the doctor was on annual leave and I subsequently asked to see the most senior doctor on duty that day. The receptionist informed me that I would have to make an appointment for a telephone consultation, but being there was only one doctor on duty, I believe she told me that her diary was full for the day. I informed her that I would wait to see her when she arrived. I was informed that they had to adhere to certain protocols and that waiting in reception was not possible.

I explained to the receptionist that sometimes certain protocols were not appropriate to certain situations and that this was one of these occasions. I proceeded to explain the reason for my actions, at which point the receptionist became accepting of my need to see a doctor. She did inform me it would likely be a very long wait, but I in turn explained that an hour or two waiting was of no consequence compared with the wait my wife was having to endure.

The doctor to whom I spoke (can't remember her name) was known to me as the doctor attending Margaret at home, as previously detailed. I explained the situation and I was informed that there was little that she could do. Eventually she said she would phone the ward and get an update on her condition. The date of this visit was Thursday 8 July.

Having heard nothing back from this doctor, not even a courtesy call to say she had tried but was unable to give me an update, I decided to repeat the exercise once more and see the doctor who normally looks after us, calling into the surgery on Wednesday 14 July.

The doctor listened to what I had to say and confirmed she would contact the hospital for an update and telephone me later on in the day.

This she duly did and informed me that Margaret had been visited earlier that day by a care worker who would be making recommendations for the immediate future. I asked the doctor what time she had spoken to the hospital and I was told about 3.15pm. I found this a little strange as I was just leaving the ward about that time. Why then did no-one on the ward deem it relevant to inform me of this fact whilst I was there?

As my son Benjamin used our allocated visiting time on Thursday 15 July to see his mum, my first opportunity to ask the question of whether anyone been to examine or consult my wife was Friday 16 July. At that time I was informed that a psychiatrist had looked at Margaret and that it was likely that they would be looking to transfer her to a residential assessment centre.

Whilst visiting my doctors' surgery on the first occasion, a gentleman, who I now know to be a retired doctor, was directed to me by the receptionist as someone that may be able to help me. I had previously spoken to him when looking for assistance in finding a care firm to care for my wife at home. It was on his recommendation that we were able to secure the services of the care organisation, who in turn through the owner of the business, 'J', has been supportive in assisting me with speaking to her contacts and providing advice throughout this traumatic time.

The retired doctor took the time to visit me at home and afforded me the opportunity, over a two-hour period, to vent my feelings about the shortcomings we have experienced.

It was regretful that approximately ten days after being admitted to Ward 3 the ward was closed completely and all patients and staff were transferred to Ward 14, which was undoubtedly a nicer environment and more modern; the downside being that any change in surroundings causes further confusion and stress to Alzheimer's patients.

Whilst visiting Margaret each day it was necessary to book an allocated time for visiting her the following day. This I did by visiting the nurses' station at the end of each visit and at the same time enquire as to whether she had been seen by anyone from the Mental Health Team. The standard reply seemed to be no; they were still waiting on a specialist doctor to visit her.

On Thursday 15 July I made this usual enquiry and again the reply was "still waiting". Imagine my surprise to receive a call from the Mental Health Clinic when I returned home (around 4.45pm), to be informed of the good news that Margaret had been seen by a psychiatrist at 11.00am that morning. This was in total contrast to what I had been told just less than two hours previously. Needless to say, the following day I made a point of asking the same senior nurse I had spoken to the day before, to enquire as to why she had given me the false information that Margaret had not been seen by a doctor, when in reality she had been seen by a psychiatrist at 11.00am.

Her response I found absolutely unbelievable. She informed me that they would not necessarily know what doctors visited the ward on any particular day or time as they were all vetted very carefully and could come and go onto the wards as they pleased without reporting to the nurses' station. I believe my response was to suggest that I did not believe doctors were incapable of losing their swipe card, and had everyone forgotten about Doctor Harold Shipman, Britain's worst mass murderer.

As I was concerned about what I considered to be a lack of interest in getting anyone to actually give my wife any treatment on Wednesday 21st July at approximately 1.00pm I decided to visit the building adjacent to the car park that was signed as "Community Office of Mental Health Services."

I believe I was very fortunate to be able to speak to the Deputy Director for Community Health Services, who gave me the time to listen to our experiences and was genuinely interested in what I had to say. She promised to speak to the Mental

Health Team and pass on my concerns. I do believe that she did as she promised and that her intervention was instrumental in the process of getting Margaret admitted to the Specialist Mental Health facility known as TOPAS on Thursday 22 July.

It was explained to me that they were going to section her under Section 2 of the Mental Health Act, due to her being unable to give her consent to being admitted to TOPAS. I objected to this and informed them that as I held power of attorney, I would give consent on her behalf. I was told that this was not possible and there was no alternative but to section her.

Again I was advised not to visit Margaret for a few days to allow her to settle into her new surroundings, and made my first visit the following Wednesday, 28 July.

PART 3
The initial impression of this specialist unit

On arrival I was handed an envelope and informed that it was a copy of her care plan. At last, I thought. This appeared to be a very positive step in the right direction with people who knew how to look after patients with my wife's condition.

On arrival home I carefully read through this care plan, but was disappointed to note there were certain anomalies that required addressing.

The care plan consisted of fourteen pages, each one itemising a different category of care need, the person responsible for providing the care as well as the current situation as was relevant at that time and a date for the next review.

I had two principal areas of concern to do with this paperwork:

(1) On analysing the review dates it became apparent that no fewer than nine categories had dates ranging from twelve to thirty-five days after the end of the

twenty-eight-day sectioning period. My feeling at the time was that these dates had been set too far into the future, and as I had hoped that Margaret could return home at the end of the twenty-eight-day period. I needed clarity on this situation

(2) The second issue was of even greater concern to me because the accompanying notes in a number of categories referred to Margaret with the use of male prefixes, being he, him, his. This was in my opinion a clear indication that the care plan was not as personal to my wife as it should have been. I could only surmise that the plan had been, at least in part, prepared by cutting and pasting from another patient's records; not the quality of care I believe is necessary to install confidence in their procedures.

In view of these concerns I compiled a list of queries and detailed the anomalies included in the care plan, with the intention of discussing these with her doctor.

On my next visit to see Margaret I approached a senior nurse to enquire as to how I should go about making an appointment to see her doctor. Unfortunately, I was informed that Dr G was away on annual leave and that probably it would be best to send him an email, so that he would get this immediately on his return. This I duly did, but the email address I had been given was incorrect and came back as not known.

Consequently on my next visit I left a copy of the email to be handed to Dr G on his return.

Before I continue by sharing the outcome of the two meetings held by Dr G and the correspondence that took place between us, I thought I'd have a quick recap of how "unlucky" we had been up to this point in time. Surely it couldn't get any worse! Could it?

- An emergency helpline number that was not fit for purpose
- The ambulance service who would not send help because it was not deemed to be an emergency
- When approximately twelve hours had passed, the ambulance crew deemed the situation to be such an emergency that they were about to call on the fire brigade to break down our front door
- After agreeing to rebook the ambulance to arrive the following morning, this was cancelled by someone else deciding to take it off the docket
- The waiting time in A&E was such that Margaret was totally distressed and began to wander around the wards, abusing me both physically and verbally
- Despite my plea for help, not one person in A&E stepped forward to offer assistance
- Likewise when she walked out of A&E, fortunately two ambulance crew members came to my assistance
- Two mental health doctors who wouldn't listen to me about talking to them in private, further distressing Margaret, and them having to agree with what I had told them
- These two doctors had no comprehension of why or how hard I'd had to fight to get her to hospital, stating that they didn't feel she could go home that evening

- Margaret was basically ignored during the first four days in hospital; food was delivered to her, but no-one seemed to show any concern when she didn't eat it
- There was no follow up by the hospital mental health team
- Their answer to not visiting Margaret on the ward was because, as she was already known to The Memory Clinic, they would leave it up to them.
- The Memory Clinic had only one full-time doctor, who was off-duty through illness, leaving only a part-time doctor and a department who was unsure of their rights to make hospital visits
- Caring for Margaret's personal hygiene and general well-being was appalling
- The allocated hospital social services person promised my son and me that she would organise a meeting between us and the doctors, but failed to do so and left on annual leave without putting this in place
- The on-duty ward doctor had no idea of the reason why Margaret was residing on the ward, so much so that she was to ask me twice what made me think my wife had a mental health problem
- The same doctor later on that day apologised to me, stating that she had not fully read my wife's notes, when in reality it was clear she had not read them at all
- Despite asking each day, after she had been relocated to another ward, I was repeatedly told that she had not been seen by the mental health team

- Finally, after subsequently discovering that eventually she was seen by a mental health doctor, this was at a time prior to a visit after which I had again asked the same question
- The following day when questioned as to why I had been told no, the nurse in charge informed me that they were not made aware of visits onto the ward by doctors who could come and go as they pleased and did not report to the nurses' station.

Had we just been unlucky? Was this to be the end of so many examples of bad luck? Someone once said to me that their success in what they did had nothing to do with good luck and was firmly of the opinion that people made their own luck.

Anyone who subscribes to this belief is, to put it politely, living in a fantasy world. If you don't believe that good luck exists then it follows there can be no such thing as bad luck. We are none of us totally in control of our own destiny. Did those poor souls who went to work on 11 September 2001, in the World Trade Centre in New York, like they had done many times before, really bring it upon themselves to have to make the choice of how they were going to die on that day? What a terrible option: die by staying where they were and burning to death, or jump out of one of the world's tallest skyscrapers.

If I had hoped that our run of bad luck was about to come to an end, I was to be sadly wrong. It was just beginning.

The really saddening aspect of all of this is that other people's actions can and do have devastating consequences on the lives of other innocent people.

Having experienced first-hand just how bad things can be for people with dementia, and indeed how such a terrible disease impacts on the lives of so many others, it is hard to comprehend why any decent person would do anything that poured even more bad luck into their lives.

PART 4
Meeting and correspondence between Margaret's doctor, Dr G, and me.
Email sent 1 August 2021 and delivered by hand

Dear Dr G,

My wife Margaret was admitted into TOPAS on 22 July, having been in Hospital X for a period of twenty-four days prior to this. My name is David Allott. I am Margaret's husband, carer and nearest relative, and hold lasting powers of attorney for her health and welfare.

Following Margaret's admission I was advised not to visit her for the first few days in order to help her settle into her new surroundings. The first time I was able to book a visiting appointment was on the following Wednesday at 3.00pm. It was on this visit that I was handed an envelope and informed that this was a copy of Margaret's care package. My immediate thoughts were that at last she was in a place that truly cared and that she was eventually in a place where she would get the help she needed, with things done in a professional and caring way.

It must be said that this was not my experience whilst she was being cared for at Hospital X; suffice to say that I felt I had to fight to get any information, or things done, and that certain staff members were totally inadequate.

My communication with TOPAS personnel has been informative when I've asked about Margaret's day-to-day progress, friendly and helpful.

On my return home from that visit I was understandably keen to read the contents of the care package put in place to look after the most precious person in my life.

Prior to my second visit, yesterday, Saturday 31 July, I prepared a brief summary of the paperwork that I had been given and asked to speak to someone about certain concerns that I had about this paperwork.

Most of my concerns are self-explanatory from the two attachments I have forwarded to you. However, what is not listed there, and this is something I brought up whilst speaking to the Care Co-ordinator, is my strong feeling that this paperwork has been prepared by someone who appears to have taken the easy road of cutting and pasting at least some of the documentation from another patient's notes. I would refer you to the use of the male prefixes, i.e. "He", "Him", "His" within the notes for the goal "For Margaret's Mental Health to be assessed under Section 2 of the Mental Health Act to cater for her needs".

Hazel was very understanding and confirmed that she would look into this, as the Care Co-ordinator who prepared this paperwork is fairly new to the role.

Please rest assured I do not wish to be critical of anyone. I have tremendous respect for the personnel involved with looking after the loved ones of other people in extremely challenging circumstances. My only desire is to get Margaret home into the surroundings of our family home and to look after her with the help of carers to assist her in things she would prefer another female to do for her.

Consequently, I look forward to having a meeting with you to discuss where we are with her medication review and progress to date.

Finally, Hazel suggested that I may be allowed to take Margaret out for an hour or so, especially as there are no visiting slots left this week until next Saturday.

Following this email I was contacted by another nurse from TOPAS, who introduced herself as the new person responsible for Margaret's care and care plan. She was able to inform me that a new care plan would be forthcoming and that the doctors would be doing an assessment with Margaret, so that she could be granted what is termed as a Section 17 leave, due to her being on a Section 2. I was also later on informed that a meeting had been arranged with Dr G for Thursday 12 August.

At that meeting, there was Dr G, two other doctors and a nurse from TOPAS with one person taking notes on the computer, and Penelope from social services. I, of course, was also in attendance with our son, Benjamin. There was no mention of us being provided with minutes of the meeting and therefore I deemed it necessary to record our understanding of what had been said by emailing Dr G with the following letter in order that this would then be a matter of record.

Email sent Tuesday 17 August as follows:

> Firstly I would like to thank you for our meeting on Thursday last, 12 August.
>
> As you will have observed from my reactions on the day, I found myself extremely distressed by some of the things you by necessity had to inform me of in relation to my wife's condition. Whilst it did not come as any surprise to me that she was unable to distinguish which was her room and how to find the toilet, it saddened me greatly to learn that she could no longer understand what the toilet bowl was and how she was no longer able to sit at the table for her meals without assistance.
>
> Whilst I endeavoured to take in all that you were saying, I did find it difficult to maintain 100% concentration, due in part to the fact that I was so upset.

However, I did take in the fact that you have released her from Section 2 of the Mental Health Act and that she now resides at TOPAS under Deprivation of Liberty Safeguards (DOLS). I also noted that you also confirmed she was now in a position to be discharged from TOPAS, either into my care at home, with assistance of visiting carers, or into a care facility, which you felt was probably the best option. You also requested me to think about what option I thought to be most suitable and to let you know which of these would be my preference by Monday 16 August.

Having now had a few days to consider what I would prefer and what is best for Margaret, I am still of the opinion that I want to try and see if we can cope together by living at home.

However, on looking back on that meeting, it became apparent to me that I had not fully grasped what the formality of that meeting was. As you know, I had a meeting on Monday 16 August with Penelope from the Adult Social Care Department and asked her what her understanding was. She informed me that the correct terminology was "A Discharge Meeting".

Over the weekend I have had the opportunity to do some further research into Margaret's rights and also those of myself and our son Benjamin, who are her legal attorneys as registered with The Office of the Public Guardian.

So much so that I questioned Penelope on whether or not having her doing an assessment on Margaret and me was not somewhat premature. I have learnt that prior to discharge a patient should be assessed by her health team for the determination of the possibility that they may indeed qualify to go forward to be assessed for Continuing Healthcare funding on the NHS. Furthermore we have the right to be present and offer our own input into that assessment and its grading under the eleven categories listed.

Clearly this has not happened and when I queried this at the meeting with Penelope and one of the nurses present, I was informed that this was not necessary at this stage and that it would be done later.

I do not believe this to be the correct order of events and, having looked carefully at the eleven categories and applied my own ratings to them, there is no question in my mind that Margaret more than qualifies to go forward for a "full assessment" at a Multi-Disciplinary Meeting.

Furthermore, I have subsequently learnt that the initial checklist should have been completed when she first entered hospital, or if done later should not take into account any improvement of her condition due to the prescribing of new medications.

I now find myself in a position with social care where they are advising not only home care visits and visits to day care centres etc., all of which is fully appreciated and no doubt needed, but also on the assumption that it is all self-funding. I am quite happy at Penelope's suggestion of a home visit by herself and the Occupational Team to visit our home to assess if any alterations/improvements are needed to reduce the elements of risk and harm to either Margaret or myself.

This all feels like we are putting the cart before the horse until we have done the initial assessment.

It had been our intention to spend today looking into what our options would be if/or when the time arrives for the need for Margaret to go into a care home.

On phoning around some of these facilities it has become apparent that they too would require copies of her assessments and notes as these would, in addition to their own assessment, be required to determine the suitability of their facility and its ability to service the needs and care of my wife. There is little point in going to the effort of looking at facilities if they do not fulfil the criteria needed to deal with Margaret's condition.

Finally, I would confirm that having raised the issue of Margaret's care plan, promised two weeks ago, that I am now in possession of same under nine different headings.

I look forward to hearing from you

Regards

David Allott

Two days later on 19 August Dr G responded with the following email, as set out below, unchanged.

Thank you David for your email. I hope you are coping well with changes with Margaret and life in general.

I have requested social services to speak to you as most of the processes you mentioned are related to placement and social matters which they would be better able to answer. In summary my view points and difference of opinion is mentioned below.

(1) The meeting we had was <u>planning</u> meeting to see what is the best future option for Margaret in discussion with family / power of attorneys. This meeting is arranged to give update on progress and express our professional opinion about future care. We take on board views of the family and come to a mutual agreement which in this case was to go home with care.

(2) Internet information can be confusing and give personal opinions which might differ from reality. I am not sure where did you get information on CHC funding being done for everyone. My understanding is that this is done only for patients requiring nursing care. Margaret does not have nursing needs like giving injections, doing dressings, nebulisers etc. Her needs

are more of a social nature and would be explored under social care funding.
(3) Both CHC and Social care funding streams have checklists / questionnaires which are done when a decision of discharge destination has been made. They are not done prior to this decision.

As decision of discharge was done only when discharge planning meeting happened, hence it was not useful to do the checklist before that. As she is not going into a care home at this discharges so again any checklist would be futile. For CHC funding, the 11 domains which you mentioned when filled by staff are then cross-checked and questioned by funding authorities. For your satisfaction, we have agreed to do the checklist, but I do not think it will have any implications on her funding or placement of discharge.

More answers about the full process can be provided by social services.

Regards
Dr G.

Before I give you my response to this communication from Dr G, I would ask you to consider how you may have responded had you been put in a similar position, or indeed, and God forbid, if you are in the future.

This was my response of 23 August 2021:

Dear Dr G,
Reference Margaret Allott
Thank you for your email of Thursday 19 August 2021 in reply to my email to you of Tuesday 17 August 2021.
I can confirm that social services plus another occupational therapist (whose name escapes me) visited our home on Friday

20 August along with my dear wife Margaret with the principal aim of establishing how she would get on at home, and to advise of any significant areas of concern that need addressing from a health and safety point of view.

I am pleased to be able to confirm that Margaret appeared to be happy to be at home and readily settled into her own chair in the lounge. Penelope sat with Margaret for the fifteen minutes or so that it took her colleague and me to look around our home and identify areas that maybe required some degree of amendment to keep both of us as safe as is possible. Fortunately, there were not many of these, some being a simple matter of removing rugs that could be trip hazards and altering grab rails etc.

The principal cause for concern was the staircase, both from a safety point of view and Margaret's ability to negotiate this even with assistance. However, I do not consider that this is an insurmountable problem.

My understanding is that they will return again with Margaret this week and we will establish how I may cope in assisting her with getting dressed. When I explained that previously she had been unwilling to allow me to help her because I was a male, I think that at that time she did not necessarily understand I was her husband. There is no doubt in my mind that she now recognises me as someone she knows and has affection for, as her face lights up each and every time I visit her at TOPAS. This may not extend to knowing I am her husband, or indeed understand what that terminology actually means, but so long as she is happy in my company I believe that she may allow me to attend to some of her toileting, washing and dressing needs etc. To that end, Jenny stated that she would look into whether or not she had been assisted at TOPAS by any male personnel, and if so Margaret's reaction to the same. If not, she would look into whether this could be addressed this week.

As you have stated, there is clearly a difference of opinion that exists between us, and in some instances these differences could have serious implications for both Margaret and me. Consequently, I will address the points you have made by reference to the three areas that you have identified.

(1) Thank you for clarifying the actual purpose of our meeting on Thursday 12 August, being that the correct terminology is that it was a **discharge planning** meeting. I am grateful for the time taken to update our son Benjamin and me on how she is doing, even though as previously stated some of these things were extremely upsetting for both of us.

It is accepted that in your professional opinion you felt that a discharge into a care home was the preference, but you accepted that in this case we would explore the other option of bringing Margaret into the comfortable environment of her own home.

I do understand that this terrible disease is incurable and, as has certainly been evidenced, there is a progressive decline in all patients which ultimately means that the patients' needs change over time. There is no doubt that Margaret's condition accelerated beyond what I had expected in a very short period of time. After nearly fifty years of marriage I am sure you will appreciate that every single additional day that we can enjoy each other's company is precious to us. I have to accept that there is the chance that a time will come when Margaret may become reliant on having care provided in a residential care home, but until that time arises it is my duty to do the very best for her, which includes fighting for her rights.

(2) I would agree with you wholeheartedly that internet information can be confusing and give personal opinions which might differ from reality, but conversely

internet information can also be educative and enlightening, dependent upon the source.

You have stated that I gave you the impression that CHC funding was available for everyone. This is simply just not true. I have looked again at my email and find no mention by me of having said any such thing.

It is important not to jump to conclusions when someone else's opinions differ from those of ourselves. As I have said, the source of information should be the deciding factor of whether or not the information is accurate or not.

If I had just been trolling the internet searching for some opinion just to suit my desires, then this would be an entirely different matter from the reality of the situation.

I am sure that given almost any scenario we could all find all manner of people that would be willing to participate in conspiracy theories.

We have in point a serious example of such misuse of the internet, with vast numbers of otherwise sensible people believing that they should not participate in the Covid vaccination programme simply because they believe the vaccines have been interfered with by government agencies to track and spy on individuals.

We live in an age of instant access to information, for which we owe a tremendous debt of gratitude to Allan Turing, whose advancement of this form of technology was founded at Bletchley Park.

We are encouraged to use the internet for all manner of sensible applications, not least by our government, professional bodies and most tellingly the vast amount of information that is provided by the NHS.

Indeed I have experienced numerous occasions when my

own GP has resorted to the internet to clarify information that he/she was not entirely 100% clear on.

No doubt you, Dr G, have likewise had the need to consult appropriate domains for further information or clarity.

In order that you are fully aware of the source of my information, I would like to confirm the following domains have been used:

(A) **The Alzheimer's Society**. If this is not a reliable source of information, then I can only say we are all of us in deep trouble, especially as the NHS constantly refers patients to them for information and indeed distributes copious amounts of literature for them.

They are well-versed in the use of the assessment forms for CHC funding and have many case histories when correct procedures have not been followed in making these assessments.

One is also able to view these and individuals' experiences as examples of how there have been many instances of wrongful interpretation of the correct procedures which have denied genuine claimants their rights within the law.

(B) **AGE Concern** also provides information of a similar nature and provides links to other domains that highlight points of law, case histories and judgements that over years have helped formulate more detailed and fair systems of dealing with assessments within the NHS, all of which has led to revisions and altered interpretations within the National Framework for NHS Continuing Healthcare and NHS-funded nursing care.

(C) The third principal source of information has been three specialist law firms who specialise in healthcare issues.

Between these law firms the stories are very similar as to the information the patients were given and not given.

- It seems first principle in the NHS is not to even mention the existence of CHC funding, presumably on the basis that someone can't ask for something they know nothing about
- There is no evidence so far as I can see of any leaflets, posters etc. directing anyone to look into CHC either in TOPAS or the main hospital
- I would liken my experience to that of a mushroom, especially in Hospital X and slightly less so in TOPAS. Being kept in the dark and a lack of communication between departments is quite frankly appalling
- On reading other people's experiences, they report being told such things as CHC is not available to persons with dementia or Alzheimer's
- There is clearly a grey area that exists between the definition of what constitutes CHC or social care and in view of the fact there is an upper limit to the latter and no lower limitations on the former this is conveniently used to assume that the majority of cases are funnelled into the social care route because this is means-tested whereas CHC is not
- It appears that the misguided opinion of one person can have a devastating effect on families because they haven't been given options or are unable to fight for the rights of their loved ones at a time in their lives when they are vulnerable and most in need of help whilst having to come to terms with such a cruel and devastating disease
- There is without a doubt a culture in this country of accepting that if the doctor says something then clearly that must be correct; after all, they are the professionals and it is hard to question their viewpoint. This places a

terrific responsibility on all doctors to know where possible that the decisions they make are done legitimately through having the correct knowledge; to do otherwise is to act in a God-like way with little feeling for the effects that their decisions have on their patients or loved ones.

It pains me to suggest that your penultimate paragraph shows little regard for some of those things mentioned above and that there exists some really grey areas in your understanding of the due process.

You state that "because Margaret is not going into a care home at this discharge so again any checklist would be futile".

For your assistance I would direct you to page 21 paragraph 63 of the National Framework. I quote: "NHS Continuing Healthcare may be provided in any setting (including, but not limited to, a care home, hospice or the person's own home. Eligibility for NHS Continuing Healthcare is, therefore, not determined or influenced either by the setting, where the care is provided, or by the characteristics of the person who delivers the care."

Clearly your statement "My understanding is that CHC funding is available only for patients requiring nursing care. Margaret does not have nursing needs like giving injections, doing dressings, nebulisers etc" is an incorrect understanding on your part.

You go on to state "Her needs are more of a social nature and would be explored under social care funding."

I believe that the very fact that the terminology "Continuing Healthcare" is in itself indicative of what interpretation should be applied to the entitlement to be considered for funding.

If your interpretation was correct then you clearly do not agree with those areas highlighted above. I would suggest that if the intention was to limit it in the way you have interpreted it, then it would have better been referred to as CNC (Continuing Nursing Care).

It then goes on to state "The decision-making rationale should not marginalise a need just because it is successfully managed; well-managed needs are still needs. (Refer to paragraphs 142–146.) Only where the successful management of a healthcare need has permanently reduced or removed an ongoing need, such that the active management of this need is reduced or no longer required, will this have a bearing on NHS Continuing Healthcare eligibility."

You may also refer to the other paragraphs in this section i.e. 64/65/66, all of which are relevant.

This section of the National Framework begins on page 19 under the heading of Primary Health Need, beginning with Paragraph 54, all of which is relevant reading.

It does seem to me that your use of the word "futile" is a poor choice of word given that the English Dictionary gives the following definitions of its meaning:

- Having no effective result – unsuccessful
- Pointless, unimportant, trifling
- Insane or foolish.

Put simply, I refute categorically that any of these meanings are applicable to this situation.

I do feel that you have inadvertently demonstrated the lack of knowledge on your part with regard to the purpose and meaning behind the initial checklist.

You summarise by stating "For your satisfaction, we have agreed to do a checklist, but I do not think it will have any implications on her funding or placement of discharge".

Whilst it does satisfy me that the checklist has been completed, this should not be interpreted for the reason for doing it; it should be because both her condition and her rights warrant it.

My response to your penultimate paragraph is that I believe my insistence on getting this initial checklist completed has been absolutely necessary, as without it my feelings are that your presumption of various factors which are misconceived would without doubt have denied both Margaret and me a process that we are undeniably entitled to.

The very existence of the screening assessment is to determine who should be entitled to go forward to a full assessment and *should not* be treated as pointless, unimportant, trifling or any other description you have used.

For my part I also wish you to know that I was clearly wrong when I stated in my email that I believed that the initial assessment should be done prior to discharge and that it should also have been done on admission to hospital. For this error I apologise and accept that having been told this by the management of a care home I wrongly assumed that they would know what was right and what was wrong. It would appear that there is an awful lot of misunderstanding from various sectors in this area.

We now move forward to the actual assessment which, do not get me wrong, I am pleased has taken place. However, again correct procedures were not followed, in that both my son and I should have had the opportunity to engage in the process, but we were not informed of it until after the event.

I received a telephone call on Wednesday evening to advise me that they had carried out the assessment. I thanked her for her information but did point out that we should have had the opportunity to be present. She explained that as I was visiting on Saturday 21 August we could discuss the assessment at that time.

As my visiting appointment was for 4.00pm we arrived early at around 3.40pm so that any discussion and explanation of the assessments would not eat into our time with Margaret. Unfortunately, no-one seemed to be aware of any meeting and it was not until over half an hour later that it was noticed that a brief footnote had been written on the visiting diary.

Eventually the Care Co-ordinator invited us into a quiet room where she set about explaining the confusion and that because of the length and detail of the assessment we may be there for at least an hour in total. As she had not yet managed to print off copies it was suggested that we go and meet with Margaret as it was fast approaching mealtime at 5.00pm.

This we did and returned to meet with the Care Co-ordinator who presented us with the photocopied forms.

I am confident that you must be well informed about this assessment form, even if it is not used as often as I suspect that it should be. I therefore feel there is little point in highlighting certain aspects of the instructions that preface the actual assessment.

You will note that the rationale for decision is for a full assessment recorded as:

1 (A), 3 (Bs), and 6 (Cs). Whereas this should have been recorded as 7 (Cs).

As we were unable to take part in this initial assessment our son Benjamin and I have had to look retrospectively as to whether or not we agree with the gradings under each heading.

We have concluded that we are not happy with the gradings allocated under the following headings:

(1) Nutrition
I learnt that there is an area of concern with regard to this as it has been observed that on occasions Margaret has in fact gone all day without any food intake and that now they are taking particular notice of this fact.

(2) Skin integrity

On visiting Margaret approximately two weeks ago I noted that she was wearing a pair of slipper socks which I knew not to be hers. When questioned about this Margaret believed the reason was because someone had stolen her shoes. When I enquired with nurses I discovered that not only were her feet and lower legs extremely swollen but she had blisters all over her feet, some in places that must have been exceptionally painful. It was explained to me that this was a combination of her putting the shoes on the wrong feet (something that I was particularly mindful of on a daily basis when she was at home) and also that she had developed a habit of not putting on socks and not realising that the tongue of the shoe was pushed inside.

All of which was compounded by the fact that Margaret is restless and spends most of the day pacing up and down the corridors. Although I sought some extra wide slippers immediately and paid an additional £8 for express delivery, they did not arrive until four days later.

I have observed that the swelling in her feet has now reduced significantly, but the Care co-ordinator informed us there is some concern over the healing of some of the blisters and consequently she thought a (B) rating was justified.

(3) Behaviour

I have experienced first-hand Margaret's aggressive behaviour, not only towards me but indeed most shockingly towards herself, not to mention damage to property through the throwing of anything that comes to hand but the constant slamming of doors, etc. The very fact that she spent almost four weeks in Hospital X with no more than two or three showers was because of her aggression towards the staff should in itself be an indicator that (C) is by no means the correct assessment.

Both my son and I believe this to be at least a (B) rating if not (A).

Whilst we are grateful for the intervention of additional drugs to calm her down, we are concerned that these are merely masking the behaviour and unless a cast iron guarantee can be given that they will continue to work in exactly the same way without any side effects to her detriment then this scoring needs to be changed to an (A) or (B).

(4) Altered States of consciousness

This is without doubt not the correct score for this category. I am surprised that anyone on your team believes she fits the criteria of (C) being either no evidence of an altered state of consciousness or that it is being effectively managed and is at low risk of harm.

On nearly all my visits to see Margaret she still displays signs of talking to people who are not there. On our last visit which lasted less than half an hour she suddenly started to whisper and got up from her chair. When challenged about where she was going she said she had been told to follow the lady. Could this be another reason why she spends so much time walking about? Could it be that these imaginary people are telling her to do things? I don't know, but I do know that there is plenty of evidence to suggest that an altered state of consciousness certainly does exist.

On each visit I try and bring with me a little treat of something I think she may like, be it biscuits, a sandwich, fruit or cake. Quite often she will break off a piece of sandwich or biscuit and hold it out for this imaginary person, whispering that it is for her.

I would conclude by saying that I have always been immensely proud of my wife and the things she has achieved in her life. I find it quite ironic that as a Senior Course Manager working at the Open University with complete dedication to her role in the School of Health and Social Care and being responsible for editing an introductory reader *Understanding Health and Social Care* along with her fellow editor Martin Robb, she now finds herself reliant upon me to make sure she benefits from everything available to her.

I do know that she still receives royalties from book sales and that this reader has been essential reading for students of social work, nursing, health and social policy as well as those in the caring professions across the health and social service sectors.

As for me, my professional qualifications and career paths have no bearing on matters of health except that I have always fought for what is right when an injustice is done. I am by nature a tenacious and determined individual.

Both Margaret and I have spent our lives working hard, paying our taxes and National Insurance contributions without any assistance in benefits from the government. If we are entitled to some form of help at this time in our lives, then we have earned it and we will fight for it. We do, however, hope that sense will prevail and those who choose to unnecessarily put obstacles in the way will look into their own conscience and do what is right.

Regards

David M. Allott

Dr G responded the next day, 24 August

Thank you, Mr Allott, for your email.

All the way from day of admission, my interest has been to look after the best interests of Margaret. As I suggested in the meeting, the caring role can be very time consuming and taxing for the carers which can lead to carers being negatively affected. At the same time, carers' stress can be detrimental to the well-being of the patient in question. I was trying to get what seemed best for both you and Margaret. At the same time, I understood the emotional connection and the impact separation will have on you, hence I agreed to the necessary interventions to come to the best solution.

I acknowledge that Margaret can be confused and hallucinating. The purpose of medication is not to take away the imaginary experience as part of her dementia altogether but is to reduce the aggression, anxiety, distrust and make the care easier for carers. In pursuit of reducing the experiences, we do not wish to embark on high doses of medications which can result in severe side-effects and worsening of cognition, hence we are mindful of medication use. She has been seen by a podiatrist for her feet and dressing has been applied to blisters.

I apologise for use of word "futile" in my email.

As the care elements are better managed by a social worker, I would let social services discuss with you about CHC funding eligibility process and related matters.

In terms of repeat OT assessment and visit in this week, may I suggest that your son Mr Ben Allott also attends the assessment so as to observe and highlight any alternatives possible.

I would copy your email to manager in relation to practices on TOPAS and for her to see if something can be addressed soon. I wish you all the best.

Dr T. Goel

My response the same day was:

Dear Dr G,

Thank you for your rapid response to my email earlier today. I do appreciate such a speedy reply and your positive attitude. As you have no doubt gathered, I am passionate about the love I have for my wife and can appreciate that sometimes I may be a little overbearing in my support for her.

Please be assured I certainly never meant to give the impression that I was questioning your medical expertise or indeed the care that is being given to her by you or any member of your team.

I am in fact extremely grateful for all that you are doing for her and should have included my thanks to you in that email.

Unfortunately Ben has to be in Manchester on Thursday, so will be unable to attend the visit for the OT assessment which I know we all hope goes well.

Thank you for your kind words, they are genuinely appreciated. With kind regards

David Allott

This concludes the correspondence between Dr G and me until I deemed it necessary to respond on 22 October to a meeting Dr G convened with me and other members of his team with no notice given to me, other than the five minutes after my arrival at TOPAS with the sole purpose of taking Margaret home for the day.

PART 5
The interim period between the OT's frist home visit and the second unscheduled meeting with Dr G.

This second visit by the two occupational therapists from TOPAS, along with Margaret was also attended by a senior social care professional, and someone from the Mental Health Clinic. The main purpose of the OT's assessment was to determine how Margaret was able to cope with going up and down the stairs. Whilst they were undertaking this assessment I was left to talk with the social care professionals, principally about NHS CHC funding as had been suggested by Dr G. I believe the social care professional was keen to make the point that unless I completed the financial assessment forms I would be deemed as self-funding. She initially stressed that it was necessary for me to disclose all our financial circumstances and immediately corrected herself by saying that she had meant to say Margaret's financial situation and not mine. As I had at one stage been informed by Penelope that Margaret would not be discharged from TOPAS until I had done this and also named a care home in the eventuality that her return home proved to be unsuccessful, I was keen to ascertain why these two elements should have any bearing on her release from TOPAS.

My view was that until a Multi-Disciplinary Team CHC assessment had taken place I would not be disclosing any financial information to anyone. (Why should any local authority be entitled through their social care services to know the private affairs of any individual prior to knowing if that person was seeking to obtain funding from them? This in my view is totally intrusive and unnecessary.) It should be said at this point that following my complaint about the screening assessment organised by Dr G that we had achieved a new screening assessment where both our son Benjamin and I were in attendance. We were successful in putting forward our strong feelings in a number of categories where the resulting re-scoring of these put it in no doubt that Margaret was eligible for the full CHC assessment.

The social care professional asked me why I thought that Margaret would be entitled to CHC funding, especially as in her opinion she had known of many patients who had been in a worse situation than Margaret and had not been successful in obtaining such funding. My reply was simply that I felt this was irrelevant, as possibly all of those cases could have wrongly been denied it and had no bearing on what I believed. I went on to give her an example of how the initial screening assessment had given Margaret a C-rating for Altered States of Consciousness, being no evidence of any such incidents. This was clearly a ludicrous misinterpretation of the reality of Margaret's condition, given her constant talking to imaginary people and hallucinations. At this statement the social care professional stated that as Margaret had not at any time been unconscious this was what was meant by altered states of consciousness. Little did I realise, but soon after I would discover that many people in positions of authority within the NHS seem to have chosen to change the meaning of certain words or phrases of the English language as defined by the Oxford English Dictionary. I informed her that having researched the meaning of Altered States of Consciousness that I did not agree with her interpretation that it was actually about unconsciousness; this to me made no sense whatsoever. At around this point in our discussions we were re-joined by Margaret and the two occupational therapists.

They reported that it had been challenging to get Margaret up and down the stairs and consequently they had concerns as to how we would manage on a continuing basis with just me to assist her on a day-to-day basis. Their suggestion was that we could possibly bring Margaret's bed downstairs into the lounge or dining room. I resisted the temptation to state that I considered this to be a ludicrous solution but did point out that it would require not only Margaret's bed to be re-sited but also my own, otherwise she would be unsupervised throughout the night. There were also the impracticalities of such a solution as there was no bathroom on the ground floor or any room to have one constructed.

I was not unduly concerned about this assessment as I had

already begun to look into the possibility of installing a lift, even though this would require a new staircase being fitted to make sufficient space to accommodate both stairs and lift.

Following this meeting I was able to bring Margaret home for 6-7 hours once or twice a week and then towards the middle of October for overnight stays.

It was on one these visits to TOPAS to pick up Margaret for a home visit that whilst waiting in reception I was told Dr G wished to see me.

I was shown into a room where Dr G and members of his team were already seated. He began by explaining that TOPAS was designed to be a facility where older people resided for a matter of a few weeks whilst their condition was assessed and would then move on to appropriate accommodation and treatment where necessary.

He saw fit to remind me that Margaret was admitted to TOPAS on Thursday 22 July, some three months ago, and that we had had a planning discharge meeting on 12 August, over two months ago. The conversation then turned to his opinion being that I needed to make the necessary decisions in order to get Margaret discharged. This seemed to take the form of me arranging to get the care plan in place with my chosen care firm and that I needed to understand that Margaret was occupying a place at TOPAS which was badly needed for other patients requiring their services.

I found it incredible that he was suggesting that it was I who was delaying my wife's return home, especially given the fact that I had on numerous occasions asked when she would be allowed to come home permanently.

It was at this point that Dr G made the statement that it was good to fight for certain rights but one should always be mindful of the personal costs involved. I remember saying that it was time for some honesty by the government and NHS. If NHS CHC is unaffordable then all involved should come clean and admit it instead of perpetuating the lie that it is available to all who are in need of it, by going through the pretence of a system that is not followed.

Dr G was keen to impress upon me that the longer Margaret resided at TOPAS the greater the chance that she may not be able to come home as her condition may deteriorate further, to the extent that he may not be able recommend her release to my care. (Now we have it; he was, in my opinion, saying that I should stop fighting for CHC funding or the result may not be to my liking. I immediately took this as a threat; whether or not that was his intention, it was certainly made to make me understand that it was he who had the power to decide on Margaret's placement.)

I went on to explain that I had ordered a new staircase to make space for the fitting of a lift which was due to be fitted in early December. This was due to the concerns of his occupational therapists and so far as I was concerned I was doing everything in my power to expedite Margaret's return home.

Dr G's response to this was to ask if I thought such expenditure was wise given the circumstances and that even if she was to return home it may only be for a limited time.

This to me was a clear indication that he was unable to grasp the reality of the situation I found myself in at

- Firstly there was nothing I would not do to expedite Margaret's return, except I would not succumb to his desires for me to forego her rights, as he had clearly intimated I should

- Secondly he failed to comprehend that any monies spent in such a way for the benefit of Margaret because of her condition was legitimate expenditure from her personal wealth. The consequence of such was in reality, should Margaret fall under social care, which is means-tested, then the cost of such works would alternatively be used for paying for her care

- There are only two reasonable conclusions I can draw from his comments:
  (1) He was divorced from the reality of the situation, being he believed I was the one who was unnecessarily delaying Margaret's return home and not the fact that it was he who had made it a condition of her discharge that I needed to
      A. Name a care home
      B. Provide social care with our financial details
      C. Effectively ignore his own OT's concerns
  (2) Alternatively was he taking me for a fool? Did he honestly believe I was some uneducated dumb fool that would easily succumb to his threats and scare tactics!

The meeting was concluded with Dr G informing me that he expected Margaret to be discharged within the following two weeks. Following that meeting I was then able to enjoy Margaret's company for the remainder of the day by bringing her home until around 6.00pm that evening.

The next day I forwarded another email to Dr G confirming my understanding as to what had been discussed at the previous day's meeting. This is the only way to properly record what took place and to give him the opportunity to dispute my account if he disagrees.

EMAIL DATED FRIDAY 22 OCT 2021

Dear Dr G,

Further to our meeting I thought it would be helpful to confirm my understanding of what we discussed, your reasons behind that discussion and how and when we can move forward in the best interests of Margaret.

You led me to believe that you had concerns about the time delay from our initial meeting up until the present time, as this had been longer than you had anticipated and that it was your view that the bed space occupied by Margaret was in demand and needed to be vacated at the earliest opportunity.

I was left with the impression that you felt that this was being brought about by my insistence on getting what I feel to be her rights under current regulations, and in so doing I was purposely slowing down the enablement of her discharge back into our home. I will confirm as stated that I am desperate to have her return home and would do so immediately if that were possible.

I was informed by Penelope some time ago, when I enquired as to when I might be able to get her home, that TOPAS (presumably being yourself) would not discharge her until I had named a care home and disclosed Margaret's financial situation.

At that time I explained the reasons why it was not possible or right to do so until we had undergone the CCG's DST assessment and received their determination in respect of this. Even though it has now been twenty-eight days, as of today I am still not in receipt of the outcome letter and have been advised that this is due to the CCG still being in discussion (negotiation) with the local authority social services over which I have no control.

I have done everything in my power to address the concerns expressed by your occupational therapists to alleviate any areas they felt were potential hazards within the home. I hope that you can appreciate that the lead time to get structural alterations to the home, in this case a new staircase to make it possible to install a lift, can be longer than one would like.

However, if everything goes to plan, the new stairs will be fitted by the week ending 6 November.

None of this has any bearing on social services working with my chosen care firm, in putting together a care plan for when Margaret returns home.

I understand that your interpretation of the criteria as laid down in the National Framework differs considerably to my own and only time will tell whose opinion is correct in this respect. However, if I was to understand correctly that your view was that the longer Margaret remains at TOPAS and any significant deterioration of her condition may lead you to revise your decision on her coming home, this would not in my opinion be in her best interests.

As you have suggested I have spoken to the care organisation who have confirmed that as an interim solution to enable us to move forward, they are prepared and able to provide care provisions for next week Wednesday/Thursday/Friday, 28/29/30 October.

I trust that this is acceptable to you.

Please confirm this is acceptable and my understanding of our discussion is also correct.

Regards

David Allott

Dr G responded the following Tuesday.

In view of the fact that I saw no point in replying to this email I have included my feelings on his response as shown in *italics* after each of his five comments.

Hi David

Thanks for your detailed email. Just a few observations.
(1) Yes, it has been longer than expected time for Margaret to go home. NHS bed constraints are always the case

but more importantly, the longer Margaret stays in hospital, more would be the chance of her finding it difficult to settle in at home. This would be counter-productive to all the efforts that have been done to send her back home. That is the reason I have been sending her on leaves with you so that she retains some memories of you and home.

How very generous of him. I wonder if I had not kept asking for permission to take Margaret out for a few hours each day rather than visiting her for infrequent one-hourly visits if he would have been so forthcoming. TOPAS allows only one patient to have a visit from their loved ones at a time. This is understandable given the nature of the patients' conditions; however, this puts a constraint on the number of times one is able to visit, only once to three times a week at best and only then if the visiting slots have not already been allocated.

(2) No, there was no implication that you were purposefully slowing the discharge. But I did not think you were fully aware of the implications of a delay in regards to future care whereby Margaret's condition might deteriorate to a degree that home care might not be possible.

It certainly felt that he was implying that I was slowing down the discharge and his admission that her condition may deteriorate further, as you will see, was not taken into account.

> That would be a waste of all the times and efforts which you put in to getting her home. Whereas if she goes soon then you can spend quality time together for longer. I also explained that in our practice we do not see Margaret as a high-need patient requiring CHC funding for care, to which you disagreed. It is good to

fight for certain rights but at the same time be mindful of the personal costs involved.

I find this statement to be truly amazing. Firstly he has completely ignored the facts I set out for him in my previous emails. It is not for him to decide who is entitled to NHS CHC. He still persists in his misconceived opinions even though Margaret was shown to be eligible for a full MDT Assessment following the results of the screening assessment, something she would have been denied of if I had not fought against his previous opinions. Probably more telling of all is his final sentence saying that sometimes it is good to fight for certain rights; he again totally misses the point that rights are rights. No-one should have to fight for them; that is the very point of having rights. He can't resist the temptation of re-stating his veiled threat about being mindful of the personal costs involved. To that I would say that is exactly what I am mindful of.

(3) In regards to your difference of opinion as to what is in her best interest about coming home even if her condition has deteriorated, it is imperative that she is not at any risk of harm and that the care can be safely provided at home. NHS teams and social services always try their best to keep patients at home provided it does not put the patient or carers at risk. And that her care needs can still be physically met at home. Risk needs, levels of care required, have to be balanced with emotional needs of the carer.

It is very commendable of him to give 100% support to his colleagues in both the NHS and social services when he says they always try their best to keep patients at home, subject to risk. Commendable but also very naïve given he probably actually knows a minute fraction of even 1% of employees in either service, and through my own experience he is wrong in his assumptions. My experiences of both these institutions has been lacking on far too many occasions for me to take comfort from his statement. Having been happily married to the love of my life for fifty years, again he makes a false assumption that he, having known her for a few moments of time spread over a few months, knows better than I what is best for her.

    (4) I have asked staff for take-home medicines to be organised from Wednesday to Saturday which is 27, 28, 29 October (not 28, 29, 30 as per your email).

    (5) I hope that funding for Margaret is sorted soon. My preferred discharge date as discussed in the meeting would be two weeks from the meeting i.e.. 4 November 2021. Unless it is for a few days either side of unexpected delays, I would suggest that private care is arranged and Margaret is taken home.

I hope this clarifies the content and intention of discussion in the meeting and helps for Margaret to move forward. Regards Dr G.

This concludes the correspondence and dealings with Dr G.

It must however be said that despite his eagerness to get Margaret discharged from TOPAS this was not achieved by the date he stipulated. I had gone to pick her up fully expecting to bring her home as arranged but could not do so as they had not arranged her discharge medicines and there were further concerns about the carers being able to shower her in the shower cubicle we had at home. This was the first time anyone had mentioned this as a problem and there was neither space nor time to consider alternatives to what we already had.

Consequently, I gave an undertaking to be the person responsible for showering Margaret, something I have done no less than three times each week since her return home. I can appreciate the difficulties for carers coming into the home to undertake this task, especially when the person being cared for still has a tendency to be aggressive at times. I accept that it is far easier for me, as I am able to get in the shower with her and by stripping down to my underwear it matters not if I get wet through in the process. By the time I have got Margaret out of bed, undressed, cleaned if necessary, into the shower, fully bathed with her hair washed and finally dried and redressed, the whole process can take between an hour to an hour and a half. I cannot pretend that it is an easy task and that looking after someone, caring for their every need almost 24/7, is not at times very tiring. However, with two carers coming into the home for an hour in the morning and half an hour in the evening, this does give me the chance to do the essential things like cleaning and just taking time out.

When asked whether there was anything that I needed and if social services should look into a period of respite care, say for a few days each month, I was grateful for that consideration. Initially it was proposed that Margaret could attend a day care centre twice per week, something I was concerned about, given her reluctance in the past to participate in group-type activities. However, after Margaret was assessed by the lady from the day care centre it was concluded that due to her condition and needs this would not be something they could cater for. Likewise, I felt going to another strange place once a month would be far too traumatic for her. I therefore asked if I could get a few hours each week, say twice weekly when someone could sit and look after her in our home, allowing me some meaningful time to myself if only to be able to get out and do the necessary weekly shop.

I am delighted to report that I have been awarded 2x six hours a week for this purpose and must acknowledge my social services professional for her efforts in achieving this for me. Thank you.

Finally when I picked Margaret up to bring her home

permanently, there were four or five plastic bags of clothes and her small suitcase ready to pick up. I noticed that she did not have on her spectacles, something that she wore permanently throughout her stay in TOPAS. I pointed this out to the nurse who completed the discharge paperwork with me who informed me they had packed everything and that they would probably be in the suitcase.

When we arrived home I gave Margaret her spare set of glasses and over the next two days set about laundering all the clothes contained in the plastic bags. It was not until I opened the suitcase to find only clothes that I realised there were far more items missing than her spectacles.

Items of a personal nature which had not been packed included a radio/cassette player, a number of story tapes, an iPod music player, headphones, an electric toothbrush and her spectacles.

On telephoning TOPAS to report these missing items I was informed that so far as they knew all Margaret's belongings had been packed and returned at her discharge. I assured the person I was not in receipt of these items and that they therefore should still be at TOPAS. Consequently I was assured that they would look for these goods and inform me accordingly. Unfortunately, I did not hear any further from TOPAS and decided to inform my social services professional and the Admiral nurse, when they next visited me. I have no doubt that they both chased up with TOPAS, especially as I had told them that my main concern was the loss of Margaret's iPod which was loaded with her own choice of her favourite songs from a time when she was fit and well. Regretfully they too seemed to be unsuccessful in eliciting a satisfactory response from TOPAS. I had also mentioned this to the mental health clinic who also had chased this up and on one of our telephone conversations she enquired as to whether I had heard further from TOPAS. I had not heard from them and informed her that she should not concern herself further. I knew they had done their best to get this resolved, but clearly I needed to now report what I considered to be the theft of my wife's belongings to the police.

The Care Co-ordinator asked me to delay in doing this and give her one last attempt to resolve this. I am pleased to report that less than one week later I did indeed receive a call from TOPAS to inform me that they had found most of the missing items and that I could pick them up at any time. Admiral nurse made a special journey to collect these items for which I am very grateful.

I will leave you to draw your own conclusions as to why items that had previously not been found suddenly came to light and, apart from the radio/cassette player/tapes and spectacles, were returned weeks after they should have been.

The next chapter covers our experiences in getting an MDT Assessment for NHS CHC funding, which anyone about to embark upon will hopefully find informative and helpful.

10

THE MULTI-DISCIPLINARY ASSESSMENT FOR NHS CHC FUNDING

Is this the end of the beginning or the beginning of the end?

Who knows? I guess that depends where you are in the process and how lucky or unlucky you have been in getting your entitlements.

Has it been easy or hard, fair or unfair, honest or dishonest, quick or slow, or any other combination of opposite meanings that express either your satisfaction or dissatisfaction for this NHS process that says one thing in the National Framework and does something entirely different in reality?

I ask these questions because one's own experiences are those things that have the greatest effect on each and every one of us. They alter how we perceive our experiences, be they good or bad. Individually they have little meaning to anyone other than ourselves except for when they are combined with the experiences of like-minded people, who have all experienced similar circumstances and in so doing become a force to be reckoned with.

I say these things at the beginning of this chapter as the MDT (Multi-Disciplinary Team) meeting, although not in itself the decision maker in the process, which falls to the CCG, is responsible for giving their recommendation which is rarely not followed by the CCG.

Do not be fooled into believing that this element of the process is any fairer than everything else you may have experienced in getting to this point. It appears to me to be merely another obstacle designed to deny you or your loved one's rights.

I hope that by detailing our experiences it will aid you in being prepared for this important meeting and at least highlight some of the pitfalls that you may encounter in your own assessment.

In an earlier chapter we talked about necessity being the mother of invention. This is exactly true in the need to find a way to get justice for everyone suffering from one of the different forms of dementia.

The problem we all have is that both the government and the NHS have chosen to not accept that they have a necessity and therefore have no incentive to find a way to solve the problem. Their collective way of dealing with the increasing number of people suffering from this terrible disease is to continue to look for ways to deny as many people as possible their rights to the help and funding they deserve and need. If we can come together and work as one, not only for our loved one's sake but also everyone else's loved ones, then the reality will change.

The necessity will arise only when there are sufficient numbers being granted their entitlement to CHC funding that they have to find the way of providing the means to make it affordable and not through the tactics they currently employ. Let us be perfectly honest: the system seems to be set up to effectively rob this ever-growing section of the population of their assets which have been accumulated over many years of hard work and through which they have already paid their fair share in taxes and NHI.

They must find a way in the short term of funding this growing need and in the long term solve the problem by investing in the science to prevent these diseases in the first place.

Once you have jumped over the various hurdles and got to the point of having a screening assessment that gives entitlement to go forward to a full assessment for NHS CHC with an MDT, this is what you may expect to happen.

Let me begin by saying that Margaret's first screening assessment (obtained only because I fought hard to get it and against Dr G's view that it was "futile") scored sufficiently high enough to go forward for recommending a full assessment with the CCG. This never happened; in other words, the result was simply ignored.

Consequently after the second screening assessment, attended by our son and me, when we were able to achieve a more realistic scoring, we made it perfectly clear that this must be forwarded to the CCG without any further delay, and through determination and constant chasing we did achieve this within a matter of days. Do not be afraid to make a nuisance of yourself. Keep asking questions and questioning their response.

The second screening assessment took place on 10 September 2021. I received a letter and information with reference to the full assessment for CHC. From the Commissioning and Support Unit dated 16 September. That letter confirmed that they had received an application from Council for consideration of eligibility for NHS CHC on behalf of Mrs Margaret Allott on the previous day, 15 September. The letter also confirmed that an MDT meeting would take place on Friday 24 September. At last there appeared to be more of a sense of urgency, and it goes to show that not only can you get some form of a result by being persistent but also they are capable of acting quickly, given the right incentive to do so.

Enclosed with that letter was a leaflet describing who is eligible for CHC, who is involved, how the needs are assessed, how they will inform you of the outcome, how to appeal etc.

Also enclosed was a form entitled *Statement of Needs for Margaret Allott*. This form asked for a summary of Margaret's medical history and current needs overview, with approximately two thirds of one side of an A4 sheet of paper on which to record this information. All this information should already have been within the knowledge of those professionals taking part in the assessment and it should not have been necessary for them to request this from us. A further two and two-thirds pages of A4 paper were given over to disclose our views on the eleven key domains that the assessment would consider along with any other additional information.

The very first thing to say is that this system is not designed to help you achieve funding via CHC. It is designed to do the exact opposite by denying you that right. How can you possibly do justice to your loved one's situation on a little over three A4 sides of paper?

Although this assessment does not have the standing in law of a court hearing, no-one is sworn to tell the truth, with sanctions for not doing so, but it does have serious implications not just for your loved one's health, but particularly for their wealth.

If this had been a dispute which needed to be settled in a court of law, then both sides would have been required to do their disclosures prior to taking the case forward. In other words both sides would tell the opposition the reasons for their claim or defence along with any evidence that they were relying on.

In this case one side (the MDT) is requesting information from the other (the patient) with no offer of disclosing how they intend to approve or deny the application for CHC. It was for these reasons that I made the decision to wait until the actual meeting before disclosing my opinions on all matters to be considered.

To this end I spent the time available to me to prepare for the assessment and gain as much knowledge as I could about the process and the meaning of each domain.

Unlike the screening assessment that has a clear definition of where the line exists between passing or failing, the MDT meeting using the Decision Support Tool has no such defined line, except where there is a clear unequivocal assessment of a "primary health need", and a domain marked as "Priority" (either Breathing, Behaviour, Drug Therapies, or Altered States of Consciousness) would generally be seen as proof of such.

The NHS website on continuing healthcare states "If you have one priority need, or severe needs in at least two areas, you can usually expect to be eligible for NHS CHC." It goes on to state "You may also be eligible if you have a severe need in one area plus a number of other needs, or a number of high or moderate needs, depending on their nature, intensity, complexity or unpredictability."

This fact alone makes it extremely difficult to determine if a patient demonstrates sufficient needs to be assessed as having a "primary health need".

There is another big "hurdle" contained within this process and within the National Framework which is important for anyone representing a patient to know about. This can probably be better explained by using the comparative example of the differences between the English and Scottish criminal law systems in arriving at a verdict. In England the verdict is very black and white: the accused will be found either "guilty or not guilty" at the end of the trial.

In Scotland there is a third option open to judges and juries being "not proven". Although a not proven verdict has the same effect as an acquittal of not guilty in the eyes of the law, it has long been felt by some to be an unfair and unsatisfactory outcome by many. This is probably why the Scottish government are currently considering the abolition of this third option.

In England the argument for not adopting this option has been that to be proven guilty this has to be beyond any reasonable doubt. In essence "not proven" is a cop out for not proving "beyond reasonable doubt" and leaves a question mark over a defendant's guilt or innocence, certainly totally unacceptable for a truly innocent person.

Regretfully the National Framework has also a third option which is equally unsatisfactory. To be clear and concise about a decision on CHC funding the answer should simply be "awarded or not awarded" with the reasons given that if incorrect it can be challenged. This is not the case because the Framework has provision for a third option of "a joint funding package" where the care is jointly funded by the NHS and the local authority social care. The agreement as to which body is responsible for a certain percentage of the costs is a matter of negotiation between them.

The framework states quite clearly the following on page six under the heading of "Executive Summary":

Paragraph 3: "At the heart of the National Framework is the process for determining whether an individual is eligible for NHS CHC or funded Nursing Care."

Paragraph 4: "An individual is eligible for NHS CHC if they have a primary health need. This is a concept developed by the Secretary of State to assist in determining when the NHS is responsible for providing <u>for all</u> of the individuals' assessed <u>health and associated social care needs</u>."

Paragraph 5: "In order to determine whether an individual has a primary health need, a detailed assessment and decision-making process must be followed, as set out in this National Framework. Where an individual has a primary health need and is therefore eligible for NHS Continuing Healthcare, the NHS is responsible for commissioning a care package that meets the individual's health and associated social care needs."

Under the heading "Legal Context", on page 14, paragraph 37 of the National Framework, is the following statement:

> "Some individuals' nursing or healthcare needs are such that the local authority is <u>not permitted</u> to meet their ongoing care and support needs, <u>and instead they become fully the responsibility of the NHS</u>. These are individuals who have been assessed as having a "primary health need" through the processes set out in this National Framework and who are eligible for NHS Continuing Healthcare. The limits of local authority provision and the concept of "primary health need" arise from the interaction between duties and limitations placed on local authorities under the Care Act 2014 and the duties placed on CCG and NHS England under the NHS Act."

The fact that there is this Joint Care Package option contained within the Framework means that there is an inbuilt contradiction of its own aims and objectives, further muddying the understanding of how a decision for CHC funding is approved or not approved. There are a number of references within the Framework that state that the patient's financial circumstances should never be a consideration in arriving at a decision for funding. E.g. Page 21 paragraph 64: "Financial issues should not be considered as part of an individual's eligibility for NHS CHC."

One of the alarming trends families are reporting is that people who have previously been assessed as being eligible for NHS CHC are being reassessed even though their needs have not reduced and are unlikely to do so. Following reassessment they are having their funding downgraded to a joint package of care. The result is, of course, that the local authority element of this is means-tested.

This is nothing short of robbing those most in need of their life savings, probably the only thing they have left if they are suffering from dementia.

If you were to rob a bank you would feel the full weight of the law and if caught you would be given free board and lodgings.

Yet here we have an institution, paid for by us all through our taxes, which through their employees is prepared to lie, cheat and steal from mainly elderly and certainly the most vulnerable people in our society.

To those despicable people who are prepared to carry out these appalling miscarriages of justice I would say this:

You are no better than someone who would mug an elderly person and you should be ashamed of yourselves. Remember Voltaire's quote: "those who can make you believe absurdities can make you commit atrocities." You know what you are doing is wrong, you know this is all about finances not about fairness and you are committing atrocities.

I would apologise to all readers if the statements made above offends anyone other than those they are intended for. I realise not everyone will share my views, but they are my views and reflect just how angry I feel about this so-called assessment procedure.

As I have previously said I used the time available to me to prepare for what was probably one of the most important meetings I would ever participate in.

There is no right or wrong way of approaching this. You will no doubt have your own views as to what best suits you and what you will be most comfortable doing. I hope that some of my experiences will be of help to some of you who find yourselves in similar circumstances. It is plainly wrong that we must fight to get what has already been established as a right, and it is this fact that is also the driving force behind my determination to try and get the changes needed to help protect our most vulnerable loved ones.

The following pages detail my approach to the then upcoming Multi-Disciplinary Team Assessment.

I started by setting out my own agenda of how I would like the meeting to be conducted in order that I had a reference point from which to ensure the important issues to me were covered.

AGENDA AND QUESTIONS FOR NHS CHC FUNDING ASSESSMENT MEETING ON FRIDAY 24 SEPTEMBER

(1) Establish the who's who in attendance
    Full names
    Professional position
    Their role in this assessment
    Who the decision makers are
(2) Whether anyone keeps minutes of this assessment meeting
(3) Seek clarification as to the format of the assessment
(4) If necessary ask relavent questions such as:
    - Are we told of the conclusions that the assessors have come to at the end of the assessment?
    - If not, why not? Who then are ultimately the decision maker(s) in this process?
    - When will we receive written confirmation of the results of this assessment and will it detail the reasons behind the decision both positively and negatively?
    - Are there any outside considerations to be factored in before a decision is reached?
    - What happens next?
(5) Before beginning, confirm I am able to make my statement and seek clarification of some other points.
(6) Some important points that may need to be made during the assessment:
    - Ben's filming clip of Margaret on Sunday 27 June

- Detailed experiences of lack of help from NHS services and social care from 31 May until referral to TOPAS. See file copy 3
- Lack of help from helpline
- Are the results from the health of the nation scale taken into consideration?

(7) Why have I been told that TOPAS will only agree to discharge Margaret when a care home has been identified and when social services has received the completed financial position form?

Two important points to make here:
- How do you identify a care home when
  (1) You have no idea when that may be needed and therefore what vacancies, if any, there will be at an unknown moment in time?
  (2) How can you identify a care home when at this moment in time it is not known how it is to be funded?
    (a) NHS CHC?
    (b) Social Services
    (c) Self-funded

The CHC nurse assessor introduced herself and stated her qualifications as being RMN. This was followed by all others in attendance doing likewise, being:
Social Worker Manager
Student Social Worker
Staff Nurse from TOPAS.
Margaret's husband
Margaret's son.

It should be noted that contrary to the recommendations laid out in the National Framework on page 38 paragraph 121, "the

MDT should usually include both health and social care professionals, <u>who are knowledgeable about the individual's health and social care needs and, where possible, have recently been involved in the assessment, treatment or care of the individual.</u>

Neither the nurse assessor, nor social care manager, had met or even seen Margaret prior to this meeting. As you will note during the actual assessment certain things were admitted by both of these individuals which gives rise to my belief they were not knowledgeable about Margaret's health.

Upon introducing myself I requested that I be permitted to read out a pre-prepared statement prior to the start of the assessment. This request was granted and I proceeded to read out the following statement.

PRE-NHS CHC ASSESSMENT MEETING STATEMENT

Before we begin the assessment of Margaret Allott's conditions and needs, I would like to make a statement which I find necessary in order that you are appraised of various factors that have a bearing on why I find it important to ask you a number of questions prior to beginning.

(1) Some of my experiences with the services provided by the NHS in both Hospital X and Hospital Y have been nothing short of abominable. These encompass my own treatments for pancreatitis and on a separate occasion for the treatment of kidney stones.

On both occasions I was left in agonising pain, the latter for no less than nine weeks after the operation and unable to walk.

Today is not about me but about the serious lack of care and treatment given to my dear wife and her experiences.

In the summer of 2020, following two trips to Hospital X and three trips to Hospital Y due to her screaming in agony on all five occasions, she was eventually diagnosed with gall bladder stones. She had her gall bladder removed in late autumn of 2020 at Hospital X.

As Margaret was already suffering from Alzheimer's, she was unable to properly communicate her needs and express her condition to the doctors involved.

On one occasion at Hospital Y after she had been initially seen by the A&E nursing staff, we were shown into a room with one bed and a chair where she was put on a drip for her pain, awaiting a visit from the on-duty doctor.

On entering the room the doctor took one look at me and said in an angry tone, "What are you doing in here? You are not allowed to be here."

I was left with no alternative but to explain that my wife had Alzheimer's and as such was unable to communicate her needs herself, and that was the reason why I was with her.

This elicited the following response from the doctor. I was told in an offhand and abrupt manner "That I needed to understand that people were walking into the hospital and leaving in body bags". I do feel this demonstrates a complete lack of understanding of the effects of Alzheimer's from a professional clinician who should at the very least have read Margaret's notes prior to seeing her and should have adopted a much more reasonable and conciliatory tone.

(2) Looking back with hindsight, her condition had been getting progressively worse since that time and reached a new

milestone at the end of April/beginning of May. It was at this time she was refusing to get out of bed for a period of three weeks, complaining of stomach pains and claiming not being able to walk, as well as referring to herself in third person. Following a visit from our GP practice I was advised that there was nothing wrong with her physical condition and to give her paracetamol.

Despite her condition not improving, the GP practice would not revisit and informed me that there was nothing further they could do for her.

Despite a very good experience with an ambulance crew, who I have nothing but praise for, following a call to the 111 service on 31 May, I can say in all honesty from that moment on, our experiences with all aspects of the NHS services and social services have been abominable with the exception of Deputy Director for Community Health Services and Penelope from Social Care.

There is far too much that went wrong for me to go into detail here, but rest assured I have documented all our dealings from that time onwards with the 111 service, 999 service, our own GP service, A&E Department, and Hospital X in-patients.

(3) I would now turn my attention to the time Margaret has spent in TOPAS.

In the main I do not have cause to complain too much and certainly, by comparison with Hospital X, I believe this to be on a completely different level of service and care.

Unfortunately, there are areas of concern that impact in a very negative way that I am compelled to mention and from which you will hopefully understand have a bearing on this assessment.

(a) I was not happy with the original care plan that was given to me approximately five days after Margaret was admitted to TOPAS. My comments are well documented and were passed onto TOPAS, which produced a change in the allocated nurse and a revised care plan.

(b) A couple of things were not noted quite as quickly as one might have hoped for but in the main I am happy with the care she has received whilst detained in this facility.

(c) My main concern is centred firmly on a lack of knowledge with the NHS Continuing Healthcare assessment.

Who it is for?

What it is for?

When and where it is used?

How to administer it?

Who is responsible for it?

What is the criteria?

Why is its existence not publicised?

I will assume you have copies of the various correspondence between myself and Dr G. If not I will happily read to you the exchanges that took place between us. In my opinion this goes to the very heart of the matter with regard to this assessment. It must be said that had I not been so thorough in fighting for my wife's rights I do not believe that the screening assessment would have taken place and consequently this assessment would have been denied to us.

I wish to make the following observations.

(1) There appears to be a complete lack of publicity about NHS CHC. I could find no leaflets or posters to advise anyone of its existence in either Hospital X or TOPAS. Presumably this is intentional and obviously significantly reduces the number of people that may benefit by its existence. This is contrary to the roles and responsibilities of CCGs who are tasked with "Promoting awareness of NHS Continuing Healthcare" (page 10, paragraph 21, item h) as set out in the National Framework. To put it simply, one is unable to ask about something of which they have no knowledge.

(2) Not one person from the NHS has mentioned to me the existence of CHC, prior to me mentioning it to them.

(3) Once a person has discovered the very existence of NHS CHC it appears that the next obstacle put in place is to deny eligibility for it. In this country we have a culture of believing the experts, especially when it comes to matters of health and wellbeing. Again put simply, we have an innate feeling that the doctor knows best. If the doctor tells you something you expect him/her to be correct in what they are saying.

When a doctor tells you something that is incorrect this can have a profound impact on that person's life.

The question is WHY? Was it through:

(a) Ignorance?

(b) Misunderstanding? Or was it

(c) Done on purpose to serve another need?

I would refer you back to the correspondence between Dr G and myself. I am not and have not questioned Dr G's abilities as a medical practitioner, but his understanding of what the criteria are for NHS CHC is completely incorrect. As stated to him to pass judgement on someone's eligibility for CHC is to act in a God-like way, which is totally unacceptable. His incorrect understanding of CHC on so many counts could be interpreted at the very least as worrying.

The Alzheimer's Society states that people with dementia experience particular difficulties accessing NHS CHC for three reasons:

(1) The health and social care system discriminates against people with dementia. Despite dementia being a medical condition, the needs of sufferers are often seen as social care needs rather than healthcare needs.

(2) The design of the NHS CHC system is not appropriate for people with dementia. The application process is difficult for them. It calls for independent experienced support and advocacy and assessments to include a care professional with experience in dementia.

(3) The performance of NHS CHC system is poor. There is a concerning lack of performance data, clear processes and weak enforcement of the National Framework.

Finally I wish to state that my experience could be likened to travelling a long and uncomfortable road with the need to have fought my way along its entire length in order to get the help needed for my beloved wife.

At the end of this road is a "T" junction with a signpost pointing one way – "Social Services This Way" – and no sign as to where the other road leads.

The assumption all along has been based on us being led towards Social Care and that we would be "self- funding".

It is for all of the above reasons that I feel compelled to ask you the following questions:

(1) Are you completely familiar with the National Framework for NHS CHC from October 2018 and how it is to be used? Page 3.

(2) Do you believe that Alzheimer's conditions can be seen to be "a primary health need?" Quote Page 19, paragraph 55.

It became apparent that two people at the meeting were not entirely happy with the questions I was asking of them. So much so that both stated they had carried out many such assessments and were well versed in how to conduct them.

It was for this reason I decided not to carry on with the remaining questions. This turned out to be a serious error on my part.

It was clear that they felt aggrieved at me asking such questions and rather than antagonise them I felt it was better to accept their assurances, which in hindsight I should not have done.

(3) Do you accept that there is no cure for Alzheimer's and that it is a condition that will inevitably get progressively worse and not better?

(3) Treatment, control, management, or prevention of disease, illness or disability and therefore the aftercare of a person with these needs? Quote page 17, paragraph 50.

(4) Is it accepted that the four characteristics of nature, intensity, complexity and unpredictability may alone or in

combination demonstrate a primary health need? Quote page 20, paragraph 63-65.

(5) Do you accept that the important principle of making this assessment is that it should be done in totality, not on a patient's condition as it might appear in a snapshot of time like to-day? A well-managed need is still a need. Page 21, paragraph 63; page 43, paragraph 142.

From this point on the assessment began with reference to the Decision Support Tool being made under the eleven named categories.

To duplicate all that was said during that meeting would be extremely difficult and indeed probably not that helpful given the fact that our opinions did not always differ in looking at each domain in turn.

I had however, along with our son Benjamin, done our own assessment using the DST to arrive to what we considered to be a realistic assessment of Margaret's condition, along with the rationale for arriving at our conclusions. Although this is produced below in the form of a letter to the Commissioning and Support Unit, as previously stated I did not send this prior to the meeting or indeed whilst awaiting a decision.

NHS
Commissioning and Support Unit
Statement of Needs for Margaret Allott 203634

Background Information
And summary of Medical History

Up until Margaret was diagnosed with breast cancer in 1989, I would describe her as being a fit and healthy person with few ailments other than common colds or sore throats etc. At that time she underwent a mastectomy of her right breast and approximately one year later received reconstructive surgery by way of an implant.

During the following twenty years prior to her being diagnosed with breast cancer in her left breast she remained reasonably fit and well, with the odd period of sickness. This second diagnosis was depressing for her and again resulted in a mastectomy of her left breast in 2009.

Since that time there have been additional periods of unwellness, such as acute bronchitis, chest pains, cystitis etc., prior to her diagnosis of Alzheimer's in 2017. In the summer of 2020 she began to suffer from acute abdominal pain which was eventually diagnosed as gall bladder stones and was operated on by removal of that organ in the autumn of 2020.

For further background information see attached "The History of Margaret Allott's Development of Alzheimer's Disease". Please note the attachments referred to and numbered 1-9 are not attached but should be available in her medical records.

I also have a fourteen-page narrative of our experiences from 31 May up until her admission to Hospital X and subsequent transfer to TOPAS. This narrative highlights not only the abominable treatment or lack thereof which she endured but also some serious and potentially dangerous shortcomings within the system.

Current Needs Overview

To provide a summary of Margaret's current care needs is best served by looking in detail at her past and the comments made in each of the categories as listed below.

Margaret is reliant on others for her well-being in almost every category but fortunately not at the present time in the domain of breathing.

Breathing

Currently there are seemingly no issues in this category but in time we understand that it is not uncommon for this to become an issue.

For this reason and in view of the fact that the National Framework (page 42, paragraph 139) clearly states "Where deterioration can be reasonably anticipated to take place in the near future, this should also be taken into account, in order to avoid the need for unnecessary or repeat assessments", we have given this category a rating of LOW.

Nutrition Food and Drink

Margaret is able to consume food and take in fluids when they are placed in front of her, providing they are things that she now likes. Her range of taste has altered significantly over the past few months, so much so that once favourite foods are now completely off the menu. She has to be shown to the table and the food or drink put in front of her. Where necessary, items need to be cut up into manageable-sized pieces. She now appears to struggle with the use of a knife and prefers the use of a spoon to that of a fork, in most instances.

The prompt to eat or drink has to come from a third party, otherwise she would seemingly not question whether or not she is hungry or thirsty.

It is clear that this category falls within the definition of well-managed needs, as clearly without this she would not be getting sufficient nutrition or fluid intake. Clearly she is in fact not able to assess her own needs and is not capable of obtaining food and drink for herself. We therefore rate this as Low to Moderate.

Our concern here would be if she continues to have any further decline in her likes or dislikes of certain foods within her diet, this would inevitably require further intervention.

Continence

TOPAS reports double incontinence in this category and in view of the fact that Margaret is unable to find the bathroom/toilet room on her own, she is not capable of assisting herself in this area. When in the bathroom she needs to be directed to the actual toilet and assisted in sitting down. Dr G reported at the Discharge Planning Meeting that she had in fact no longer recognised what the toilet bowl was for. I have personally experienced three occasions of taking her to the toilet when she has suddenly turned through ninety degrees and sat on the floor. She currently recognises when she has a need to urinate and will whisper "Pee pee", but getting her to the toilet on time is reliant on there being someone close enough at hand to hear her softly spoken word.

I would be unable to quantify just how often each cry for "Pee pee" is actually a need as one of the nurses/carers at TOPAS has informed me that she can quite often whisper this every fifteen minutes or so. My own experience has been somewhat similar as I assisted her, on one occasion, no fewer than seventeen times in a seven-hour period.

We would believe that for these reasons there is at the least a level of need in the Moderate range.

Skin tissue viability

During Margaret's time at TOPAS the staff report that she would be constantly wandering the corridors with little time spent sitting down. She had got into a habit of not putting her socks on before putting on her shoes and that they would often be on the wrong feet. (This was something that had become a common occurrence well before she was admitted to hospital and one that I was mindful of on a daily basis.) Couple this with the fact that the tongue of the shoe would get pushed into the inside of the shoe, which would undoubtedly be a most uncomfortable situation.

These factors were not noticed immediately, until she had developed severe blistering on both feet, including swelling of the feet and lower legs. Despite her continuing habit of constantly walking the corridors Margaret was unable to associate the pain that she most definitely must have been in with the need to request help.

As some of the blisters have been particularly slow to heal, and as recognised by Hazel from the TOPAS team, this is the reason we would rate her risk in this area as at least Moderate but possibly High.

Mobility

Margaret could be said to be completely mobile as evidenced by her continuing walking of the corridors within TOPAS. However, whereas this gives the impression that possibly a score of NO needs may be appropriate, the following factors must also be considered:

(A) The TOPAS facility is located on the ground floor with no stairs to be negotiated.

(B) As one might expect with such a facility there are no trip hazards to contend with either on a permanent basis (apart from the door into the garden) such as door thresholds, or occasional hazards such as someone leaving something in the wrong place, or spillages etc.

(C) Toilet and shower facilities offer no challenges to the patients.

   Dr G has pointed out that Margaret tends to shuffle along in her movement and looks straight ahead of herself without seeing the need to look down at her feet when moving about.

Whereas the elimination, where possible, of trip hazards in the home have been undertaken, there will inevitably be the need to assist her in her movements at all times around the house, not least due to her not knowing where each room is located or indeed the purpose of that room. So mobility is not necessarily limited so much by her physical ability but by her mental ability. Her movements have certainly got much slower and unsure, a deterioration which is likely to further decline in the future. Level of need we consider to be Moderate.

Communication

We believe that this is a particularly difficult area to assess and one that could easily be misinterpreted. Firstly it must be understood as to what is meant by the word. This can, in our opinion, best be served by looking at the how it is defined by the English Dictionary:

(1) The act or an instance of communicating, the imparting or exchange of information, ideas, or feelings.

(2) Something communicated, such as a message, letter or telephone call.

(3) Something functioning as in sing, the ways in which human beings communicate, including speech, gestures, or systems as in publishing or broadcasting.

(4) A connecting route, passage or link.

The power of speech or indeed the ability to use sign language or gestures is not in itself sufficient to state that an individual can communicate. There has to be mental as well as physical ability to be able to communicate. One is of no use without the other.

An extreme example of this would be Professor Stephen Hawkins. Had it not been for the invention of some wonderful technology, his sharp and undoubtedly genius mind would have been locked away for ever. So his abilities were constrained by his physical abilities. It could also be said that his needs were well managed by him being able to interact with his computer. His need was still a need no matter how well managed it was.

On the other hand if the mind is incapable of understanding what is required for the needs of the body then how can it be communicated to someone else? If it doesn't understand what pain is (e.g. blistered feet) or that they are hungry or in need of the toilet or any other feeling of desire then communication does not exist.

Too often communication is seen to be a physical thing, not a mental one. To use the opposite analogy of that of Stephen Hawkins, a physically fit body is of no help to a person suffering from Alzheimer's in their ability to communicate.

For these reasons we cannot believe that any assessment other than High could be seen to be correct. Again we would point out that this situation will not get better, it will only get worse.

Psychological and Emotional

Every human being has P&E needs on some level, some of which are essential for survival, not least of which would be air, water, food and sleep, as well as clothes and shelter.

Following which health, personal security and emotional security are all high on the list.

Love and social belonging with family, friendships, intimacy, and esteem are all needs, as well as cognitive and aesthetic needs which have been given their own category in the assessment tool.

Emotional needs are part of being human; having family and friends who like and admire you, being loved and appreciated, with motivations and a sense of purpose, self-esteem and feelings of worth should never be underestimated.

So many of these basic needs are taken for granted by those of us fortunate enough not to be inflicted by such a terrible disease as Alzheimer's, but for those who are it robs them of those things most precious to them.

The description for the level of need under the heading of High is unarguably and regrettably correct in every way possible in the case of Margaret.

There can be no other assessment other than High.

Cognition

The mental act or process by which knowledge is acquired, including perception, intuition, and reasoning. Sadly, Margaret's cognitive abilities have all but been eliminated entirely. Every single descriptive word that is written in the DST to warrant a rating of severe regretfully describes Margaret to a T.

Without doubt this category must be classified as being nothing less than (S) severe.

Behaviour

I have struggled with finding the right words to describe Margaret's behaviour. To be totally honest about this, it feels like I am betraying her and that the Margaret I have loved and cherished for the past fifty years is deserving of much better than how I am being asked to describe her now.

I am shameful of the fact that on one particularly bad occasion when she attacked me I felt the need to telephone the police, having been advised by our GP that this was the only way to get assistance. I received a call back to say that a police officer would be calling round later in the day, but on reflection I called them back to say I did not want them to take any further action and to withdraw my notification. This they duly did and followed up with me the following day to request my confirmation that I definitely did not want to take the matter any further.

However, I realise that her behaviour is and has been nothing to do with the woman I love but is a result of this terrible disease. Prior to Margaret entering hospital her behaviour could be erratic, unpredictable, violent and disturbing. Her demeanour could change within seconds from being peaceful and loving to one of great aggression and hate towards myself. These episodes increased in their frequency and length of duration and were accompanied by both verbal and physical violence towards me, and later towards herself by attacking her own body.

The location of such attacks was not in any way a restraint on the physical abuse with three such incidents taking place whilst I was driving the car. Damage to property was never a consideration, which included the throwing of anything that came to hand, slamming of doors etc, and mainly accompanied by bouts of severe screaming.

I would refer the persons making the assessment to page 21, paragraph 63 of the National Framework.

I quote the relevant passage: "Only where the successful management of a healthcare need will this have a bearing on NHS CHC eligibility." This should also be considered alongside the statement within the Framework.

Page 43, paragraph 142 - Quote: "Well-managed needs are still needs." It then goes on to restate the sentence as given above.

Clearly the time spent at TOPAS has, amongst other things, been to establish a regime of medication to calm Margaret and make her care more easily attainable. Dr G has stated "we are mindful of medication use."

Given these facts and the criteria as laid out within the National Framework, we conclude that the only reasonable scoring within the category is at least Severe or Priority.

Drug Therapies

In view of what has been stated in the previous category, it seems to us that if Margaret were to be denied continuing medications there is a strong likelihood that her condition would go back to its former state of aggression, anxiety, and distrust.

Her behaviour is now inextricably linked to her medications which makes them paramount in the management of her behaviour and overall calmness.

I am unable to list what drugs have been prescribed to Margaret or what their side effects may be but no doubt this is well documented in her medical records. The only additional thing I can mention is that since Margaret's cancer she has always relied upon me making sure she takes the correct dosage at the correct time and that she has never posed any problem in taking her medications.

For this reason drug therapy must be seen to be a High to Severe level of need.

ALTERED STATES OF CONSCIOUSNESS

There appears to be certain misunderstandings about what this phrase actually means. Social services initially informed me that as Margaret had not experienced any unconscious episodes, this would indicate that she had not suffered any state of altered consciousness. I informed her that I disagreed with her understanding as to what this phrase actually meant and went on to state that in a similar way to autism the spectrum was wide-ranging and consequently covered various states from self-inflicted, with or without the use of drugs, to natural occurring conditions such as dreams, and non-awareness of a change in state from what would otherwise be described as a natural state.

These altered states of consciousness fall between:

The altered state being a state of consciousness without being unconscious either intentionally created by such things as meditation, hypnosis, psychedelic drugs, religious chanting or praying etc.

Or

An un-intentional state such as dreams or daydreams. Then there is the altered state of consciousness that I believe is the one being referred to in the context of the NHS CHC assessment. This is most certainly unintentional and a severe change to the person's state caused through that person's illness, in this case Alzheimer's disease.

Margaret has been suffering from this altered state of consciousness for probably over a year, during which time the condition has manifested itself in varying degrees of seriousness and durations.

For a number of months now the following things have become daily worries for her.

To give just a few examples, she has been convinced of the following things.

(1) That giving our grandsons weekly pocket money must be stopped or we would be giving away all our money.

(2) That everything we owned belonged to her, be it money, house, car, possessions etc. and that I had nothing.

(3) That she had promised to give away our various collections of items to a woman in the village who was building a museum. This at one time included her beloved Juke Box.

(4) She was convinced that I had another woman living in one of the upstairs bedrooms.

(5) Items of clothing which were hers she didn't recognise as such.

(6) She believes she has two young children to feed, wash and care for and that she has a house in the village where they are waiting for her. When I have tried to convince her to the contrary she becomes very aggressive and violent.

(7) She is often seen to be talking in whispers, apparently to another woman or women, trying to share her food with them and believing they are asking her to do things.

(8) At times she believes she or they are trying to kill her and becomes tearful and scared. Even though Dr G has confirmed that he has prescribed medication to reduce these incidents they still exist. Even during my visits to see her, she will suddenly start to whisper and get up to go. When challenged Margaret will often say that the woman was asking her to go with her.

(9) The other disconcerting thing was the period when she would refer to herself in third person. I would ask Margaret a question such as whether she would like a cup of tea, and she would reply "she doesn't like tea".

Again we believe these hallucinations which still continue would be almost impossible to manage without the medications she is now receiving, and for these reasons we consider this category to be at the very least High but more likely to be Priority given that there is no Severe option.

Additional Information

I will use this opportunity to place on record a number of salient points I believe need to be addressed in respect of NHS CHC in relation to its use, especially in the context of those people suffering from dementia and in particular Alzheimer's, and my observations from the experience of having to deal with this.

(1) I believe that even though there are an ever-increasing number of people suffering from the effects of Alzheimer's, there is very little knowledge of the reality of what it means within the general population. It is one of those conditions that generally receives very little publicity about its truly devastating effects and tends to be regarded as simply a loss of memory. How often does a member of the public who has no personal experience of what it encompasses simply say, "Oh poor dear, they are losing their memory, they're having senior moments", thinking it's a pity but they are just losing the ability to recall memories, nothing more.

(2) Compare this with a diagnosis of cancer and there is a completely different reaction. Firstly, it gets much more publicity which in turn provides greater knowledge within the population. It is seen as scary, devastating, frightening, life-limiting, and one of those diseases that no-one wants to hear they have been diagnosed with. Yet even though it can still be a killer, it is treatable and there is still hope that it has been caught in time with the possibility of full recovery. In many cases, granted not all, there is still the possibility of leading a fairly normal life. Not so with Alzheimer's; it is life-threatening, there is currently no cure, it robs the patient of not only their memories, but also their very being; they become totally reliant on others for their very existence. All these things are painfully obvious, especially to professionals working in the health and

care sectors. And so I would pose this question: "Why is it that a diagnosis of dementia of any kind is seemingly taken less seriously than almost any other disease?" This has without doubt been my experience, from my GP surgery, the 111 service, the 999 service, A&E, Hospital X, mental health team and in-patients wards.

(3) I would pose this question: "Why is it that it is a constant battle to get help for a person suffering from such a devastating disease?"

Is it because:

(a) It generally affects older people (although not always) so who cares? We're all going to die at some time.

(b) There is no cure so what's the point?

(c) It's not contagious, so why spend precious resources which could be used elsewhere to seemingly greater effect?

(d) It is such a massive problem that the simplest thing to do is play it down in the hope that the less the general population knows about the reality and the facts, the less the need to do something about it?

It appears to me and obviously to many others in a similar situation that there is an obstacle course that has to be undertaken to get what should be provided as a matter of right and fairness. This at a time when probably the greater proportion of those in need are least able to undertake such a task. After all, the greater proportion of those affected are elderly and so too are their carers, but where this is left to their children to undertake, on their parents' behalf, this is limited by the time they have available, with their own busy lives to continue getting on with.

So what are these obstacles to which I am referring?

(1) National Framework (NF), page 32, paragraph 32: "CCGs should make the public information leaflet available to members of the public, hard copies on hospital wards, through primary care outlets etc." It then goes on to state that any individual being considered for NHS CHC at the screening or referral stage should be given a leaflet, local information contact details etc:

(a) I could find no evidence of any leaflet or poster displayed in either Hospital X or TOPAS with reference to the existence of NHS CHC even though the CCGs are responsible for "Promoting awareness of NHS CHC" (NF, page 10, paragraph 21 b).

(b) How can any person avail themselves of help if its very existence is denied to them? This is simply a case of what you don't know, you can't ask for.

(c) To suggest that a leaflet is handed to anyone being considered for screening or referral is simply totally ineffective. How can anyone know about their rights if the person they are relying on telling them about them has the ability to deny them of them? This is like giving someone a locked box and telling them the only way to open it is to read the instructions that are inside it.

This was indeed my own experience with Dr G who had already made up his mind that an initial screening assessment was in his words "futile" (a word he used and subsequently apologised for).

(2) Not one person within the NHS had ever uttered the words "Continuing Healthcare" until they realised I was aware of its existence.

(3) My experience of getting an initial screening was the obstacle of overcoming one individual's belief that my wife was not entitled to it because in his opinion she had no nursing needs. Firstly it should not be left up to one individual to make such a decision, especially as his understanding of what CHC is was actually (or hopefully was) completely wrong.

The (NF) last paragraph on page three states "all those involved in the delivery of NHS CHC should become familiar with the whole National Framework."

(4) Having reluctantly agreed to carry out an initial assessment Dr G advised me that it was for my satisfaction and it would not in his opinion have any bearing on Margaret's funding or placement.

I should not have had to point out to Dr G that doing an initial assessment was not simply to satisfy me but because Margaret's condition and her rights warranted doing an assessment.

(5) Regretfully an initial screening assessment went ahead without our knowledge and although it produced a result that confirmed that it should go forward for a full assessment, neither my son nor myself were happy with the conclusions reached in a number of categories. Consequently we had to ask for a further assessment which was carried out to our satisfaction.

(6) All along this journey it has felt like coming to a fork in a bumpy road with a signpost pointing one way saying

"social care this way" and no indication at all of where the alternative leads to.

(7) It seemed to me that the social care sector had also made an assumption that not only will we not be entitled to NHS CHC but also that we will be self-funding. They have, since my attendance at the meeting of 12 August, been requesting me to divulge Margaret's financial situation, which to date I have refused to do, based on the fact that I feel this is premature, given that we have not until this time been assessed for Continuing Healthcare. Again due to statements made by a senior social care worker, I am led to believe she too has already determined that we are not entitled to it. I have now learnt from Penelope, the other social care worker involved, that TOPAS has made the determination that Margaret will not be discharged until I have completed the financial assessment and named a care home for use in the event that her condition deteriorates to such a degree that she would ultimately be required to go into such a facility.

I find both of these conditions to be wholly unwarranted. It feels like moral blackmail.

(a) There is nothing lawful about demanding that I divulge financial information which may not be necessary.

(b) How can anyone name a care home when it could possibly be dependent on who is funding the cost, or indeed when the time for the need of the services of such are unknown? It could be weeks, months, or years and ultimately will be dependent upon vacancies that exist at a particular moment in time.

DAVID MATTHEW ALLOTT

SIGNATURE ————————

Relationship HUSBAND

I Confirm I am Margaret Allott's lawful representative and hold lasting power of attorney for both financial affairs and health and welfare.

Date: ————————

I have produced here a table showing the assessment under the 12 domains.
(1) As listed above DA.
(2) As notified to me (eventually) by the CCG MD

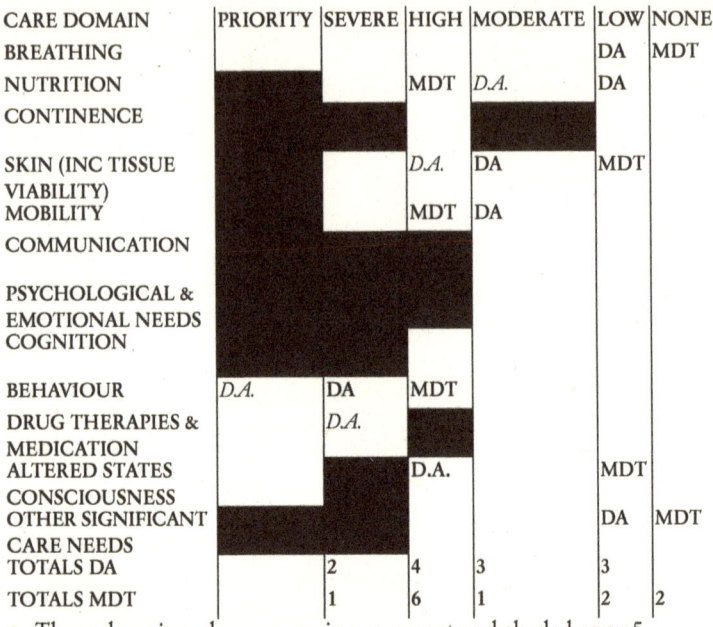

CARE DOMAIN	PRIORITY	SEVERE	HIGH	MODERATE	LOW	NONE
BREATHING					DA	MDT
NUTRITION			MDT	D.A.	DA	
CONTINENCE						
SKIN (INC TISSUE VIABILITY)			D.A.	DA	MDT	
MOBILITY			MDT	DA		
COMMUNICATION						
PSYCHOLOGICAL & EMOTIONAL NEEDS						
COGNITION						
BEHAVIOUR	D.A.	DA	MDT			
DRUG THERAPIES & MEDICATION		D.A.				
ALTERED STATES CONSCIOUSNESS			D.A.		MDT	
OTHER SIGNIFICANT CARE NEEDS					DA	MDT
TOTALS DA		2	4	3	3	
TOTALS MDT		1	6	1	2	2

- Those domains where we are in agreement and shaded grey: 5
- Number of domains where MDT has scored above DA: 2
- Number of domains where MDT has scored below DA: 5

Obviously there exists no dispute in the seven domains listed in the first two categories.

Whilst I see no point in taking any issue with the difference of opinion in regards to the breathing domain, I also do not take issue with the scoring under "skin" as this was caused by a lack of care whilst residing at TOPAS and has subsequently cleared up to my satisfaction.

This leaves us with three domains that I most certainly do not find acceptable for the following reasons:

- BEHAVIOUR: Whilst the MDT scored this as a high need this was somewhat watered down by the fact that although significant discussion took place on this subject and over a full page of notes was made in relation to some of the things said, it appears to me that again procedures laid down in the National Framework were not followed as they should have been.

Five of these comments were made by the TOPAS nurse and included the following:

(1) Every morning Margaret is aggressive towards her carers both verbally and physically whilst carrying out personal care.

(2) Two staff members are required for personal care due to her aggression.

(3) Initially on her admission to TOPAS three staff members were required to deal with her aggression.

(4) Always two staff members required for continence care.

(5) Margaret is not normally aggressive when not requiring personal care.

Three comments were recorded highlighting the medication given to Margaret particularly to address her aggressive behaviour. There appears to be no recognition of the fact that this has reduced the care numbers required from three to two, but most importantly the principle of "needs are still needs no matter how well managed" as laid down in the National Framework has been completely ignored.

- Five incidents of Margaret's aggression as detailed by my son and me, including video footage of her self-harming, were recorded in the notes but these were by no means the sum total of our examples discussed

The DST notes under behaviour also included twenty recorded incidents from TOPAS. No fewer than sixteen of these were recording aggressive behaviour and four or five reported on her continuing walking in the corridors. Margaret was admitted to TOPAS on Thursday 22 July.

It should be noted that there is just one entry in the TOPAS notes for July being the day of her admission and the next entries were not until four weeks later on 18 and 19 August. There followed a further gap in these notes of over two weeks until an entry appears on 4 September. Again a further one week passed until an entry was made on 11 September which was followed by daily entries all but for two separate days leading up until the assessment on Friday 24 September.

It is relevant to note these dates in relation to

(A) The date of the first screening being 18 August

(B) The date of the second screening being 12 September.

To put it bluntly it would appear that the MDT only really had sight of the notes from TOPAS when it was apparent that a full assessment was to be undertaken and therefore only reflected Margaret's condition after she had already been on a course of medication for over one month. This is again contrary to the conditions laid out in the National Framework. In addition to this the NF also states that:

- "Determining whether an individual has a primary health need involves looking at the totality of the relevant needs". Page 19, paragraph 54.

- "Where deterioration can be reasonably anticipated to take place in the near future, this should also be taken into account, in order to avoid the need for unnecessary or repeat assessments." Page 42, paragraph 139.

Both my son and I made the MDT aware of these facts but they were seemingly ignored.

It was our firm belief that the description given for the level of need identified as Severe was appropriate to the needs of Margaret. "Challenging behaviour of severity and/or frequency that poses a significant risk to self, others or property. The risk assessment identifies that the behaviour(s) require(s) a prompt and skilled response that might be outside the range of planned interventions."

I sincerely believe that due to the fact that the previous domain of cognition was undeniably scored as Severe, the MDT purposely would not give a Severe rating in this domain as it would automatically trigger the conclusion that Margaret did in fact have a primary health need and therefore be entitled to CHC funding. It is further apparent that there is without doubt a determination to deny as many people as they can for this funding, and their determination to do so seemingly knows no bounds.

The second domain that we totally disagreed with, was that of altered states of consciousness.

For the sake of completeness I have decided to duplicate the sum total of what was reported to the CCG from the MDT.

Checklist dated 14.09.21

- Margaret hallucinates occasionally and requires support from staff to minimise risk of harm

MDT Discussion
- The nurse reported that Margaret has vacant episodes the whole time; unless you are directly in front of her, she will not see you
- The nurse reported that the team doctors are aware of these episodes and have reported that this is part of the dementia
- No rescue medication prescribed.

Level of need – Low
CHCNA agreed
Staff nurse agreed
Social Worker agreed

Description
History of ASC but it is effectively managed and there is a low risk of harm.

I find it difficult to know where to start in responding to this blatant disregard for the:

(1) Rules as laid down in the National Framework.

(2) The fact that considerable discussion took place over the meaning of ASC which was incorrectly interpreted by the MDT who were adamant that the NHS defined it as being a state of unconsciousness, which Margaret had not suffered from.

(3) The fact that the document did not even record our views on this subject in any way whatsoever.

(4) The fact that it appears that because our views were so at odds with their own they omitted to even state that the family did not agree with them.

(5) To make the statement that "the team doctors are aware of these episodes and have reported that this is part of the dementia" is absurd. It implies that because they know and it is common in patients that have dementia then it has no relevance. By the same logic one could argue that any symptoms of any disease are irrelevant because it is known to the doctors and is common in similar cases. This is not the point, the point is to ascertain the level of need, no matter how many doctors know and how often it manifests itself in people in similar circumstances. The National Framework is quite clear about the fact that the assessment has nothing to do with the diagnosis of a particular disease but is about assessing the level of needs of the patient. Yet here we are

with the nurse assessor, failing to grasp the meaning of what she has reported.

As I have detailed earlier on the true meaning of ASC, I can assure all readers that my son and I did not give up lightly on trying to get the other parties to understand just how wrong their interpretation of the meaning was. As their belief was that it was to do with unconsciousness, we suggested that surely then it would be defined as such. But we were merely told that this was how the NHS defined the meaning of ASC and therefore Margaret was at low risk. I enquired as to how it was that the NHS had the power to alter the meaning of a word or set of words that have been defined in the English language and appears in the dictionary. Again the response was simply that this is how the NHS defines ASC. Why did the formatters of the National Framework use such a group of words if they had meant them to be interpreted in exactly the opposite way?

The NHS website can be very informative when looking up certain conditions or their definitions. To try to understand how this anomaly could possibly have taken place I thought it might be helpful to consult the said website.

What I found was no reference to ASC but six pages of information on what the NHS terms as "Disorders of Consciousness".

Here are just a few of the things stated about this condition:

"A disorder, of consciousness or impaired consciousness, is a state where consciousness has been affected by damage to the brain."

The main disorders of consciousness are:

Coma, vegetive state, minimally conscious state.

So the reality is that the NHS already has a set of words to define the meaning of how they have chosen to define ASC. They therefore have no need to steal, borrow or make up their own definition of an already established and known definition by using ASC in such a way.

Again I would argue that the formatters of the NF would have used the terminology "disorders of consciousness" if this is how they wished this domain to be interpreted.

Finally on this subject, it is plain to see that the nurse assessor had got herself tied up in her own lies by reporting a descriptive level of needs as Low, citing "History of ASC but it is effectively managed and there is a low risk of harm". She has clearly demonstrated that she did understand the true meaning of ASC as the element of unconsciousness is dealt with in its worst form only under the needs heading of Priority.

I can now turn my attention to the final domain heading which is listed as Other Significant Care Needs.

This is the only comment made by the assessor of the DST:

- "No other needs were raised outside of the previous eleven domains when asked and it was felt that the assessor had been comprehensive in the completion of this Decision Support Tool."

This is nothing short of a blatant lie and highlights the dangers of a system that allows the assessor to be the sole arbitrator of what did or did not take place prior to it being forwarded (with their own recommendation) for a final decision to be made by the CCG.

Firstly there is again no record of what my son and I discussed under this heading; it is reported as though we said nothing which is completely untrue.

Earlier on I made mention of the fact that those involved in the assessment should, as laid out in the NF, (page 38 para 121) "Whilst as a minimum requirement an MDT can comprise two professionals from different healthcare professions, the MDT should usually include both health and social care professionals, who are knowledgeable about the individual's health and social care needs and where possible have been involved in the assessment, treatment or care of the individual."

As previously stated neither of these two professionals had even seen Margaret prior to the assessment let alone been involved in her care or treatment. The above makes it clear that they should "be knowledgeable about the individual's health and social care needs".

So far as I can determine, in order for them to become knowledgeable about Margaret's needs, they would need to digest her medical records to achieve a comprehensive view on those needs. (This being due to the fact that neither one had seen her in person.)

I had taken the time and effort to get Margaret's medical notes, which brought to my attention that since being diagnosed with Alzheimer's she had been assessed no fewer than nine times under an NHS assessment procedure formulated by doctors of psychology and known as "The Health of the Nation Outcome Scales" (HoNOS).

I brought this up under the 12th domain and stated that we wished to discuss this with the analysis of how her condition had been seen to decline over this period of time.

We were informed by the nurse assessor that this was not relevant to this assessment especially as she had never even heard of HoNOS, a sentiment also expressed by the social care manager.

It is clear to me that this is proof beyond doubt that neither party had bothered to get Margaret's medical notes prior to the meeting because had they done so there would have been no way they would have denied any knowledge of HoNOS.

I would have to ask the question:

If they had not seen sight of Margaret's medical records and the notes from TOPAS were limited to the ones provided and shown in the DST (where no fewer than seven weeks at the beginning of her time at TOPAS showed no entries) then how could these so-called professionals be fully knowledgeable about my wife's condition?

Within the notes on recommendation, they start with an overview about Margaret. I cannot express my anger sufficiently at what was stated in the second sentence which again confirms beyond any reasonable doubt that the CHC nurse assessor was in my opinion negligent in becoming knowledgeable about Margaret's situation. I quote what she wrote: "MA was admitted to Hospital X hospital on ward 14 following concerns about her physical health."

This is absolute rubbish. How dare she state such a thing after I had been informed by our doctors that there was nothing wrong with Margaret's physical health and therefore they could not offer any further help? This was also followed by ambulance crews having attended to her and doing all the necessary tests which also confirmed that they could find nothing physically wrong with her. Indeed as previously stated we had to fight hard to get her into hospital because the ambulance service did not consider her to be an emergency case.

She then has the audacity in her next sentence to suggest that it was while in hospital that they noted that she showed signs of deterioration in her medical state. This makes my blood boil given the fact that the doctor on the ward, after being there for over a week, asked me why I felt Margaret had a mental condition. Given the fact that the CHC nurse assessor was the person responsible for assessing Margaret's needs, the very least she could have done was to read her medical notes and truly understand the nature of her condition. To be so negligent when holding such a position of power is no small misdemeanour. She is unfit to hold such authority and therefore I would repeat the saying: There are little things worse than holding a position of "authority without accountability". It should never be allowed to happen.

I am left with no alternative but to suppose the whole procedure is nothing short of being a farce. Did the nurse assessor and the social care manager get together prior to the meeting to formulate their response in advance?

Finally on this subject, had we been made aware that what we had to say on altered states of consciousness would be totally ignored, then we would have also asked for this to be recorded under the 12th domain, as our concerns in this respect were not addressed at all.

The NF states that the findings of the CCG should be known to the patient within twenty-eight days of the MDT meeting. They again failed by being unable to reach this deadline.

Approximately six weeks after the MDT Assessment I received a telephone call from Penelope (the student social care worker) informing me that they had received the determination from the CCG. Naturally I asked her what their findings were, but Penelope stated that she was uncertain if she was permitted to divulge this information to me and would have to consult with her manager. The response was that I would have to wait confirmation from the CCG. How utterly shameful; the CCG could inform social services but they couldn't inform me. Why did they believe it to be acceptable to withhold this information from me?

A number of telephone calls took place which resulted in me finally making contact with a person who could help me by giving me a link to download the full MDT notes and recommendations, but not until I had forwarded another copy of my power of attorney forms.

This document, after having completed the twelve domains assessment, goes on to list where a difference of opinion existed between the CNCNA and staff nurse who scored a Moderate under "psychological and emotional needs" as opposed to the social services manager and us who believed it to be High, which was ultimately the score ascribed to it.

There then follows a three-page summary under the four headings used to identify nature, intensity, complexity and unpredictability, finally culminating in the decision, which was:

Not eligible – joint fund (community placement).

This is what was stated:

"MA's needs do not meet the criteria for NHS CHC because taken as a whole their needs (which should obviously read *her* needs) are not beyond the power of an LA to meet, however some specific needs have been identified in the DST that are not of a nature that an LA can solely meet, or are beyond the power of an LA to fully meet."

(Well, in the words of the likeable Cilla Black, surprise, surprise.)

This is the result of the ambiguity of having the third option, like not proven.

So desperate are these "civil servants" who are paid for by the taxes you, I, and the majority of the population pay to deprive as many people as possible of our rights, that I suspect that this joint funding package is their fall-back position in the vast majority of cases where it is seen as the final hurdle that can be put in place to deny us our rights.

Maybe they take the view that some people will finally fall at this hurdle and not pursue what is a legitimate claim for CHC.

It's possible they think more people will give up their fight for their rights if they throw a few crumbs from their table to give us a sense of having achieved something.

There can be nothing more abhorrent than those who make the rules or enforce the rules to take it upon themselves to treat the rest of us like idiots, knowing full well that if the boot was on the other foot and if it were their loved one who was being treated in such a way they would be the first to make sure they got their full entitlement.

The final page of this recommendation is probably the thing that causes me the greatest amount of anger, because it highlights the very fact that there is nothing they won't do to achieve their goal of denying my wife her rights.

This page is basically a confirmation from the MDT to the CCG that "the professionals" involved are all speaking from the same song-sheet in giving the recommendation that they have.

Just to put the record straight, there were only two professionals in attendance at that meeting.

The CHC nurse assessor.

The social worker manager.

The student social worker who was in attendance at the meeting, did not contribute in any way to the discussions that took place throughout. In fact from recollection other than stating her name and her position as student social worker this was the only time she spoke.

I wish to make it 100% clear that I mean no criticism of Penelope, so far as we understood she was there to observe and learn from the experience; nothing more. I am all in favour of students in any profession being able to experience as much as they can whilst learning their trade; in fact it is essential if we are to see the next generation move forward. The only proviso is that they need to learn good practice, not bad practice.

What was demonstrated to Penelope was bad practice at its worse. It was obvious that her manager had asked her to sign the form, stating that she was in agreement with the conclusion reached on joint funding. This should never have happened. In Penelope's position this was wholly inappropriate, and she had little choice other than to follow her then-boss's instructions.

Why then did he take such a stupid and inappropriate decision?

I believe there is only one conclusion that can be drawn from this, and that would be that he was not confident in his or CHC nurse's conclusion and therefore having a further signature would reinforce it for the benefit of the CCG.

It must also be noted that CHC nurse, being the one responsible for sending their findings to the CCG, should also have spotted the inappropriateness of such an action and should have spoken out against it. Maybe she was in fact the one that instigated it in the first place. One can only guess as to what went on in this respect.

Of one thing I am entirely sure: I do not believe Penelope took it upon herself to sign this document. So incensed was I about this that I spoke to Penelope and explained that in life people enter different professions for a variety of different reasons; some undoubtedly do so with a genuine desire to help and improve the life of others. As far as I was concerned I believed that she more than likely fell into this category as my dealings with her had always been very cordial and helpful with a real interest in listening to what I had to say. As she was in the process of returning to university from her work experience placement, I explained that in life one will inevitably come across other people in higher positions that do not demonstrate the same desires or standards you would wish them to follow. The hardest thing to do in these circumstances is not to fall into the trap of blindly following instructions that are in conflict with one's own beliefs and personal humane feelings. Not to acquiesce and lower your own standards, when all around you people are telling you to do something that is clearly wrong, is an extremely difficult thing to do, but remember one simple principle: the cream always rises to the top. It is too often hard and can be at personal cost to oneself but doing what is right by yourself and to those who are reliant upon your humanity is not only a mark of your own goodness but highlights the inherent badness of those that would have you believe their way is the only way.

Whilst doing my own fact-gathering in preparation for this assessment, I came across an article on The Alzheimer's website which had been written by Peter Garside in loving memory of his wife Pauline and as a tribute to her in the hope that detailing their experiences may be of help to others.

The eighteen-page detail of Pauline's story is certainly enlightening and reflects many of the experiences I have experienced and talked about in this book.

For me to just include the odd snippet of what Peter has written would not do justice to what he has to say and therefore I would implore you to read the whole story by visiting the website. However, there is one part of the story that I feel compelled to share with you.

Peter informs us that Pauline's initial assessment was to deny that she had a primary health need and did not therefore qualify for NHS CHC. This necessitated an appeal, the narrative of his experience in this process I have duplicated below.

Peter writes:

"Decision Support Tool (DST) At Our Appeal.

The questionnaire used to note all the above categories of domain is called the DST by social workers and NHS assessment staff. The initial assessment meetings were not as detailed as far as I was aware. Pauline was not given any "Priority" or "Severe" scores at the appeal tribunal, but was graded with four "High" needs and five "Moderate" Needs. The other three categories were either "Low" or "No Needs". The overall result was well above the required score to achieve NHS CHC. Indeed two "High" and three or more Moderate levels of need would have been sufficient to qualify as far as I know

The Appeal Panel sat on 12 August 2015 and agreed that Pauline's health needs were such that without my care at home she would have to enter a nursing home immediately. Pauline was therefore properly assessed as being eligible for NHS CHC, and it was confirmed that her Alzheimer's disease was identified as a "primary health need."

The panel warned me that her health would continue to decline, and so the funding would require monitoring so that the actual costs of the provision of care at home in the future would be fully covered by the NHS long term. A specialist Continuing Healthcare nurse (CHC nurse) was present at the appeals tribunal and she took personal charge of our case thereafter. The CHC nurse dealt with the financial requirements in an exemplary manner via the Clinical Commissioning Group (CCG) local office. The cost of care at home was financed via a Personal Health Budget (PHB)."

Their original assessment meeting took place on 12 December 2014 and Peter admits he had done no preparation for that meeting in the mistaken belief that their case for NHS CHC was a matter of routine. He informs us that he received the decision letter from the CCG by 7 January 2015 (within the twenty-eight-day period stipulated by the National Framework. This letter informed him that Pauline had been refused NHS funding because Alzheimer's disease was not considered to be a "primary health need", and Pauline did not meet the criteria for help.

I believe that Peter's story highlights a number of important points which begs even further questions to do with the fairness, consistency and effectiveness of the whole process:

- It appears that the CCG took a similar stance to that of many other CCGs in believing that Alzheimer's disease did not constitute a "primary health need" at the first assessment. Now I can understand that the disease in itself does not give automatic entitlement to CHC funding; it's what the disease does to the patient and in turn how that affects the level of care required to look after them that is important. Conversely, it does not give automatic non-eligibility for funding which many in the NHS believe to be the case

- At least they responded with the decision letter in line with the timeframe set out in the NF. More than can be said of our CCG

- Is the vast difference in the scoring of the domains purely down to the difference in interpretation of the "National Framework" by different CCGs? If it is then this is clearly an indisputable fact that the system is not achieving its stated aims of consistency. In some places you may well have a better chance of winning the "Postcode Lottery" than getting a fair assessment for CHC funding

- Even the staggering differences between the scoring levels and the corresponding results beggar's belief

Compare Pauline's four "High" and five "Moderate", at appeal stage with Margaret's one "Severe", six "High" and one "Moderate". This is not a game; I am sorry to have to make such comparisons. I do so only to highlight the hypocrisy of such an inadequate system

- Thanks must go to Peter for highlighting the importance of doing the necessary preparation prior to any meeting, because there is one thing you can be sure of: they will pull the wool over your eyes at the first opportunity they get.

The next logical step for me was to appeal their decision and although I would very much have liked to have done this myself, I did realise my time would be somewhat limited as Margaret's return home with myself as principal carer would put time constraints on what I'd be able to achieve.

While my chosen law firm, were getting up to speed on all that had happened (or so I thought), my next obstacle was to ensure that I completed the necessary financial forms and information required to get help from the local authority social services.

I include in the next chapter some information which I hope you will find useful in the event you find yourself in a position that social care is the only option open to you. Obviously I hope and pray that this will not be the case.

11

WHO PAYS: SELF FUNDING OR SOCIAL SERVICES?

Although I had spent many weeks resisting the pressure to complete the necessary forms to disclose Margaret's financial position, the time had now come to undertake this task.

Before I go into the whys and wherefores of the detailed information, I think it may be of some help to some of you to remind you of the criteria of who qualifies for social funding and who through their circumstances will inevitably be deemed to have sufficient funds to be what they term as "Self-funding".

- If the patient has over £23,250 in cash, savings, income, benefits, pensions and property then the chances are they will be self-funding, but with certain provisos (figures and criteria are different in Scotland Wales and Northern Ireland)

- The value of the principal residence cannot be taken into account if:
  o (1) The patient is being cared for at home
  o (2) Their spouse or partner is still living in the property, irrespective of where the patient is being cared for, even if that is in a care home
  o (3) No debt can be accumulated against the patient's share of that property if one or two above apply

- Unfortunately second homes do not enjoy the same degree of protection and the patient's interest in that property will be taken into account in assessing their means

- Belongings often referred to as chattels are also not assessed for value

- There is a second limit of £14,250 which comes into play once the patient's wealth has been reduced to only £23,250. Between these limits the funding of care is shared equally between the patient and social care until their wealth has been reduced to the lower limit. (Not much to show for a lifetime of work, paying taxes, being frugal and thinking you have something to leave for your children or grandchildren to help make their life a little better)

- All other savings are considered in the assessment including building society accounts, ISAS, even premium bonds and of course personal bank accounts. Any joint accounts that are held with spouses, partners or others are deemed to be owned directly in proportion to the number of people named on the account

- Income from pensions is also assessed, but if the patient's pension allows for the spouse or partner to still enjoy a share of that pension after the demise of the pension holder (usually 50%) then only 50% will form part of the calculation.

It would be unwise to try and cheat the system by transferring monies from these accounts in order to purely reduce their assets to below the threshold figure. I understand that in so doing, this could be perceived as attempting to defraud the LA, and at the very least could negate any responsibilities they may have for funding of any kind.

The financial declaration form is quite detailed, but I have no idea if this is a standard form used by local authorities throughout the country or if each one is left to their own devices in determining the questions to be asked. Even if the latter is the case, I would suspect that each one will be quite similar.

Most of the questions asked are self-explanatory and easy to answer. The first section details the patient's regular income from benefits and pensions, but bear in mind that some of these are paid on a four-weekly basis, having the effect that there are the equivalent of thirteen months' payments.

The next section deals with income from all other sources including employment, lodgers, court orders, maintenance payments etc.

This is followed by the person's capital reserves details including building society accounts, banks, national savings, shares, cash, unit trusts and details of properties owned. (Note: this is why it is so important to make sure your principal property is registered in the correct way.)

Next comes details of standard household expenditure such as council tax, gas, electric, water, rent, insurances, loans, telephones, TV licence, other fuels etc.

All of the above are so regular in payment terms that it would be difficult to forget any of them; however, the next section is the most demanding, in that you are required to disclose absolutely everything else you spend, along with amount and frequency.

Obviously all of this expenditure is a shared expense, some of which is only incurred once a year or possibly less frequently. Don't forget things such as Christmas cards and stamps, charitable donations, subscriptions such as Sky TV, National Trust, RSPB etc. Think about car expenses, road tax, repairs, new tyres, fuel and Christmas and birthday gifts, window cleaner etc.

The single biggest expenditure is probably that of the weekly shop. The forms that I was required to complete stated that all claims for expenses must be accompanied by receipts and proof of purchases. Easily said but not always easily done. I personally know nobody who keeps the supermarket checkout receipts or indeed receipts for those incidental purchases such as coffee, the odd pub drink, newspapers, magazines, parking charges, to name just a few.

Because of this I chose to deal with this by listing every conceivable supermarket commodity that I knew we purchased and not necessarily items that were weekly purchases. Such things as condiments, table sauces, accompaniments and the like may be purchased infrequently but they all cost money and they all add up. There was the added complication that during lockdown periods our son and daughter-in-law would do our shopping for us and we would repay them with cash; other than the bank statements showing withdrawals there was no other record of what this had been spent on. Furthermore Margaret was in hospital for over four months and therefore this also impacted on our usual spending trends.

Having completed the supermarket spending list, I compiled a typical seven-day menu to arrive at an average weekly cost for food and drink purchases. Likewise for all the other non-food item expenses, such as cleaning materials, washing powders and fabric conditioners, dishwasher tablets, dishwasher liquid, paper towels, toilet tissues.

Even though I thought I had covered everything, I have subsequently been making a list of those things I did forget, such as replacement lightbulbs, batteries, printing paper and ink, eye drops, toothbrushes, razor blades and shaving gel. Bin bags, Brillo pads, and many more.

For the food shopping I took the weekly average x 51 weeks and did an additional week to cover the added expense of Christmas to arrive at the annual expense.

Because most of my expenditure was paid for on my credit card, which I have a direct debit to pay in full each month, I was able to highlight the different forms of spending and show this on the bank statements. Although I was only required to provide copies of three months' statements from Margaret's own account and our joint account, I chose to provide a full six months for these, along with copies of six months' statements for my own credit card. I felt it was necessary to provide this level of detail to ensure that it was clear to those doing the assessment that my disclosures were 100% factual and provable.

I would point out that I also confirmed, with copies of invoices, the expenditure incurred to overcome the concerns expressed by the occupational therapists in reference to the stairs and all other purchases that were required to ensure Margaret's safety and comfort on her return home. All such expenditure which was necessary due to her condition is a legitimate outgoing that was and still is paid for out of Margaret's own accounts and income. This has reduced her personal wealth below the thresholds to the extent that her social care element of the "Joint Funding Package" is now rightly paid for by social services.

Once again this highlights the importance of having in place the power of attorney documentation for both health and welfare and in this case that of property and financial.

Imagine just how much more complicated this would have been if I had had to resort to dealing with these things by applying to the Court of Protection for their permission to undertake these purchases, not only from the timing delays this would have incurred but also the added expense of getting these agreements.

I keep detailed records of all the ongoing expenditure incurred to make Margaret's life safer and more comfortable, including such things as cameras, so I am always able to keep an eye on her whenever I am in another room or the expense incurred for incontinence underwear prior to finally getting these approved on the NHS. There have been many other items such as over-chair/bed tables, night lights, motion detectors, pressure pads, slip sheets, specialist crockery and cutlery, additional towels and flannels for cleaning etc.

I hope some of this information is useful and helpful to the reader. I know some of it may appear to be common sense but there again what you don't know is only something that you haven't learnt through experience or by gaining the knowledge from someone else.

The next chapter will deal with a variety of other aspects of the minefield created by those whose wish is that you don't gain the knowledge to challenge their aims of denying your loved ones their rights. It also sets out my own personal wishes and desires and hopefully how you can contribute towards a fairer and better society for us all.

12

PEOPLE'S RIGHTS AND WHO REALLY KNOWS WHAT ABOUT CHC FUNDING

I wanted to start this chapter by talking a little bit about rights and what we understand this to mean.

There are numerous examples throughout history where individuals have been constructive in changing the thinking of others, simply because things weren't right, and if it's not right then the obvious and only conclusion is that it is wrong.

Words have little meaning if the actions which should conform to the words don't happen.

Thomas Jefferson 1776 is credited with penning this phrase in the *Declaration of Independence*:

"We hold these truths to be self-evident, that all men are created equal, that they are endowed by their creator with certain unalienable rights, that amongst these are life, liberty and the pursuit of happiness."

Strange to believe that this was penned at a time when slavery was so common place in the southern states.

In 1848 Elizabeth Cady Stanton, the American Suffragist, rightly believed that the phrase should read "All men and women are created equal."

Winston Churchill wrote "The American Constitution declares all men are born equal, the British Socialist Party add all men must be kept equal."

All words with undeniable good intentions but nevertheless just words on a piece of paper, when the actions don't match the intention. I say this because the National Framework even in its highly detailed attempt to treat people with fairness and equality, without prejudice, and with compassion, is in effect just more words where the actions don't match.

I remember being privileged to visit Montgomery in the southern state of Alabama and visit the actual spot where Rosa Parks bravely refused to give up her seat on a bus to a white man, a deed that resulted in her arrest and became the catalyst for the Civil Rights movement. It is hard to comprehend that this took place as recently as 1955, but there again here we are in the twenty-first century and there is still so much prejudice against people born with a different colour of skin to that of the perpetrators of this injustice. Whilst visiting this city we sought out The Dexter Avenue King Memorial Church, a building which sits on the former site of a Slave Traders Pen (named as such because the slave masters would pen the slaves inside, pending their sale). Although the building is only open on certain days, we learnt from the plaque outside that Martin Luther King Jr, after whom the church was renamed, was the Pastor of this community from 1954 to 1960 and subsequently his son has preached there on regular occasions.

We know that Rosa Parks's actions resulted in a boycott of all the buses, which went on for eleven months, during which time the busses ran almost empty until the Supreme Court ruled segregated seating to be illegal. Truly amazing how powerful this peaceful protest against this injustice turned out to be.

Just one street up from the church is the site of The Civil Rights Memorial, a simple but appropriate way in which to remember and pay tribute to those who gave their lives in the fight for what should have been their unalienable right since they were born.

The memorial is in two parts: a large circular black granite table which is inscribed with the names of the martyrs and chronicles the history in lines that radiate from the centre like the hands of a clock. Water emerges from the centre and flows evenly over the table, and behind stands a curved black granite wall with more water flowing gently over the words inscribed there:, Martin Luther King's paraphrase of Amos 5:24 - "We will not be satisfied until justice rolls down like waters and righteousness like a mighty stream".

There can be little doubt that Martin Luther King Jr was an inspirational person and achieved recognition for his peaceful protests and work during his lifetime. His name and his "dreams" live on through the hundreds of streets in America named after him, and of course there is the lasting honour of having a public holiday named after him to celebrate his life.

How sad it is that the things he fought against, the inequalities, the prejudices, the racism, the whole unfairness of a system that allows these things to happen, still remains to this day.

Although our fight for justice is not comparable in terms of the numbers of people affected or the length of time throughout their lives that they had to endure such a terrible miscarriage of human justice, I sincerely believe that in its own way our cause in fighting for the rights of our loved ones is no less important because of their inability to fight for their own rights and the sheer hypocrisy of those in a position to do the right thing.

Our cause is not about the colour of one's skin, their gender, their religious beliefs, their nationality, age, or anything else one might use to define a group of people. No, the only defining factor for us is that our loved ones have so sadly been inflicted with such a cruel disease that has robbed, or is robbing, them of their past, present and future and we are the only ones able to fight the injustice of them not being cared for in a time of their greatest need.

I cannot get away from the thought that once rights are enshrined in law then those who are guilty of denying them to others are doing so either illegally or at the very least unlawfully and should be held to account under the law. Consider the fact that someone who is arrested for whatever reason no matter how large or small the alleged offence is, is given the courtesy of having their rights read out to them and to understand what their options are. Compare this with the number of people who don't even know about NHS CHC because no-one wants to tell them of their rights to be considered for this type of funding.

Let us contrast this with a female being refused her right to cast her vote at a polling station and being told that, by a misconceived official, "The right to vote did not include them because he/she had heard that the voter in question had self-identified as a "Star Trekker" from the planet Klingon." Outrageous yes, unlikely yes, but not necessarily impossible as it appears that a change is happening to allow anyone the right (there is That Word again) to self-identify as neither male nor female. Does a gender-neutral person lose their rights?

There are many groups, organisations and charities fighting for the rights of numerous different causes simply because some of these do not have the protection of the law, but also because the law is impotent in defending those rights where they do exist.

The Act of Parliament of 1946, "The National Health Service Act", brought into being the NHS on 5 July 1948.

The Act provided for the establishment of a comprehensive health service for England and Wales. The Act stated that "It shall be the duty of the Minister of Health to promote the establishment of a health service to secure improvement in the physical and mental health of the people and the prevention, diagnosis and treatment of illness". The Act stated that "the services shall be free of charge".

It is unequivocal that the service was and still is not only there to help in the treatment of physical ailments but importantly also for mental health.

The English Dictionary defines the meaning of the word "treatment" in the following way: "The application of medicines, surgery, psychotherapy etc. to a patient or disease or symptom". It would be my contention that it is paramount that a person who is suffering from any physical or mental disease cannot be devoid of the need for care at all stages of their treatment; in other words, the actual act of caring for someone forms a serious part of the treatment for that person. To deny the rights to that care by the NHS would in my opinion be a serious breach of the obligations placed upon it when it was conceived.

I would further contend that relying upon social care for this element of the treatment of someone with a diagnosed condition or illness is wholly inappropriate and should be confined to assisting those people in our society who have needs that are not of a medical nature or caused by an illness or disease.

To use a modern day analogy, one would not expect the owner of a new electric car with the benefit of a guarantee of quality to be denied the necessary repairs if any one of the many things that could become faulty are expressly denied their rights to have them put right at no cost to themselves. To argue that the basis for such a denial being that the very reason why they don't work is because the computer is faulty, not that the individual elements of the car are faulty, just the computer.

Is this not what is being argued in the case of people with dementia, because the brain is faulty (i.e. the computer). All the other bodily functions that don't work are of a social nature purely because we don't yet have the capacity to fix the brain and therefore aren't covered by the NHS (the guarantee).

I sincerely believe that the powers that be, be they politicians, the senior judiciary or NHS management and doctors are fully aware that what is happening is undeniably wrong. Yet they all seemingly conspire to avoid not only the obligations they have but the very denial of a full and detailed investigation of such abuse. As we have learnt from the sterling work done by Ex-Rear Admiral Philip Mathias all of these bodies – the NHS, police, judiciary, politicians and even public bodies formed to protect the rights of the people, have all turned their backs on the most vulnerable in our society.

I find it extremely galling to read how any member of any of these bodies can use such strong terminology to describe the action of others, without the realisation that in a similar way the same could be said of themselves. The front-page headline article of the *Daily Mail*, in describing the war in the Ukraine, on 10 March 2022, reported that Boris Johnson is quoted as saying "There are few things more depraved than targeting the vulnerable and defenceless". He is undeniably correct in making this statement, but can he not realise that this is exactly what is happening in targeting the people with dementia in the way they are doing?

Please be assured I make no reference by comparison to the dreadful atrocities that the innocent victims of this war are or have been enduring, and I am not comparing the actions of our own bodies and organisations with those of Vladimir Putin, as obviously these are on a completely different scale. I do however wish to point out that if one is to look at the treatment of any human being on a one-to-one basis without looking at the magnitude of how each one forms a part of the total then the treatment of our loved ones, who through no fault of their own, in being struck down by this dreadful disease are also worthy of our help, compassion and consideration.

The fact that this injustice is of such magnitude, that it too, on a less newsworthy day should also warrant being headline news in our own press and TV coverage, shows it is clearly of interest to millions of people in the country.

Figures often speak louder than words, even though there is that ever-popular phrase "Statistics, statistics and damned lies", depending upon who's using the information and to what end the statistics are being used. In the following table I merely reproduce the figures provided by the London School of Economics in their report on the numbers of people suffering from dementia as at 2020 and their projections for the future, along with the costs.

	NUMBERS OF PEOPLE SUFFERING FROM DEMENTIA 2019	NUMBERS SUFFERING FROM SEVERE DEMENTIA	NUMBERS SUFFERING FROM MODERATE DEMENTIA
ENGLAND	769,200	461,900	198,900
WALES	48,100	28,700	12,600
SCOTLAND	67,900	38,500	19,400
N.IRELAND	22,700	13,500	6,000
TOTALS	907,900	542,600	236,900

The preceding table omits those numbers associated with mild dementia as obviously at that stage in its development there is little impact on the need for care.

The LSE have provided the following forecast of people likely to be suffering from dementia in the future

BY 2014	1 MILLION PEOPLE
BY 2040	1.6 MILLION PEOPLE

The next table gives the costs of providing care and who funds these. In view of the fact that the Nation of Scotland enjoys a far better and fairer system of apportioning the burden of care by the state taking on a greater proportion of this cost, I have only shown the figures combined for England and Wales and also omitted the figures for Northern Ireland as I am unsure of their individual arrangements.

			2020 £ millions	2025 £ millions	2040 £millions
NHS HEALTHCARE			4,570	5,630	11,230
SOCIAL CARE	LA-funded	39.4%	6,040	7,746	16,284
	Self-funded	60.6%	9,290	11,914	25,046
UNPAID CARE			12,970	16,250	31,870
OTHER			222	276	570
TOTAL			33,092	41,816	85,000

In order to put these figures into context, the following table gives the breakdown of who pays what in percentage terms. It should also be noted that in the case of NHS healthcare and LA-funded social care these are not funded by some magical money tree; they are funded by all those who pay their fair share through their taxes, which include NHI and council taxes.

	2020	2025	2040
NHS H/CARE	13.85%	13.46%	13.21%
LA FUNDED S/CARE	18.25%	18.52%	19.16%
SELF FUNDED S/CARE	28.07%	28.49%	29.46%
UNPAID CARE	39.19%	38.86%	37.49%
OTHER	0.66%	0.66%	0.67%

I would pose these questions:

"Do you find it strange that the very body purposely set up seventy-four years ago to look after the health of the nation (at no cost to the individual) is by far the smallest contributor when help is required?"

"Do you find it absolutely shocking that the state element of this total cost is less than one third and yet over two thirds of the cost is born by the patient and their families and/or friends?"

Let no-one suggest that we have either a perfect model in how to look after our "vulnerable and defenceless citizens" or that these human beings don't deserve to be treated more fairly by the rest of our society.

I believe we sit on the "Horns of a Dilemma".

We all know that this country is capable of great things when the chips are apparently down. Let's just consider what great things were achieved in the Second World War with some incredible inventions and how as a nation the populace worked together to overcome the forces of evil. The design and build of some amazing machinery like the Spitfire and Lancaster Bomber, the invention of a bomb that could bounce its way to the target, the cracking of a code used by the Nazis that was thought to be unbreakable, which gave way to the modern computer. We saw the selflessness of thousands of young men and women who gave their lives for the common goal of freedom for us all. Just to remember the spirit of the Armada of small boats and their crews who set sail into the jaws of the enemy to help save the lives of our brave forces, trapped on the beaches in Normandy, is still an inspiration to us all. So many examples of determination to overcome adversity, so many brave and selfless individuals, so many ways in which the accepted norms in society were changed forever. We were able to put faith in our young and old generations, we saw that women were more than able and capable of working in hard manual job environments, doing tasks previously thought only as male domains. They dug for Britain and for freedom by growing more of our own food; the list is endless. The reality was that each person regarded the person stood next to them as just as important as their own brother, sister, mother or father. That was just how important the task in hand was for the generations of that time.

Of course we have other more recent examples of what can be achieved when the needs for solutions are presented to us. The speed with which the whole world worked together for the solution to the Covid-19 pandemic was incredible. Britain did not stand alone in finding a vaccine that ultimately must have saved millions of lives, but it was able to contribute in part to the success in helping find a way to offer help and treatment to so many people.

Sadly we have seen evil rise its ugly head once more with Putin's desires to turn back the clock, and once again we see the atrocities that have been committed purely because he has been able to convince enough people of the absurdities of his beliefs of what is right from wrong. But even in the face of such terrible actions we are witnessing the bravery and determination of the Ukrainian nation in standing up for their rights and their beliefs. We are once again witnessing the coming together of an alliance of nations who are helping in some way to come to the aid of this nation in their time of need. We also witness the generosity of the individuals who have shown the spirit of human companionship and generosity by donating money, goods, and physical help to those in need. In doing so I believe that these individuals as a whole have reacted in many ways quicker than their own elected bodies and effectively forced the machinery of governments to do what is right at a far quicker pace than would have been the case.

Why, you may be asking, am I writing about these things? Maybe you are thinking this is just the ravings of a mad man. Well, you would be correct to think so. I am mad, not in the sense of being of unsound mind but mad as in enraged about the treatment of our loved ones who through no fault of their own are being neglected and abused by the system.

It has to stop, and we are the only people who can make it happen. We have the will and the incentive to ensure we aren't treated as the third option because of their indecisiveness and their desire to take the easy way out.

We have seen the monetary figures of who pays for what and the percentages which show the true extent of the scale of this injustice. We have to ask ourselves why this situation has arisen and how we can change it for the betterment of society as a whole.

We must look at the treatment of mental diseases in comparison with how other terrible diseases are also treated. Do they compare? If not, why not?

We need to understand how change can be brought about by forcing a change in one area which can also be the catalyst for an even greater advancement in another area.

Let us compare the treatment of cancer which is undoubtedly another terrible disease which brings physical pain, worry and changes in the ability to enjoy life to the full or indeed life at all.

I have read comments from some cancer sufferers who accuse some of the advocates fighting the cause for dementia suffers that because cancer can affect all manner of different organs of the body there may be a tendency to compare all dementia suffers with only one type of cancer sufferer, such as lung cancer or skin cancer or kidney cancer or pancreatic cancer or breast cancer. It is important that we do not enter into a battle between different serious conditions. We are all inevitably paddling the same lifeboat, trying to survive whatever illness we have been inflicted with.

Cancer overall has a much higher profile and probably therefore a greater knowledge within the population. It's scary to be diagnosed with cancer; so too is dementia. The principal difference being that cancer is not necessarily the death sentence it used to be, and greater advancements have taken place throughout the last few decades to find cures and/or effective treatments. Cancer has far greater investment in finding cures, be it through government funding for research or through charity work to raise monies or awareness of things to do or not to do to reduce the risks involved.

Regretfully, the same principles have not been applied to the various forms of dementia both from a funding for research point of view or greater knowledge of the hows and whys of this disease. I believe there are a number of reasons for this.

- A greater proportion of the sufferers of dementia are in the older age bracket; not all by any means, but it is certainly regarded as a "senior" disease in the general population as a whole

- Why invest heavily in finding a cure for an age group who have enjoyed a life and have lived long enough to be inflicted by such a disease? They're going to die anyway

- It appears we still know so little about the human brain and because of the complexities of it there is a tendency to shy away from carrying out procedures that could be more devastating than leaving well alone

- Charitable fundraising tends to have a life and soul of its own; the greater the profile the greater the level of support.

Maybe, just maybe, the establishment takes the view that while they can get away with off-setting the true costs of looking after those people suffering from dementia by getting the families to shoulder the burden of the majority of the costs, then there is less demand to seek a solution in finding this through research.

The lower the amount that the state has to fund (32% of the cost by 2025) and the higher the amount funded by families (including unpaid care, 67% by 2025) then there is little chance that the situation will alter and little chance that more funds will be made available for the badly needed research.

Imagine if the state had to pick up the bill for the self-funded element, even without the costs involved for unpaid care; would this not give the impetus to get the research done? I believe it would.

My own view is that it is imperative to get the funding which, let's face it, is morally and legally justified, not just for the sake of our loved ones suffering today, but for the benefit of all generations of the future.

To look at it in another way, the onset of dementia is being turned into yet another taxation band which would not be tolerated in any other situation. It would be akin to the government of the day announcing that anyone who has worked hard and accumulated any wealth in their lifetime must pay death duties on anything over £25,000, oh and by the way not just a small percentage but we'll have the full 100% thank you very much. I realise this is such a stupid statement to make, but sometimes one has look at things in the extreme to shine a light on the true reality as to what is actually happening. Actually I accept that this is a bad analogy, as it would at least be fair in the sense that it would apply to the whole population. Maybe a more realistic analogy would be to say it would be done simply as a lottery draw, draw a ticket, keep your money or lose everything you have over £25,000.

As I have previously mentioned my wife Margaret's doctor, Dr G, stated in his email to me that for her to have even an initial screening assessment would be a futile exercise because in his words, "This is only done for patients requiring nursing care. Margaret does not have nursing needs, like giving injections, doing dressings, nebulisers etc." I am drawing attention to this yet again because not only is this statement outrageously untrue in its contention, but also because it gives the impression that nurses are employed to carry out only specific tasks, unrelated to actually caring for the patient. The true reality is that all nursing personnel don't spend their entire working time carrying out procedures like those as described above by Dr G. No, the act of nursing encompasses a wide range of duties, not least of which is caring for their patients, looking after their basic needs and ensuring they get the best possible treatment through what could be described as medical procedures and, equally importantly, their basic human needs. In fact I would suspect that the majority of their time spent is spent doing the later rather than the former.

If one was to look at a typical job description for a nurse it is apparent that the role is varied and challenging and is described as "Ranging from purely clinical care to a wider one of emotional and social support".

In an attempt to educate myself further with regards to what our politicians really know about what is happening I availed myself of the published details (17 January 2018 by authority of the House of Commons) of the findings of the Committee of Public Accounts on NHS Continuing Healthcare funding.

This report consists of two main elements:

(1) Being evidence given by various interested bodies;

(2) Minutes of the meeting following the evidential session, which records the answers given to a variety of questions posed by those in attendance.

As the document runs to over fifty pages it is not possible to duplicate everything here, so I will limit my summations to what I consider to be the most important points. I will, however, reproduce in full the following two sections:

(A) INTRODUCTION

NHS (CHC) is a package of care provided outside of hospital that is arranged and funded by the NHS for individuals who have significant ongoing healthcare needs. Such individuals are eligible for NHS funding if their healthcare needs go beyond what can legally be provided by local authorities, but this is a highly complex and sensitive area, with potentially significant cost implications for the individual. If someone is assessed as eligible for CHC, the NHS is responsible for funding the full package of health and social care. However, if someone is not eligible for CHC, they may have to pay for all or part of their social care costs, depending on their financial circumstances.

The Department of Health (the Department) is responsible for the legal framework for CHC, including setting criteria for assessing eligibility for CHC through a national framework. CCGs are responsible for determining eligibility for CHC and for commissioning this care. NHS England is responsible for making sure CCGs comply with the National Framework. People can access CHC funding through two processes: a standard CHC process and a fast-track process for people with rapidly deteriorating conditions who may be nearing the end of their life. The number of people assessed as eligible for CHC funding has grown by an average of 6% over the last four years. In 2015-16, almost 160,000 people received, or were assessed as eligible for, CHC funding.

(B) SUMMARY

NHS CHC funding is intended to help some of the most vulnerable people in society, who have significant healthcare needs. But too often people's care is compromised because no-one makes them aware of the funding available, or helps them to navigate the hugely complicated process for accessing funding. Those people that are assessed spend too long waiting to find out if they are eligible for funding and receive the essential care that they need. About one-third of assessments in 2015-16 took longer than twenty-eight days. In some cases people have died whilst waiting for a decision. There is unacceptable variation between areas in the number of people assessed as eligible to receive CHC funding, ranging from 28 to 365 people per 50,000 population in 2015-16, caused partly by Clinical Commissioning Groups (CCGs) interpreting the assessment criteria inconsistently. The Department of Health and NHS England recognise that the system is not working as well as it should but are not doing enough to ensure CCGs are meeting their responsibilities, or to address the variation between areas in accessing essential funding. NHS England wants CCGs to make £855 million of efficiency savings in CHC and NHS-funded nursing care spending by 2020-2021, but it is not clear how they can do this without either increasing the threshold of those assessed as eligible, or by limiting the care packages available, both of which will ultimately put patient safety at risk.

I think this summary gives a clear indication that CHC funding is failing in many ways starting from the very beginning that there is acceptance that "it remains the NHS's best kept secret" through to admission that it is complicated, inconsistent in its awards, and that it lacks fairness and accountability. Bear in mind that this report was commissioned back in 2017-18 and that during a two-year ongoing period they expected to see a reduction in costs of £855 million from the then projected cost for that period. When you look at the NHS healthcare 2020 costs of £4,570 million, £855 million represents a saving forecast of 18.7% Here we are talking about getting justice for our loved ones who have lost their memories and a real sense of reality and yet we are looking at an organisation that believes it needs to make improvements on what it is achieving whilst at the same time looking to save 18.7% of its forecast. Without meaning to sound in any way unsympathetic to anyone who is suffering from mental illnesses of any kind, this would certainly lead any sensible person to believe in that well-worn phrase "that the inmates have got hold of the asylum". In this case the asylum being NHS England and the inmates the management of such. Unbelievable; on one hand they give hope that maybe, just maybe there will be improvement in the system for the benefit of the needy, only for them to take it all away by suggesting they can perform miracles in doing what is necessary for an ever-increasing number of needy people for 18.7% less. In reality what they are suggesting is more akin to suggesting they can find 25-30% savings.

I will confine any further information to what I have noted in the minutes of that committee and show my personal comments in this type of text.

The Committee of Public Accounts consisted of the following personnel:

Meg Hillier (Chairperson) (LAB - Hackney South & Shoreditch)
Sir Geoffrey Clifton Brown (CON - The Cotswolds)
Chris Evans (LAB - Islwyn)
Caroline Flint (LAB - Don Valley)
Shabana Mahmood (LAB - Birmingham Ladywood)
Nigel Mills (CON - Amber Valley)
Stephen Morgan (LAB - Portsmouth South)
Bridget Phillipson (LAB - Houghton & Sunderland South)
Gareth Snell (LAB - Stoke-on-Trent)

In addition to the above stakeholders present to represent patients were the following witnesses:

Matina Loizou (Continuing Healthcare Alliance) (CHC)
Brian O'Shea (Spinal Injuries Association) (SIA)
Dan Harbour (Managing Director Beacon) (BEAC)
Elisa Hoardley (Hospice Director Sue Ryder) (S/RYD)

(If your MP is listed above you will have some reassurance that at least your MP is knowledgeable about the difficulties with NHS CHC. I think it is a pity that either Age Concern, Dementia UK or The Alzheimer's Association were not similarly represented.)

The report also lists no fewer than twenty-four individuals and/or organisations who also submitted written evidence.

Under the heading of "People's Experience of Accessing NHS CHC", additional information was noted and included:

- CCGs reported that about 10% of assessments took longer than 100 days on average during the period November 2015–October 2016

- CHA stated that some people had waited up to three years for a decision

- S/RYD reports some people are left to die in a place not of their choice because they cannot get an appropriate care package in time

- SIA noted that delays in funding CHC are treated differently to other NHS services, giving the example that it would not be considered appropriate for someone needing dialysis to have to wait months for a treatment on which their life depends upon

- CHA says around two thirds of people did not find out about CHC until very late in their journey through the system. People are not being signposted to CHC funding in cases where it may be appropriate to them, and only 3% of people find out about it through their GP

- Independent Age told us that older people are not always aware of CHC funding and that health and care professionals do not always identify people who need an assessment

- A 2016 survey found that people with motor neurone disease found that 30% of respondents were receiving CHC funding but that 33% did not know what it was
- SIA says there is a real lack of ability to communicate in simple terms the purpose or consequences of CHC assessments
- Written evidence indicates 78% of health professionals believe the CHC system is difficult for patients and families to navigate
  - My own experiences suggest that it is not just patients and families who find it hard to navigate, but the same can be said of those same health professionals
- The Department admitted that the National Framework could be communicated more simply and that it is being refreshed so people can more easily understand their entitlement
- The Department when asked what it was going to do to make sure people from all socioeconomic groups and backgrounds are made aware of CHC and are able to navigate the system responded in the following way. "It believes the easiest way of reaching out to people is to ensure that the health and care professionals understand who is eligible for CHC, rather than increasing public awareness
  - *What an absolutely appalling statement to make. Firstly it is already their responsibility to ensure that the professionals know and understand who*

should be eligible and look at how well they have done in achieving this. Likewise it is also their responsibility to advertise the existence and purpose of CHC funding by providing and ensuring posters and leaflets, displayed in hospitals, on wards, in reception areas, in waiting rooms, doctors' surgeries etc. and again look at how efficient they were at achieving this. They have never had any intention of increasing the public's awareness or knowledge about CHC and here we are with the same negative response designed to maintain the status quo and keep the public in the dark. Why not get some enterprising private firm to take up the challenge of paying for and distributing these leaflets and posters which could be funded by selling advertising space to local businesses and appropriate national companies such as manufacturers of disabled equipment etc.

- *It is imperative for a balanced checking system that information is equally available to both the end user and the provider in a knowledgeable way. I suspect that the individuals who provided this as a solution on behalf of the Department are possibly doctors with a God-like complex or management who are conceited in believing their way is the only way.*

- The Department and NHS England both confirmed that the variations in eligibility and spending differed significantly between different CCGs. It was confirmed that eligibility ranged from 28 to 365 people per 50,000 population in 2015-16 and the spending ranged between 1% to 10 % of their total budget. NHS England went on to say that some of these variations were down to the demographics and difference in the cost of care packages from one area to another but did not account for such a wide-ranging variance. NHS England went on to say that variance in access had already reduced by 6% for standard CHC and a 19% increase for fast-track CHC and expected this trend would continue to narrow as a result of improvement work underway on assessment processes and on training

▫ *This has absolutely nothing to do with improvements of any kind; it is merely putting (yet again) a positive spin on a negative set of figures. Any fool can see that if you deprive genuine claimants of their entitlement to standard CHC funding then this automatically increases the numbers of those who will be entitled to fast-track funding when those persons' conditions have deteriorated even further to the point of reaching end of life. Obviously there will be more people applying for standard CHC funding than for fast-track and therefore 6% will represent a higher figure in actual numbers than the numbers relating to fast-track which will be lower but a higher percentage. Again I think it is just indicative of the contempt that these people treat others when they believe they think they are cleverer than those listening to their rubbish*

- NHS England noted that the national guidance was very complicated for frontline nurses, therapists and other clinicians to apply and had led to variations in the way it is applied

- Beacon agreed to these variations across the country but went on to point out that some assessors were setting additional arbitrary rules, such as that the person needs to have healthcare needs that carers cannot manage, or physically challenging behaviour, to be assessed as eligible, both of which are incorrect

- CHA found that around 60% of healthcare professionals are assessing people without sufficient specialist knowledge of the medical condition that they are looking at.
  - *You wouldn't ask a mechanic to analyse the problems you were having with your boiler or a plumber to diagnose faults in your motor vehicle, would you? Yet the NHS are prepared to not only put your loved one's health at serious risk but they are also potentially costing them tens, if not hundreds of thousands of pounds.*
  - *Maybe there should be a warning on all NHS literature. Warning: "The NHS can seriously damage your health and your wealth"*

- Witnesses highlighted cases of good practice. Beacon noted Oxfordshire assessment teams are composed of people that have recent experience of looking after the patient and understand the condition being assessed

- S/RYD noted where the CHC team had good links with the palliative care team, they find the fast-track process works well.

- NHS England highlighted Great Yarmouth, where a team of nurses connected with care homes discuss the range of care options with the family including CHC and social care services

- The National Audit Office found that NHS England had limited assurance processes in place to ensure that eligibility decisions are being made fairly and consistently, both between and within CCGs. Their analysis suggests that on average people are receiving funding for a shorter period than they did previously, but NHS England does not have data on why this is happening. Similarly, NHS England does not collect data on the number of local appeals or their outcomes.

> *This is a classic defence strategy of any organisation that does not wish their shortcomings to be highlighted in any way. It is easier for them to spin the findings and experiences of others if they don't provide them with further information which would prove the realities. What is that saying? "Give them enough rope and they will hang themselves." The problem here is that NHS England is in charge of the rope supplies.*

- The Department and NHS England gave their assurances that there was no quota or cap on access to CHC funding and they had no intentions to change the eligibility criteria
  > *How very reassuring. Can such organisations really be relied upon? They appear to put more effort in finding ways to deny the rights of those that need it.*

This assurance is given even though between 2011-12 and 2015-16 the proportion of people assessed as eligible for standard CHC has reduced from 34% to 29%.

When confronted with these statistics, NHS England (here comes their usual spin policy) claimed that the trend suggests assessors are probably becoming better at making accurate judgements earlier on about whether people are likely to be eligible and need a full assessment. (Yet another off the hoof statement in trying to defend their position.) However, if this was the case, then we would expect the proportion of people assessed as eligible to increase, rather than decrease. It told us that the data for 2016-17 showed that the number assessed as eligible for standard CHC reduced by 6% and the number of those eligible for fast-track CHC actually increased by 5%.

NHS England seem to be incapable of accepting reality when it stares them in the face and keep on digging their hole deeper and deeper to try and defend their position. NHS England considered that this may show that awareness and use of fast-track assessment is going up. (Of course fast-track is going up; if you limit the supply of those who are eligible for standard CHC and therefore take them out of the pool of those requiring it at the end of their lives you have conversely increased the numbers requiring fast-track.)

- The stakeholders expressed their concerns that CCGs are in fact increasingly placing arbitrary financial caps on the cost of care packages and may be forcing people to accept lower cost packages that do not meet their care needs. Specifically, they told us that some CCGs are limiting how much they will spend on someone's first choice of care package where it costs more than the cheapest possible option. For those people who wish to live at home, this may mean that they are forced to accept packages with fewer hours and unsafe levels of care.
    - *Here comes NHS England response, God forbid that they could ever admit to getting anything wrong.*

NHS England confirmed that it is aiming for people to get the right care for their needs in the right setting. (Here it comes.) However, it noted that there is variation in the rate that is being paid by different CCGs for care in different parts of the country and that there may be differences in the care packages people receive, compared to what they wanted, because CCGs may fund cheaper packages that deliver the same outcomes.

- The Equality and Human Rights Commission told us that it has recently written to forty-four CCGs because it has concerns that they have policies that restrict funding, which may result in disabled people facing institutional care against their wishes.

All of the information contained above is recorded in the minutes of the meeting held on 10 January 2018. However, prior to this meeting another meeting of The Public Accounts Committee took place on 1 November 2017 which was watched by the eight MPs as listed previously but also included:
Bim Afolami (CON - Hitchen and Harpenden)
Andrew Jones (CON - Harrogate and Knaresborough)
Gillian Keegan (CON - Chichester)
Layla Moran (LIB DEM - Oxford West and Abingdon)

In addition to these MPs also in attendance were:
Robert White - Director, National Audit Office.
Jenny George - Director, National Audit Office.
Adrian Jenner - Director of Parliamentary Relations, NAO.
Marius Gallaher - Alternate Treasury Officer of Accounts, HMT.

Witnesses were as stated in the meeting dated 10 January but also included were:

Sir Christopher Wormald, Permanent Secretary, DOH.
Simon Stevens, Chief Executive, NHS England.
Jane Cummings, Chief Nursing Officer, NHS England.
Jonath Marron, Director General, Community Care, DOH.

There were 113 questions posed of which 1-33 involved the four witnesses representing the stakeholders working with the patients trying to get or currently receiving CHC funding.

The remaining questions 34-113 were addressed to the four persons as named above, representing NHS England and the Department of Health.

As there are forty pages of minutes and a considerable proportion of both questions and answers have already been addressed and commented on. I include here only information that is of interest and over and above that already noted.

Andrew Jones, Exchequer Secretary to the Committee, gave the following commitment:

"I assure the committee that the government will always endeavour to deliver fully on the Committee's recommendations. I agree with the Committee that important issues should not just be treated with lip service. This is an important government commitment that has been a part of performance in the past and will always be a part of performance in the future."

Brian O'Shea reported that he believes the vast majority of the variations in both rates of eligibility and levels of support across CCGs arises from the interpretation and application of the assessment tools. He states: "I think that they are unclear, and if I can go so far as to say this, I actually think that they are not fit for purpose".

Matina Loizou CHA reports that with 66% of people only finding out about CHC really close to the end and only 3% finding out about it through their GPs it is indicative of the fact that people are not being signposted to the service when it is the most appropriate thing for them. "When people come through to us, they really are exhausted and distressed. They have been through such a complex and baffling process that by the time they get to us, they are at their wits end.

"We want a radical overhaul of the assessment tools, because that is leading to some really strange, different decisions and a lot of variation across the country."

Dan Harbour from Beacon reports that they had taken 8,500 calls in the previous 12 months and in a lot of the assessments attended they found that the MDTs are minimally constructed and have never met the individual before. "We often see that those informed health and social care professionals who are familiar with the individual's needs are cut out of the process."

The next question to be addressed was the one of the effect on patients and families in the delays experienced in doing the assessments.

Brian O'Shea says, "I am always amazed that CHC somehow sits apart from so many other NHS services." He uses the example of someone in need of dialysis not having to wait but in some instances people requiring CHC funding are having to rely on informal care for the delivery of complex care that is the responsibility of the NHS. He goes on to make the strong and undeniable fact that NHS CHC is a matter of law; it is laid down in statute. Despite this he goes on to talk about there being a lot of talk from the NHS about benchmarking and how this is not an optional extra for the NHS. the primary benchmark is the law, yet the NHS is making people wait.

Elise Hoadley (Sue Ryder) adds to the discussion by making the additional point that the impact is also to the relatives and survivors who maybe go on to suffer in their bereavement because they felt they could not offer their loved one the best care.

Geoffrey Clifton Brown referred to the Couglan case which became case law following the findings of the Courts and

Tribunals Service who had said that Pamela Couglan would likely be eligible today for CHC funding. He asks of Dan Harbour if the blurring of 100% of what should be provided under CHC is allowing the CCGs to not provide the service in some cases because there is no clear legal base.

Dan Harbour responds by stating that where they have noted very poor practice the answer would be yes. "Assessors will tell us if you don't have physically challenging behaviour you cannot be eligible, whereas others will claim behaviour is not a care need and not a nursing need and cannot be taken into account. On this basis Pamela Coughlan would never achieve a score to achieve eligibility for CHC funding."

Dan Harbour goes on to explain the absurdity of this illogical statement in that this would imply that of the thousands of people in care homes eligible for CHC that these homes would be unable to care for them. This ends up distorting the original intention of the primary health need which gets its authority from law and the Couglan judgements.

Geoffrey Clifton Brown asks if anyone would like to comment on assessments having taken place without families being involved and/or where they have not been given copies of the assessment. Brian O'Shea replies where this is the case it leaves the individual effectively doing battle against the NHS, which is a behemoth. This is especially so when appealing against a decision of ineligibility, because the resources that are thrown at the individual by both the NHS and the CCGs are fundamentally unfair. On one hand you have a well-resourced CCG and on the other an information-poor and resource-poor individual attempting to answer very complex questions which are often framed in too complex a way and almost designed to distort the issues.

The Chair asks the question: "The NOA investigation found some disturbing incidents of people not getting care in places they would prefer, the implication being that this is a rationing process, even though there is a statutory duty to offer this. Does anyone have any examples of this from palliative care?"

Elise Hoadley (Sue Ryder) made the point that many people believe that people want to die in the hospice, but the majority would prefer to die at home. She explains that even those with CHC funding are denied this outcome due to being unable to get an appropriate care package.

Brian O'Shea (CHA) reports an increasing number of CCGs placing arbitrary financial caps and cites his involvement in some research done by the NHS a couple of years ago. It found that the primary driver of delayed discharges from neurological specialist care centres across London was the lack of specialist residential care beds. Yet CCGs are effectively saying, "If the cost of your care goes above the cost of a residential setting bed, we will expect you to live in a residential setting." He goes on to recount the story of a Manchester man which aired on "You and Yours". The fifty-three-year-old man has four children between the ages of four and fourteen and had been running his own business from his hospital bed for six months, and yet he was expected to move into a nursing home and not be allowed to go home to his family. Quote: "What we believe is happening is that CCGs are not actually serious about incarcerating people in nursing homes, because we don't believe that there are enough nursing home beds available. What they are doing is using it as a tool to blackmail people into accepting unsafe levels of care and funding to live in their own home or their preferred setting of care and relying on informal support to pick up the rest of the care.

Martina Loizou (CHA) says "I echo what my colleague is saying. In Leicestershire we have seen a shift in policies, they are trying to bring in a settings of care policy. They are moving their 25% cap over and above the cheapest possible care option down to 10%. As an example for 100 hours of care a week, rather than 168 that they have been assessed to need, or move out to a care home, regardless of whether or not that is a place they want to be or if it is assessed to be the most appropriate place for them."

Chair asks all four witnesses what their two or three things are that would make the biggest difference to the people they are representing today, and what they would like the people who set the framework to consider in the next part of the session.

Elise Hoadly (Sue Ryder):

(1) Overall measuring of assessments, with people being held accountable, with more targets and a more robust process to be more equitable across the country.
(2) More training for those carrying out the assessments so they understand the diseases they are assessing.
(3) That MDTs, both social and healthcare, working together to work in the patient's best interest.

Dan Harbour (Beacon)

(1) We need to get into the mind-set of changing the culture and unpick the bad practice with better quality control.
(2) Introduce really robust national training.
(3) Good quality assurance and accountability.

Matina Loizou (CHA)

(1) We need to get serious about how we fund CHC, with an ageing population we need to talk about how we put a support system in place.
(2) We need to radically overhaul the assessment tools.
(3) Make the system more user friendly and transparent. By the time people come to us they are exhausted by it.

Brian O'Shea (CH advisor)

(1) Assessors are by nature, generalists, they need to involve those with condition specific knowledge in the assessment process.
(2) Simplification CHC, is simple, there is a lawful limit on what an LA can provide, if the health limits go beyond that then it is the responsibility of the NHS.
(3) Stop reassessment of those people with non-improving and deteriorating conditions. To continue with these is often a waste of money.

This concludes the comments of relevance made during the first part of this session, which reflect the experiences and comments of the four witnesses representing patient groups.

The first part of the second session mainly concentrates on funding issues including the then proposed 1% pay increase and the already embarked upon efficiency programme.

S.S. talks about holding three truths at once:

(1) NHS is arguably already the most efficient of any of the western industrialised countries' health services. We spend £23 billion per year – less than the French or the Germans.
(2) There is waste and inefficiency in the NHS.
(3) Improving the health service over time will need the injection of further funding to maintain and improve the service.

These three things can all be true at the same time.

Sir Chris Wormald wished to re-emphasise that any set of pay discussions in any sector also has three truths:

(1) What is fair for the workforce?
(2) What is affordable?
(3) The Productivity Question?

The Chair raises the issue of fraud in the NHS and the comments made by Sue Firth, the Chief Executive of NHS Counter Fraud Authority. Her team did an analysis that estimated that £1.25 billion worth of fraud is being committed each year by patients, staff and contractors, representing 1% of the NHS budget. She asks Mr Stevens if this is high up on his agenda of things to tackle?

S.S. confirms that it most certainly is but wished to caveat what the chair had said. (I quote in full his statement on this subject because I believe it is important for you the reader to understand exactly what he said.) "The £1.25 billion is at the far end of their estimate, as against the almost certain or highly likely quantification. The highly likely quantification is more in the £300 million zone. (So what he is saying is that in effect he doesn't believe the findings of the analysis conducted by the NHS Counter Fraud Authority and his estimate is just shy of being £1 billion less, or to put it another way more than 75% less than stated. I suppose no CEO of any organisation would like to hold their hands up to such a high level of fraud within their organisation and therefore maybe it is human nature to try and be defensive on such issues. He continues.) Nevertheless, the biggest single item is their assessment that there may be patient fraud going on with the help with healthcare costs scheme, which they size at £400 million, but there are other big items that they estimate around dental contractor fraud and other procurement-related items. From our point of view this is great, because we want to go after this, and every pound we save in this area is a pound we can put into patient care."

I would comment on his last statement first. I am surprised at his poor choice of words for a person in his position. There is nothing great about discovering there is fraud being carried out on such an enormous scale.

Secondly his contention that the likely quantification of the true scale of the fraud is more than 75% less than the estimate by the NHS Counter Fraud Authority is a mere £300 million and yet he chooses to use that authority's figures (£400 million) to the full when trying to lay blame at the door of patients defrauding the healthcare costs scheme. Surely he should at the very least have proportionately reduced this amount, which would be in the region of £100 million.

Thirdly he gives no other figures for the two other major areas he has identified. Why not? Why has he chosen to make a point of highlighting healthcare costs?

Finally on this point I would ask this question. How is such a magnitude of fraud being committed in a sector which is coming under such scrutiny for not delivering on its obligations to provide care to those genuinely in need? It suggests to me that he doesn't consider the fact that too many people are being incorrectly assessed as not having eligibility for CHC funding as a problem, but more that it is one of too many being approved for it. Frankly I think this beggars belief and epitomises just what we are up against.

At this point in the proceedings the Chair asked for the panel to kick off with the main topic starting with:

Bridget Phillipson summarised the findings of the pre-panel, whose view was that the process for CHC was that it was difficult to navigate, unclear, exhausting and baffling and asked Mr Wormald what his views on the experience is.

Sir Chris Wormald stated that he believed The National Audit Office had basically identified the right set of issues which concurred with the pre-panel which was those around complication and variation issues. He went on to add: "I do not think we are coming to say we think there are any simple solutions, but in terms of what we need to improve and the processors we have" (The Chair intervenes with: "So you acknowledge there is a problem with the process now?") "Looking at the variation in numbers from the NAO, I do not think any of us think that is where the system should be."

Bridget Phillipson asks S.S. if he wishes to add anything but he confirms that he agrees completely with Sir Chris. He is then asked about how confident he is that CCGs are complying with the National Framework.

Simon Stevens's belief is that we have ended up with a complicated set of guidance for frontline nurses, therapists and other clinicians to operationalise and he believes it is not completely unpredictable that there will be variation. He goes on to say that this is the reason that they are reviewing the way the checklist and the assessment process is structured, and at the same time they are taking direct action with CCGs to ensure that we standardise more of the way they go about their job.

I personally see this as a somewhat woolly answer to the question. My view is somewhat simpler and is more a question of making sure that those charged with such a life-changing responsibility should at the very least have full knowledge of what is contained in the Framework and the meaning of each and every aspect of it. In any other professional capacity, with responsibility for people's lives, we all expect that those in charge know what they are doing and fully understand the operational systems which are there to protect everyone. Using again my aircraft analogy, the expectation of us all is that anyone involved in the operation of an airline flight is fully conversant with all the correct procedures. This includes pilots, cabin crew, maintenance personnel, refuelling teams, caterers, airport staff, air traffic controllers etc. but not least of all, the management. To get things right it is ultimately the responsibility of the latter to ensure that everyone is properly trained, retrained, updated and proven to be fully competent in the role they play. We all know the devastating results of the management taking shortcuts in training purely through corporate greed. The management of Boeing Airlines took a decision not to retrain their pilots when they introduced what was meant to be an additional safety feature that turned out to be the cause of two airline crashes with total loss of life and all because they didn't retrain their crews and keep them informed. The NHS has a similar responsibility, and the management are the ones who must carry the burden of ensuring everyone is correctly trained and know fully the role that they are expected to play.

Bridget Phillipson: Why is it that such a small proportion of screenings would lead to eligibility being determined for CHC?

S.S. claims because they err on the side of caution, they are doing far more assessments than are likely to lead to eligibility for CHC. He claims that this is a good thing because it means that fewer people are likely to fall through the net. He goes on to say that it does have serious downsides, not least the fact that more families experience uncertainty and are given false expectations. In addition to this they are tying up a lot of nurses for no clinical benefit and this is the reason why they think this process has to be looked at again.

Here we go again. Spin the story in such a way that it is of benefit to the management in trying to make their targets. It looks like he is advocating making it even harder to access CHC funding. I can assure him and would do so to his face if I was ever given the opportunity that he is totally and utterly wrong, as this has been far from my experience. No wonder that contrary to their obligations to inform the public of the existence of CHC there is a distinct lack of publicity of what it is, who it's for and how to apply for it. The fact is plain for any fool to see that as evidenced in the first session people do not know about CHC funding. Is he really suggesting that those who have jumped their first hurdle by finding out about it are still too great in number that the hurdle needs to be raised even more?

Sir Chris Wormald had a slightly different viewpoint when he stated: "When we looked at whether you could just up the threshold of the checklist so fewer people went through, we found that people who would eventually end up with a CHC package would have been excluded by the process of having a higher threshold."

Bridget Phillipson and Jane Cummings exchanged questions and answers on the subject of the lack of knowledge of people working on MDTs. The latter confirmed that they were making e-learning involve families, carers and other clinical professionals.

Bridget Phillipson: "The NAO report identifies that the estimated proportion of people referred for a full assessment had fallen in the period from 2011-12 to 2015-16. Mr Stevens, is this indicative of CCGs restricting access, do you think?

Simon Stevens: "No." He goes on to talk about the backlog of cases that CCGs have had to deal with (63,000 going back to 2004) and that these have just finally been completed in March 2017. (I don't see the relevance of this information to the question being asked. Why would an historical case backlog impact those needing an assessment now?) He responds further: "Probably what is happening is that people are getting a bit more familiar with making more accurate early judgements about whether cases need to go through to a full assessment. As the precision of that improves, we expect to see the ratios continue to improve.

Notice the use of the word "probably". He doesn't know the reason but chooses to look on the bright side by suggesting that it is through improvement. The reality is that it is more likely to be the exact opposite with less people being given screening assessments, and more of those who do are being wrongly downgraded. No matter what SS says I have felt the reality of how the system works, a full three years on from these comments, and that was certainly not my experience.

Nigel Mills goes on to ask: "I might naively think that NHS policies were moving people into falling within this assessment, rather than staying in hospital. If you want to die at home or if you have need of complicated care in the community then I assume you need a care package of this type. Would you not expect the volume to be rising, with effectively a saving elsewhere matched with an increase in cost here?"

Probably - is for the proportion of fast-track cases to be going up" he reports that Standard assessments have fallen by 6% and fast-track has gone up by 5% ." Further exchange took place talking about actual numbers both on standard and fast-track with those who were found to be eligible.

I think by now my readers will appreciate my views on this, given the fact that if you keep denying people the right to standard CHC then it is as plain as night follows day that there will be more people falling into fast-track and that this is the reason for the switch in numbers.

The next topic to be discussed was the review process where families were not happy with the outcome and had the opportunity to appeal the decision. Understandably S.S. used the numbers and percentages to underline his belief that they show that not only can they be interpreted as a measure of success but in his view shows how accurate the assessments are.

Again I am left with no alternative but to state that there is a failing to understand why people don't go on to appeal the decisions of the CCGs in greater numbers. There are undoubtedly many different reasons: maybe the loved one has passed away, maybe the process has taken so long that they eventually were given fast-track. The process is so complex and tiring that people just give up, again for a variety of reasons: lack of time, inability to keep fighting, lack of upfront funds to pay specialist solicitors to carry on on their behalf, or most likely of all is a complete and utter loss of faith in a system that is so blatantly unfair and uses such a multitude of different techniques to deny them their rights that they just give up.

Bridget Phillipson makes this same point about people just giving up which S.S. responds to in what is becoming the all too familiar way. Firstly he agrees that he has a lot of sympathy with this viewpoint and agrees in some situations this may be correct. However, he then goes on to suggest that the figures showing the numbers of people going to appeal indicates that this is not the case. Quote: "Look, I am really not saying that everything is perfect in this world – that is not the case – but equally, if it were dramatically problematic, I think we might expect to see some of that showing up in both of the independent appeal processes." (Here again he has chosen to put his own positive spin on the figures. Is this not the very reason why the figures are so low, exactly because by this point in the process people have just given up?) The Chair responds by pointing out that "There is a difference between a problem in the decision and a problem with the process."

Bridget Philipson goes on to make the point that better data would give us a much better understanding of what is actually happening, and asks what is happening to improve this.

S.S. informs the committee that they have substantially improved data quality and range of capture, and makes special reference to fast-track and the duration for which individuals are getting CHC on a national basis.

My concerns are more to do with standard CHC assessments. As I have previously mentioned, fast-track seems to be used as a way of throwing a few crumbs at the patient when they are at the end of life and enabling the NHS to appear to be looking after people in a caring way, when in actual fact they should have been doing so while the patient still had a life.

Layla Moran cites the case of Sue from Gloucestershire who learnt of NHS CHC from her husband Bob's nurse, but was passed from pillar to post by their CCG. Sadly, Bob ended up going into a care home and died. The day after he died a CHC assessor knocked on the door and did a retrospective assessment. Seven months later Sue received a sixty-four-page document rejecting her claim and quote: "The whole process was dreadful. It was if they forgot that they were dealing with real people. S.L. asks S.S. "Mr Stevens, you spoke about families, what would you say to Sue?"

Simon Stevens: "I would say how sorry I was to hear of those circumstances." He goes on to restate his belief that no-one here believes the process is working right throughout the country and suggests the people in Gloucester spend time in Great Yarmouth and Leeds, where they are getting it right.

Layla Moran: "How many retrospective assessments are carried out each year after someone has died? That is surely heartbreakng, do you keep that data?"

Simon Stevens: "That would presumably come out of the fast-track data."

Layla Moran: "This wasn't under fast-track, this was the normal data. Do you keep the data?"

Simon Stevens: "Obviously individual CCGs will have that, whether that is tabulated nationally I would have to—"

Chair: "Are you sure, because the CCGs did not seem to have a lot of information? Are you sure they have it? I am not trying to catch you out. Do you know they have it?"

His response to this is classic. When caught out, look for a way out, blame someone else.

Simon Stevens: "As we know, the legal, statutory framework is that CCGs have to make the assessment. They cannot delegate that to someone else (here it comes) and they cannot pass it up to us."

Geoffrey Clifton-Brown asks Mr Wormald: "What can you do to really highlight the worst decision making within CCGs? For example, we know that Arden and Greater East Midlands commissioning support unit (CSU) covers three CCGs so they must be dealing with a lot of people. You have issued them with one performance notice and two fines in 2016-17 for this dreadful performance they have had. What can you do to highlight those really bad performances and drive up quality control?"

Sir Chris Wormald: "Those were NHS England problems, I think."

Simon Stevens: "We have had concerns about Arden and GEM and the way that they have handled some of these cases. There have been some substantial changes."

The reader should note the following:
(1) The date of this meeting was 1 November 2017 and yet S.S. makes claim to having already introduced substantial changes in handling of cases. If this were true then it would imply they have acted swiftly to improve performance, even before the revised National Framework was introduced in October 2018.

(2) My experience at my wife's assessment, dated 24 September 2021 being three years after the introduction of the revised Framework being introduced and four years after S.S. had made this claim, most certainly does not show any evidence of this being the case. I find it difficult to comprehend how our experience could in any way be an improvement on previous standards as, if this was the case, then the previous standards must have been totally beyond any level of competence on any scale. I think it more likely that the claims made by S.S. have no basis of reality in any shape or form. I merely ask this question: if the head of NHS England thinks things have improved or indeed will improve, then how can there ever be a real and meaningful shift for the betterment of care in the NHS which is so badly needed for those in greatest need?

The false claims seemingly go on and on.

Geoffrey Clifton Brown asks: "What can you do to drive up quality control, basically?" to which S.S. replies: "We have actually changed."

The questions and answers continued with the Chair pointing out that there was no need to keep repeating the phrase that everyone keeps saying i.e. no-one is saying that things are perfect and that there is room for improvement; the issue is how do we improve it? Talk continued on the vast variances in CHC funding between different CCGs ranging from 1% to 10% with an estimate of an average of 4%, of each one's budget. Some of this was explained away by the difference in demographics between the CCGs and the difference in costs of care packages throughout the country. S.S. uses the opportunity to suggest that these sorts of things will be contributing factors in achieving the £855 million efficiency savings.

Nigel Mills asks if he should be worried about the fact his CCG (Southern Derbyshire) is only spending about 2.2% of its budget on CHC funding and it they are setting the bar too high.

S.S. states that Southern Derbyshire does rather well on a number of the performance metrics and N.M. may like to congratulate them on that performance. He puts this down to two main things. Firstly, if a patient gets their assessment back at home or in a circumstance closer to what it would be if they were more independent, they are less likely to be recommended for care home placement and be funded in perpetuity by the NHS. Secondly, that Derbyshire has achieved a rate of only 10.9% believing that this means nurses and professionals doing the assessments are more likely to make smart judgements.

I am finding it difficult to continue making the points about Simon Stevens's constant use of everything pointing to how well they are doing, or to put it another way, his constant use of spin in every scenario. I will leave the reader to form their own opinion.

At this point Nigel Mills believes that this naturally drifts into to question of the £885 million efficiency savings and asks if they really believe if they can achieve this by doing better – by standardising and delivering a better quality process. Or is this in danger of becoming salami slicing and giving it to fewer people to save money?

S.S. responds by stating that he wants everyone to understand exactly what the £855 million is. He starts by making the statement that the efficiencies are about driving the savings proportionally about the same as the efficiencies already earmarked for NHS spending over the next several years.

Can he really be serious in believing that every department within the NHS must proportionately cut their budget in line with the need for a reduction of the total? This takes no account of where the money needs to be spent irrespective of any other factors such as which departments are doing well or doing badly, or where certain diseases or conditions are becoming more prevalent or are in decline. This would be akin to the government making proportionate cuts to every department including the NHS in the face of a pandemic; absolutely outrageously crazy. Had the government adopted this model of budgetary control where would we be now?

He goes on to pose and answer a question of his own: "Is the NHS going to get more efficient over the next several years?" "Yes, in many ways it is and this is one of the ways that we already have pencilled in. That is against our assumption as to what would have happened to spending growth had we not acted He goes on to make the point "that if previous trends had carried on going up and up what would we be spending and how do we want to moderate that growth?" "NHS spending on CHC will still be higher in 2020-21 than it is now, even if we succeed in this programme. We just want to slow the rate of growth." (Now we have it - to the slow the rate of growth.)

Further discussion took place about reduced eligibility being the likely outcome, but S.S. remains of the opinion that adopting some of the practices we see in the best performing CCGs will result in these savings, citing the fact that already CCGs have contributed £170 million against the counter factual to that, during the past year. (They may well have reduced the costs in that year, but he offers no hard evidence as to how this was achieved and at what cost, not in monetary terms but in eligibility of those in need.)

The conversation then turns to that of procurement and S.S. suggests that "although there are variations around the country maybe CCGs are not either locally and collectively engaging in smart medium-term relationships with care homes and home care agencies, rather than using the spot market, which as you well know has all kinds of pressures and problems."

Gareth Snell: "Given that there is disjointedness in the CCGs between the acute setting, the sub-acute setting and community setting, how much of this is just shunting money around the system? If someone is denied CHC funding in a timely manner are they not more likely to present at an acute setting which is a much more expensive provision?"

The Chair restates the Department of Health figures for each type of setting from the 2015 statistics. Acute beds £303 per day, an NHS community healthcare bed £89 per day, home-based LA short-term services £63 per day and home-based packages of social care £41.

Further conversations took place on this subject which culminated in S.S. saying that on average CHC funding costs £50,000 per person per year compared with a much smaller figure for social care procured services. He goes on to state that he didn't think substituting one for the other would be good value for the taxpayer.

Again I am left feeling utter frustration with Simon Stevens's views on this as to what he chooses to make reference to. I believe I can pretty much guarantee that the patients, families and friends of dementia sufferers, who are also taxpayers, would not agree with his assessment of what is value for money.

What really needs highlighting is his average annual cost of £50,000 for NHS CHC. That is less than £1,000 per week per person and he claims this is substantially more than social care procured services. We have two options here: one is to believe he is utterly naïve, and doesn't understand what he is saying or how the system works, or secondly, he knows full well the extent of his deception and his continuing use of smoke and mirrors to make his point.

When did he last enquire as to the costs of a private individual who is self-funding their own care? I think that the vast majority would feel that a figure below £1,000 would be an absolute bargain. Why? Because they are also subsidising the cost of providing care to those who are funded by social services. This is like comparing apples with bananas (not even pears as at least there would be some degree of likeness).

Regretfully I cannot continue to keep quoting the he/she asked this and he/she responded on this way, because the vein that runs through the entirety of this meeting is in simplistic terms that the question posers accept there is a major problem with the system but the providers seemingly just want to defend their current position and try hard to justify their belief they can achieve more for far less.

Further discussion took place on the £855 million proposed savings and how it might be achieved. It was suggested that there will always be problems associated with NHS CHC as it sits at the very border of a system where on one side there is a fully funded free-at-the-point-of-delivery system trying to match onto a means-tested system. *This is undoubtedly true, but that border is not one of equal dimension; it cannot be seen as a line in the sand where one can easily step over it from one side to the other, given a fair assessment of the facts and reality of an individual's needs. Imagine the border to be three-dimensional instead of being on an equal plane; the patients are stood only a step away from the line that defines the two but they start from the presumption that they are going to fund their own care and start on the side termed as social care. The real problem is that NHS CHC funding sits at the top of one massive high cliff and therefore to get over that border they must first climb this massive cliff. No assistance is given in the form of having the correct equipment to undertake such a task. One can liken it to trying to climb a mountain in a pair of flip flops. Along the way there are all manner of other obstacles to be overcome: falling rocks, maybe the odd snake or two, birds nesting and of course the weather. There is no-one from the NHS who stands at the top of this great mountain to throw you a lifeline to assist in your climb; no, if you are going to do this, it will be with help from your family and friends. It's up to you to find the equipment (knowledge) to scale this seemingly unsurmountable obstacle and even then do not be surprised if those standing at the top don't look for other ways of making it more difficult.*

13

MY HOPES AND ASPIRATIONS FOR THE FUTURE

It has been really difficult to find the right words to express myself in a meaningful way about what I hope for in the future.

I think that the very word "hope" is as good a place to start as any other as it sums up a feeling that each and every one of us must have, both as an individual and as a member of society. What do we have if we lose the ability to be able to hope for something better than is currently available? Hope is the cement that binds us all together in the belief that things can be improved upon, it gives us a sense of purpose, something to aim and fight for, to enhance the lives we live and those of our loved ones. Without hope we truly are devoid of a reason to exist. Spare a thought for those poor souls who thought their only way out of a life without hope was to take away the thing most precious to us by committing suicide. Hope is never enough on its own, it has to be seen as the catalyst that gives us the determination to find the ways of putting right those things that are clearly wrong, to call out those instances and people who would treat others with contempt and without feeling or compassion.

It would be natural for most people to take the view that hope is driven in the first instance by a personal and maybe a selfish desire to the betterment of our own or our loved ones' lives. Whilst this is understandable, it is by no means exclusive; the beauty of hope is that there are no limitations to the range of things that any one person or persons can hope for at any single point in time. Maybe some people have alternative names for hope; some may call it wishful thinking, daydreaming or purely having your head in the clouds. It doesn't matter what it's called, it only matters that it really does exist and while we retain that ability to hope we also retain the ability do something about it, whatever the desire is to change something that is unfair, unfeeling or plainly wrong.

This book has grown out of my own hopes for trying to do the best I can for the love of my life. It really started when I began to keep notes of our experiences and lack of help, when I had a feeling of being unable to cope with a situation that was beyond my knowledge or capabilities.

In my search for knowledge to fight for our rights and to get justice for Margaret, it involved me making copious notes, finding and printing the information needed and collating it into some sort of sensible order. As time passed and the more I read, it became obvious that our situation was not unique, far from it, and it actually started to feel as if it was the norm. I guess that it was the MDT Assessment meeting that really became the catalyst to spur me on to think a little more deeply about the whole process. If there were thousands of people going through similar experiences to ourselves, I started to wonder how they were managing to cope. I am by no means a "brain box". I'm not highly intelligent, but I do have a certain ability to be able to look for ways to resolve problems or situations. So due to the enormity of the injustice I was experiencing, I wondered just how some of the other people were managing to cope, some who may be less fortunate than myself for whatever reason. I could imagine that a son or daughter with busy lives of their own and the need to work must find the prospect of trying to do their best for their parents in such a situation almost impossible. Then of course there are elderly people like myself who are having to look after their spouse and are unable to do the sort of research I had done either through lack of time or resource. Whatever their situation, maybe, just maybe, I could be of some help to them by putting my own experiences down on paper in the hope that it may help them to find a way through this maze of obstacles designed to not help them make their lives better but to do the exact opposite, by denying them their rights under the law.

Gone are all those plans we had for our retirement, the ability to go away on holiday, to enjoy BBQs with family and friends, dinner parties, celebrations, family gatherings, days spent pottering about in the garden, going for days out, visiting the seaside, places of interest like National Trust properties, having a weekend away or the simple things like going to the shops together or just the odd run out into the countryside to enjoy a picnic. So many things we enjoyed doing together like eating out, going to the cinema, having a game of ten pin bowling, Margaret enjoyed going for walks with her friends and I enjoyed the odd game of golf. None of these things and many others no longer form part of our present or future but for me they lay firmly in my past with just the memories of happy times together. For Margaret even these have now been denied her because of this dreadful disease with only a glimmer of recognition when looking through our photo albums.

The present and the future is very different from what we had expected. Margaret spends at least twelve hours in bed with the other twelve hours being cared for in all her daily needs and either staring at the TV, which she is unable to follow, or listening to music which does spark certain recollections and the occasional look of happiness on her face.

This book has mainly been written in the hours between 4.30am – 7.30am when Margaret remains asleep and after I have woken up due to going to bed around 8.00 – 8.30 each evening. It has given me a certain degree of purpose and satisfaction in my life as it now is. I have always subscribed to the belief that if you can help someone in need and you have the time to do so and maybe the resources and abilities, then why wouldn't you? I believe in the bank of human kindness: when you help someone without pay or reward, no matter what it is, then you are making a deposit into that bank. There will be times when maybe you will be in need of help and you hope that someone will come to your assistance. More often than not, someone will be willing to do so; this is them making a deposit and you making a withdrawal. It really does work, and the beauty is there are no greedy bankers demanding their share of your goodwill. There is no doubt in my mind that we are, in the main, a nation of people who come together in a time of need, not necessarily our need but someone else's. One only has to look at the vast funds raised through charitable donations or the giving of time to see that when the populace understands there is a need for help it can flow like water from a tap. I truly believe that if more people are aware of this massive injustice and the total hypocrisy of those in high places, be they politicians, NHS management, assessment personnel, law enforcement, judiciary, or anyone that is involved in the practice of denying seriously ill fellow human beings of their rights, then something really can happen to make changes to a system that is currently inadequate, unfair and morally bankrupt.

Here I list my personal hopes and aspirations:

- I hope that I will be successful in my endeavour to get CHC funding for the love of my life

- I hope that I will be able to find a way to get this book published so that the information it contains can be out there and helping others

- I hope that I am able to market it in such a way that it becomes a bestseller and provides the means with which to fight against this corrupt system. I have no interest in doing this for personal gain and pledge every single penny of profits towards fighting for a change

- I hope that if we fail to fight it from the top down that we can fight it from the bottom up. Let every person who is willing to participate in this hypocrisy understand that no matter what their reason for so doing they may be held to account on a personal level

- I hope that anyone reading this book will find it useful and helpful in fighting for the rights of their loved ones

- I hope that having read this book it will give the reader the incentive to spread the word and get more people to understand the need to join the quest and also spread the word. The power of growth by exponentially telling more people will give us the opportunity to right this wrong

- I hope that this book will find its way into the hands of some good people who are in a position to help us make a difference. Hopefully there may be members of the legal profession, law enforcement or politicians and members of the NHS who are in a position to take up this challenge by making their own deposit into the bank of human kindness

- I hope that some of the proceeds from the sale of this book can be used to send every single member of parliament their own copy. Maybe then we will see just how many of them truly want to make a difference to people's lives!

- I hope the media in its various forms will take up the challenge and question those same politicians, so there is no place for them to hide in respect of our quest for justice

- I hope that you the reader will engage in a thinking-out-of-the-box opportunity to help find solutions to this and other problems that beset us all. Make it fun: have a dinner party or a BBQ, get some friends round and ask them their views on how they would solve a particular problem, but please include our most pressing challenge. How do we get the establishment to change their administration and realise that NHS CHC needs to deliver on its promise of free at the point of access to those in need. No more lies, no more cheating and above all no more hypocrisy. Let's put an end to this postcode lottery that allows one person to be correctly cared for in one area, but not so in another

- I hope that we can all come together and get justice not only for our own loved ones but for those of our fellow sufferers, and provide the seed that forces government to not only find the funds to pay for the care of all in need but also make them realise the true solution to ultimately reducing the costs is to find a cure for dementia.

14

JOINING THE FIGHT AND SPREADING THE WORD

Take a pen and write on a piece of glass or a window the letters NHS. Now view this from the opposite side (this is like looking into a glass box from the outside). What you read is SHN. This is our badge of honour.

A long time ago I worked for a steakhouse restaurant chain named Berni Inns. In today's world it would probably be considered as a bit of an unusual concept. Each "inn" consisted of two or three restaurants and anything up to six bars all within the same premises. The menu in each restaurant consisted of only three or four items: there was normally a "Steak and Plaice" offering fried plaice, sirloin steak and gammon & egg.

The "Steak Bar": Three different cuts of steak in different sizes and a fish option of Dover sole.

The "Steak and Duck Bar": 10oz rump steak, half roast duck or scampi.

Each menu offering came with the choice of either ice cream or cheese and biscuits included in the price. The description under ice cream stated "Our ice cream is made from 100% non-milk fat". I cannot begin to tell you how many customers would delight in telling us that there was a printing error on the menu. Barely a day went by without this being pointed out on a number of occasions. They thought that the menu should have read "100% non-fat milk". They took some persuading that the fact was the ice cream was as it stated: made from non-milk fat, as in it had never been anywhere near an animal's udder.

The moral of this story is that people love to point out that they have spotted an error that they think no-one else has noticed.

This is another reason why I have decided to order lapel badges made in the same colours and size of an NHS badge but with the letters printed (incorrectly) SHN. Not only will the wearing of these lapel badges indicate someone else can be identified as a fellow advocate for the cause and could enable an exchange of ideas or experiences, but it could also spark a conversation with someone who is unaware of CHC funding or how to apply for it.

SHN stands for "Stop Hypocrisy Now".

If you would like to order one of these badges, they are available inclusive of ten information cards that can be handed out to anyone you feel could benefit from the knowledge.

Order online at [www.dementia-crisis.co.uk]

PLEASE HELP US SPREAD THE WORD.

15

SOME ADDITIONAL FOOD FOR THOUGHT

This final chapter is written to address two further thinking-out-of-the-box subjects, both of which have some relevance to the way successive governments have chosen to deal with the scandal of not addressing the issues surrounding looking after the most vulnerable members of our society.

Before we come on to these, I would like to take this opportunity to update you on the NHS CEO's achievements in driving down the costs of CHC funding, since that House of Commons meeting back in 2018. This was to be achieved by increasing the efficiency of the system (Simon Stevens's words).

Remember that the Public Accounts Committee stated: "The funding system is failing people with continuing healthcare needs and there is unacceptable variation between areas in the number of people assessed as eligible, ranging from 28 to 356 people per 50,000 population. NHS England is not adequately carrying out its responsibility to ensure CCGs are complying with the legal requirement to provide CHC to those who are eligible."

Remember his belief that he could save £855 million from the then-projected cost of the CHC budget by increased efficiency. Well, it would appear that since he became CEO of NHS England, 20,000+ fewer people are eligible for CHC funding than would have been the case, given the increase in numbers of the ageing population, and this only reflects the numbers up until 2020.

It would appear that the majority of the members taking part in that committee were concerned about the very low numbers of certain CCGs (i.e. as low as 28 per 50,000) being eligible for funding. But conversely S.S. has adopted the exact opposite viewpoint, being that his concern was there were too many people being found to be assessed as being entitled to funding (356 per 50,000).

Bear in mind that S.S. said that the average cost of providing CHC funding was £50,000 per annum per person, so his target of £855 million in savings is equivalent to no fewer than 17,100 people being denied CHC funding. Obviously it would appear that the establishment is extremely grateful for his work in ensuring that an even greater number of people are subjected to the trauma of the hypocrisy of this system and can effectively be robbed of their assets from a life of work. So grateful in fact, that his reward is to have bestowed upon him the title of Lord.

To think that the committee was considering how they could ensure CCGs were complying with their legal requirements to provide CHC to those who are eligible and yet the outcome has been not to improve the system but in reality make it even worse than it was then. As is evidenced by the facts of those discussions, many members participating were knowledgeable about some of the shortcomings of the system, but the CEO Simon Stevens, with his determination through his unbelievable spin on every negative put to him, has achieved his goal of the exact opposite.

In life we recognise that there are some people who are good and some who are bad. That is not to say that some good people may not be good all the time and can have a degree of badness at times. Likewise there are bad people who also are not bad all the time and can have a degree of goodness at times. For these reasons it could be said that there are two separate scales of goodness on the one hand and badness on the other.

At the extremities of these scales it could also be said that on the goodness scale lay those people who are seen to be saintly, by virtue of them never wavering from their actions of kindness, love and devotion in doing good for all living creatures at all times. At the extremity of the bad scale we would probably define these types of people as being evil to their very core, not having any regard for the feelings, well-being, or care for any living thing at any time.

I believe that no matter where one sits within either scale, we are all motivated by something. At the saintly end we see people whose sole motivation is to improve the life and comfort of all living things. These types of people are not motivated by self-gain or glorification; their sole interest is helping others for no reward of any kind. They truly are saintly.

At the other end of the scale we see the true meaning of evil. These types of people live only for themselves, having no regard for anyone or anything other than their own life. The only life that is of any consequence to them is their own. They are in fact cowards. It would appear that their motivation in life is solely centred on just one person: themselves. Maybe they have a desire to be remembered in history as the most evil human being that ever walked on this planet. Who can possibly figure out how such an evil mind works?

What is of interest to us is what was and is the motivation behind all those "in charge" that allows them to not only break the law with impunity but to do so with the result of denying thousands of very vulnerable people their rights by denying them access to NHS CHC funding?

Greed often plays a big role in the motivation of many people, wanting something more than they are truly entitled to, which comes at the expense of many others. In their way of thinking it matters not what they deprive others of or indeed how many people suffer, but what enhances their own lifestyle and personal enjoyment of their life.

Maybe S.S. was motivated solely by a promise of being made a Lord of the Realm and all the privileges that such an honour bestows upon him. This truly is high up the scale of badness.

What needs to be asked is how have they managed to engineer the system and more importantly the many hundreds if not thousands of people involved to carry out his calling?

I am truly amazed that so many people in what is regarded as a caring profession have been persuaded to act in such an unprofessional way and have been willing to lie and cheat, to deny our loved ones of their rights, all at the bequest of their boss and for his glorification.

This begs a number of questions on how this has been achieved. Some of these questions may seem outrageous and unpalatable; maybe there are other questions that are nearer the reality and have more reasonable answers. Whatever these are I don't think anyone can deny that there is something seriously wrong that needs to be fully investigated.

How do you persuade good people to move from the good scale of assessing them as a human being and converting them to join the bad scale? It defies logic.

What is that old saying often used to describe the different ways of teaching children right from wrong? "The stick or the carrot".

We are all aware of the high turnover of staff within the NHS and so the first question must be, why? No doubt there are numerous reasons why people leave any profession, many of which are perfectly legitimate and understandable. What interests me are those previously dedicated individuals who had become disillusioned with the role they were being asked to play as part of their job within the NHS. Logic suggests there must be a significant number of people who had started out with a real desire to help others in need only to discover that what was being asked of them did not fit with their personal desires, beliefs and standards and felt the only option for them was to no longer subscribe to the hypocrisy of the institution we know as the NHS.

Maybe they felt that they were unable to speak out about the wrongdoings of an institution that we are constantly being told is beyond reproach, but whatever their reasons were, be it fear of retribution, a fear of betraying their friends and colleagues or a belief that no-one would believe them, there must be many ex-employees of the NHS who hold a key to shining a light on the true scale of this injustice.

Imagine the power of testimony given under oath by anyone who has experienced first-hand how that institution manages to continuingly break the law and get away with it. If any reader recognises themselves to be in this description then all I would ask is to help us in our campaign; after all, you too are a victim of this abuse, given the fact you have been deprived of a job or career that through circumstances you have felt the need to leave.

What needs to be asked next is how those remaining in the system and still contributing to its inadequacies have been persuaded to become part of this bad practices. To them I ask you these questions:

- Are you a bad person or have you just fallen into a system over which you feel you have no control?

- Do you genuinely not care what happens to seriously ill people or the cost to them or their families because of your participation in this corrupt system? Remember this is not solely about who pays for the care, it is so much more than that. It affects the health and happiness of entire families.

- Would you pass the ultimate test of asking yourself, if this was happening to my own mum, dad, gran, grandad, brother, sister, husband, wife or best friend, would I behave differently?

- Are you living in fear of your superiors who have ordered you to tow the party line, do as you are told and don't rock the boat?

- How have they motivated you to be part of their calling?

- Have they used the proverbial "stick" to frighten you into doing the wrong thing? Maybe you felt that your job was in jeopardy or that you would get demoted with less pay? Maybe your chances of promotion will be curtailed. Is it the fear of not getting a good reference if you are looking to move on to pastures new?

- Or was the size and deliciousness of the "carrot" just too tempting for you to refuse?

- Have your principles been compromised by an increase in pay, more friendly hours, no weekend work, maybe less hours for the same money?

- Does carrying out assessments involve receiving bonus payments?

- Are you given incentives to keep down the numbers of people being assessed as in need of CHC funding?

- Are you effectively being blackmailed into towing the line? Maybe someone knows something about you that you would prefer was not shared with others. Is the price you are willing to pay for their silence the cost that is being paid by those seriously ill patients who do not get the care they need?

- If you are involved in assessments, have you been told not to worry about how to conduct these properly and within the law? Were you told it doesn't matter, the only guiding principle is to make sure the patient doesn't get the funding?

So many questions and no doubt many more worthy of being asked.

Of one thing I am absolutely convinced, and that is these continuing deviations from what should be happening are in no way coincidental, they are far too frequent and have such commonality running through them that they can be nothing short of being engineered.

This is nothing short of a massive Ponzi scheme, and like all such schemes they eventually fail due to their magnitude getting harder and harder to cover up and the management of the numerous and increasing number of players and their lies becoming more and more difficult to control.

As I have previously mentioned, Retired Vice Admiral Philip Mathias is to be admired and thanked for his determination in trying to get this issue resolved by taking the logical route of bringing to task the very people at the top of the tree who need to be held to account. However, his efforts have been thwarted by a closing of ranks of the very people who have it in their power to not only perpetrate this injustice but also to actively protect their fellow conspirators. It appears they have taken a lesson from other criminals in the way it is said that there is "honour amongst thieves".

So adept are they at protecting each other, we have in my opinion no other alternative but to open this can of worms by taking the players further down the chain to task.

It would be my view that with determination and effort we can bring private prosecutions against those individuals who can be proven to have told lies at any stage within the process, be they nurses, doctors, social workers, MDT members or CCG members. I do not profess that such a task will be easy, as no doubt the NHS will with their massive resources fight to protect their legions of followers doing their bidding in an attempt to maintain the status quo. It will no doubt be expensive but we must bear in mind we have right on our side and if we are confronted by the need to give evidence in court, there will (in my experience) be some of those foot soldiers who, even just to protect what dignity and integrity they still have left, will find it more difficult to lie on oath and run the risk of committing perjury. Maybe then the truth will come out and justice can prevail.

I urge each and every reader to consider that we would be working together as one. It matters not whose cases get selected to go forward to a private prosecution. The important thing would be to select those cases where written evidence can be produced. The intent would be to expose the system to scrutiny by suing individuals for relatively small sums of money (not for the costs of care packages) and any settlements after costs would go into the fighting fund. By taking this approach it is hoped that rather than become embroiled in an expensive legal battle at this stage we can get the publicity we need and argue our case time and time again in front of different judges. Who knows, maybe some of the plaintiffs would want to settle out of court rather than face the scrutiny of their lying ways. This would have to be done on the basis that they admit to how they were persuaded to ensure that patients were refused NHS CHC funding.

Please bear in mind, the longer this hypocrisy continues the greater the number of seriously ill people are deprived of their rights and the greater the number of families will be subjected to the trauma.

Please help us raise awareness of this injustice. Tell as many people as you can what is really happening and remind them that this dreadful disease can happen to anyone. It could be them or their loved ones next. Remind them that all donations no matter how small will enable us to keep fighting. We will win in the end, because good will always eventually prevail over evil.

This chapter was to address two other out-of-the-box thinking subjects, both of which I stated have some relevance to our main subject matter:

1. Government and how it works or doesn't work.

2. The question to be addressed is, is there a better way of doing it?

Put quite simply, there must be. We could hardly believe that we have reached perfection in the way the country is governed. There are many faults with the system we currently have, but before we can think about what we can improve upon we need to identify what areas are not working as well as they should.

As all governments come from the result of a general election, this would seem to be a good place to start. Back on 5 May 2011 we were given the opportunity, through a referendum, to vote for the way we choose our MPs. The question was a simple one: "Should the alternative vote system be used in place of the "first past the post" system currently used? Yes or no? Only 42% of eligible voters expressed their view in the ballot, of which 67.9% said no. The real question is, was this a sensible way to determine what the population really felt about this issue?

Firstly, there appeared to be a certain amount of apathy from the public. Was this because they were not interested? Maybe they didn't think it was important. Perhaps they didn't understand what an alternative voting system was and how it works, or was it that they didn't think that with such a simple Yes or No question it was highly likely that the status quo would be maintained. After all, a this or that question can only produce an answer which is in itself a first past the post answer. Maybe the question should have had more alternatives! Why was a halfway solution not offered? For example, in a similar way to how the Scottish parliament is elected.

The question could have been, "Please indicate your preference to how you would like members of parliament to be elected in the future." Enter 1 – Your first preference with 1. 2 – Your second preference with a 2.

(A) Maintain our current system of first past the post

(B) Alternative vote system where members of parliament are elected on a system that takes account of people's 2nd and 3rd preferences

(C) A system that is a mixture of first past the post where 50% of the MPs are elected in the same way as they are now, but the remaining 50% are elected in proportion to the number of votes cast for your preference of political party.

I am not advocating an exact replica of the Scottish system where they vote for their chosen party candidates for their constituency, of which there are seventy-three, and a further vote for their preference within a region, of which there are eight in total. Each of these regions are represented by seven SMPs, selected by a proportion of the votes cast.

So my out-of-the-box suggestion is:

(a) Double the size of each constituency, to be represented by one MP and one partner (on a lesser salary than an MP and funded out of the current allowances given to MPs). The partner will not attend parliament or have any voting rights; their sole responsibility would be to engage full-time within their constituency through surgeries and other methods of engaging with the public to gauge what is important to them. This information can be fed back to the sitting MP for that constituency.

(b) The remaining 325 seats would be allocated to what we could refer to as Party Members of Parliament. These would be selected as a direct number of votes cast to each party from both constituency votes and Party Member votes in the same ratio, to determine how many seats are allocated.

(c) My suggestion would be that only Party Member MPs are within the Parliamentary Whip, not the Constituency MPs who would then not have a conflict of interest with the wishes of their constituents and would vote in line with their interests.

(d) Each political party would name in advance their complete list of candidates to potentially become party MPs in a pre-specified order.

(e) No constituency nominee can also be nominated on the party list.

It is my belief that such a system could have some distinct advantages over the simple first past the post system currently in use:

(1) It addresses the issue of those people who feel their vote will not count if they vote for some of the smaller parties. This in itself could encourage a higher turnout of voters as indeed every vote will count towards their voice being heard.

(2) It allows the electorate to vote for the candidate they feel will serve them best even if that candidate is not from the party they would like to vote for, as indeed their Party Member would still receive a vote from them under this system. Again a reason to vote and not feel their vote is wasted.

(3) It opens up the possibility that there may be more co-operation across party lines where Constituency MPs with similar concerns or needs can legitimately disagree with a party line.

(4) It forces potential candidates to make a choice as to whether to stand as a constituency MP or a party MP.

I have no doubt that there are many people who would fiercely oppose such a change and no doubt that there will be many who will identify the pitfalls I may not have considered. There may also be others who feel they can see other ways of improving the system. Good, let's hear them and start a debate, because there is one thing that is certain: we all know we don't have the perfect model and this constant game of kicking difficult decisions into the long grass and playing ping pong between the different parties is allowing atrocities on a frightening scale. Anyone who has had dealings with NHS CHC know this to be a truth.

Another point on political issues is the question of Scotland wanting to gain their independence. Having lived and worked in Scotland back in the seventies, my experience was that there are many, many proud and good Scottish people, but due to historical incidents there seems to be an everlasting distrust of the English by an ever-increasing number of them.

I have no beef with them; we had some very good friends and enjoyed most of our time spent there. We loved the country and the traditions, the food and the drink and in the main the people, so why are they so desperate to have their independence?

One can be fiercely independent without being enemies; in fact, our differences should be celebrated, not argued over. Where differences of opinion are evident, this drives a wedge between two nations who should be living in complete harmony with each other and it should be incumbent upon politicians on both sides of the border to do their best to foster better relations, not argue about who's right and who's wrong.

What would be so drastically wrong or bad about allowing Scotland their independence? Surely an amicable divorce where both parties agree the terms of a settlement must be better than one party wanting something different and the other refusing to a divorce simply on historical grounds.

Yes, I know that there are complications over the transfer of goods over the border, currency, EU membership etc. etc. It strikes me that we hear so much from our English MPs that the Union must be maintained, but very little justification other than it has been good for both countries. At the moment we hear from only one partner in this long-lived marriage of convenience; why aren't the English asked if we would be happy to have an amicable divorce? Who knows, the answer may be a surprise to both parties!

Finally, I pose this question. Why do we believe that politicians are inevitably wise just because they managed to convince a small section of the electorate that they are the best person for the job? The one thing that has always been a puzzle for me is the fact that the great and not so great departments of state are run in some cases by people who do not always have the necessary qualifications to undertake the responsibilities that have been assigned to them. I realise there are numerous civil servants who work behind the scenes in helping to develop policy and try to keep these ministers in check. However, from time to time we are subjected to management of some of these departments by people who would seemingly have difficulty in organising a day trip to the seaside.

When was the last time you saw an advert for a multi-conglomerate organisation seeking a new Chief Executive Officer under the heading of "No Experience Necessary"? Probably never, and yet under our current system we are confronted too frequently with seeing inexperienced members of parliament being elevated to such dizzying heights of responsibility.

My second subject for-out-of-the-box thinking has got to be about the police, judiciary and prison system.

There appears to be so much wrong with these three interconnected institutions that I wouldn't know where to start, or probably more to the point I would probably find it difficult to finish.

Let me say I am not wanting to belittle any one of the many good personnel involved in these three institutions. Actually, although as is always the case, there will be good and bad in any large collection of people, and in the main the majority do an amazing job that we should all be grateful for and for which I have tremendous respect.

I believe the police must get very frustrated in their endeavours in bringing criminals to justice, only to see that the perpetrators of the crimes committed are let off with a metaphorical slap on the wrist and are back out on the streets committing the same crimes again.

I have great sympathy for the victims of crimes and in the worst cases the families of loved ones who have died at the hands of murderers. If anyone is deserving of getting justice it must surely be them. Alas we constantly hear of the injustice they are subjected to, such as a family member who was murdered by someone who was let out of prison early by a parole board who didn't recognise the danger this person posed. There are so many innocent good people who have lost their lives at the hands of evil people.

What amazes me is the length of imprisonment given to these murderers. Then the fact that in half the time they have served they can be released back into society.

It is not unusual to hear of instances where prisoners are using the system to obtain additional benefits for themselves based on their "Human Rights" and the so-called "Do Gooders" brigade fighting on their behalf telling us society can't do this or that as it would be against their "Human Rights". We are told by these advocates for some of the worst of the worst that prison is not about punishment but should be about rehabilitation, so that these people can be released back into society and be a contributor rather than a burden.

If this was truly the case we are in deep trouble, but quite simply it is a massively flawed argument as it should be about both.

There has to be a serious element of punishment incorporated into the sentence, otherwise it is no wonder that when prisoners are released back into society some will just continue with their lives of crime. Too often we are told that the punishment is simply being deprived of their liberty and that in itself is sufficient.

Why do we bother trying to bring people to justice, especially cold cases, if it was only about trying to rehabilitate them? Why was so much resource put into getting Ronnie Biggs (one of the Great Train Robbers) back into a British jail? It could be argued that he had rehabilitated himself and subsequently enjoyed a family life for many years before it was known where he was. The truly enlightening thing was that in the end he was happy to give himself up, so that he could benefit from this society's compassion towards seriously ill prisoners with treatment administered in a humane way.

Let us contrast this with the sufferers of dementia. On the one hand, in R. Biggs's case, we have someone who was a net taker from our society. He, together with others, robbed the country of over £2.6 million (nearly £56 million in todays currency) and at the same time was prepared to seriously injure the driver to achieve their aim. What was the cost of trying to bring him back to justice after he was successful in breaking out of prison? In the end he was quite happy to surrender himself because he knew he would be well looked after by a society he had robbed and turned his back on for the majority of his life. On the other hand we have thousands of seriously ill people who have paid their taxes and NHI payments who, in their hour of need, society has turned its back on. Where on earth is the justice in this seriously flawed system? Maybe people diagnosed with dementia would be better off robbing society prior to getting seriously ill! This could seem to be a win/win situation. If they get caught then the state will lock them up and give them all the trappings of a reasonably good life with free board and lodgings, recreational facilities, the company of other people and importantly the care and compassion at no cost to themselves when they need it most. The other win side is if they don't get caught then they will at least have some additional funds to add to their own assets when the state decides to rob them.

I make this analogy, ridiculous as it is, merely to highlight the stupidity and injustice built into a system which allows the state to break their own rules, to lie and to cheat and steal from a section of the good citizens whilst at the same time spending hundreds and thousands on the bad citizens.

Getting back to the out-of-the-box thinking, my suggestions for improvement are:

(1) The length of sentence needs to be more appropriate to the seriousness of the crime. The Great Train

Robbers initially received up to thirty-year sentences. Today the common phrase of "you get less for murder" is sadly so true.

(2) Each sentence should be viewed as comprising of three equal parts of the total sentence:

Part one should be the punishment phase: this should be a denial of not just their liberty but also denial of the luxuries of life such as TV, computers, games, limited menu choices, restricted social communications etc.

Part two should be the rehabilitation phase inclusive of all of those items excluded in part one now being permitted.

Part three is the parole phase, where providing the prisoner has been a model prisoner then they can be released on licence back into the community under certain conditions. Failure to comply would see the prisoner serving out the remainder of their time under part one conditions.

Moving from part one to two and two to three would all be subject to their behaviour during each period.

I offer these thoughts on the above two subjects for out-of-the-box thinking, not in the belief that I am foolish enough to think I have all or any of the answers, but simply in the hope that sowing such a seed may see it germinate and grow into something bigger.

Good luck with your personal journey. I wish you the very best for your future and the future of your loved ones. I hope that you will find some help through the reading of this book and that you will join with us in fighting for the change to a corrupt system.

THE END OF THE BEGINNING!

Post Script

Should you the reader be a member of the NHS family, I would ask you to understand that I realise there are some amazing people working in the NHS in so many different ways and that the contents of this book in its criticism of your employer is not aimed at you.

The problem is that, as the saying goes, "One bad apple can affect the whole barrel".

To those good people I offer my thanks for the work you do and the dedication you have in your role of caring for the sick and needy within our society.

To those amongst your colleagues who, for whatever reason, have chosen to do the bidding of their masters in helping them to deny the most needy of their fellow citizens, I say this:

Shame on you. How do you sleep well at night knowing the role you play in perpetrating one of the most atrocious miscarriages of justice and that your actions have a profound effect on the lives and happiness of hundreds of thousands of people who have done you no harm?

It is never too late to change your ways. Now is the time to move back from the dark side to the good side. Speak up about how they managed to get you to believe their absurdities and involve you in their atrocities.

Take your NHS badge and wear it upside down so that it reads SHN (Stop Hypocrisy Now). Do not be afraid to help everyone stand up for what is right. Remember you will be helping to protect the NHS from the stain of shame they have brought upon this service through their illegal activities.